P9-DGT-921

MARBORO
6-22
1.98

THE SHAH

THE SHAH

The Glittering Story Of Iran and Its People

Edwin P. Hoyt

Paul S. Eriksson, Inc.

New York

Paul S. Eriksson, Inc., 119 West 57th Street, New York, N. Y. 10019. Published simultaneously in Canada by George J. McLeod, Inc., Ontario. Library of Congress Catalog Card Number 75-16501. ISBN 0-8397-7753-1. Manufactured in the United States of America.

For George Weller and
Reynolds Packard
In memory of
times past.

Contents

Illustrations

Between Pages

THE SHAH

1

Journey Into The Past

To Rome, the jet was loaded with international traffic, some passengers bound for holidays, some on business; a variegated crowd of excited and tired people moving across the Atlantic. From Rome to Istanbul the character of the passengers changed; there were a few home-bound wives and relatives, but for the most part the travellers were enroute to the Middle East on errands, business, or government, or press.

It was the spring of 1975, the Middle East had supplanted Southeast Asia as the cockpit of world politics.

The plane was half full to Istanbul, but here we picked up connecting flights from Frankfort and Central Europe. By the time we took off for Ankara, the international and local traffic had filled every seat, and an air of expectation had also come to the jet, in spite of the tired ministrations of the attractive young Pan American stewardesses who had done it all so many times before.

For now we knew each other: destination Teheran. Every seat

was taken as we headed for the hottest spot in the Middle East, the center of intrigue; the country whose ruler was even then boasting he would bring his nation into the forefront of world powers within a generation. And the reason we were there, all of us aboard that Pan Am jet that fine spring day, was to take advantage, as we could, of the opportunity that growth and ferment offered us in Teheran. Among us were college professors, going to lecture at Teheran University on modern business techniques, experts bound for a biochemical conference in Isfahan; others for a petrochemical meeting in Teheran. German, French, Italian, American, Dutch, British—businessmen from every walk of life coming to investigate the possibility of selling goods to a government that was spending money as if the world was going to end tomorrow.

I was heading back to Teheran for the first time in more than a quarter of a century, beckoned by the changes that had come to what was once little more than a Middle Eastern dungheap. For five years the Shah had been trumpeting his song of change, and in the past two years the rising price of oil and the international crisis caused by the awakening of the oil producers had made the Shah's words seem more prophetic than before. The Shah boasted he was taking his country out of the Middle Ages and into the forefront of modern society. I was coming to see if it was true.

We flew over mountains all afternoon, high, snow clad reminders that there is so much of the world about which we know so little, and as dusk turned to darkness the mountains grew more barren, less populous. We moved from Asiatic Turkey into the Iran that is really the bridge between west and eastern worlds.

Night fell, a dark clear night, as we headed down toward Teheran, which sits at the foot of its own mountain *massif* in Central Iran. So clear was the air that we could see the ground below, and the occasional flickering of a fire or even a dim scatter of lights that represented a town. A town it must be, for the villages outside the Teheran ring still were unremarked by electricity. Below us, mile-upon-mile was darkness, and yet those who knew the country could tell one that life teemed down there; a life still regulated for the most part by the sun.

How true this was as the jet approached Teheran. Suddenly, out of the blackness popped light—villages on the electrical circuits around the city, few enough of those, but the brilliance of the lines, squares and crosses that represented Teheran and its streets and lighted houses and buildings. The capital stood like an oasis of brilliance in a sea of dark.

And then we were coming to the international airport, the great international airport, prepared to accomodate any craft that flies. Again anomaly. For around that airport unseen by us that night, crisscross the sheep and camel trails that lead up to the mountains, and the jet pilot flying in daytime may see a caravan as he approaches the end of his runway, a caravan as old as time can remember, camels and donkeys and men, heading into the mountains in strength, aware of the possibility of brigandage even in this day.

On the ground we were soon out of the jet and inside the air service terminal, an unlovely structure, more like a warehouse than a reception building. And there was reason for the plain ugliness. The building was a temporary terminal.

In its story lies a deep truth about the Iran of the 1970s.

A few years earlier, in the fervor of the building program, the Shah, his courtiers and planners, had decided that Teheran must have as fine an international airport as any capital in the world. And so the handsome arched-roof building that was to be the terminal was laid out on paper, and foreign architects and engineers and contractors were invited to come and bid. Italians and British and French and Americans vied for the contracts, and eventually various firms got various parts of the work, for the Shah and his minions have long played a careful game to keep the industrial powers of the world at their beck and call. And when the beautiful new terminal was built with its Persian floors and hangings and woodwork, and broad glassed expanses, it was a sight to behold.

All was well. The Shah was pleased, and that being so, as Allah willed it, all Iran might be pleased. And there is another truism of the Iran of the 1970s, Allah be blessed, but the Shah is the people's God.

All was well until the cold winter of 1973, when the snow piled up in the mountains and around the city of Teheran, taxing even the modern removal equipment bought with all those petrodollars from the Americans and the Russians and the other bidders who would do business with one of the richest countries in the world.

Then, in the aftermath of a spring storm one day, the roof of the handsome new airline terminal collapsed, killing and injuring several people. The world laughed at the foolish tribesmen of a backward country who thought they could compete with the civilized west in a 20th century that seemed to belong to Europe and America. Another example of pride and the pretense of the fakirs.

The Shah was furious. The disgraced terminal was blocked off, the substitute building pressed into service, and a long judicial investigation begun. It was ending as I arrived, and soon it was to become the scandal in Teheran for a moment in time. The investigators discovered the cause of the collapse of the building. The European contractors blamed the Iranian maintenance personnel. The Iranians blamed the Europeans; the foreigners were trying to cheat them, they claimed. And in the detail, which became apparent during my stay (and is related in context,) lies one of the great contradictions and great problems of the burgeoning Iran of the 1970s. Just how can one nation drag itself into the twentieth century in what the mathematicians of Teheran University like to regard as one gigantic exponential leap? Reduced to its essentials, the problem is that the people of Iran, the vast majority of them still illiterate, are a thousand times removed from the benign, hawklike face of the Shah, that tired aristocrat.

And yet therein is another of the anomalies of Iran. The tired aristocrat is not of the line of Cyrus and the kings of the Peacock Throne. Not at all. The dynasty he represents is scarcely half a century old and he is its second king, no more. Had history taken a slightly different turn he might be scrabbling in the dust of some village for his living, or best eking out his life as an officer in the army of another ruler.

This is all a part of what I had come to see and judge for myself, the romance and mystery of a once forbidden land now opening like a date palm blossom, nurtured by the sun of western knowledge and the liquid of oil beneath the ground.

In the temporary air terminal, I had more glimpses of the conflict between past and present. Soldiers in Iranian gray flocked in the terminal, and special police in black, and while I waited briefly in line for a check on my visa and health certificate, they dragged a young Iranian stiffkneed to a police office near the entrance to the building, and the door clanged resolutely shut. What was his crime? It was something I would never know, for the ways of the police are a secret of the realm. As I was to learn in my month's stay, the activities of the army and the various branches of the police are one of the keys to the police state that is modern Iran. And that salient fact of the monarchy must never be forgotten. The Shah does not only reign, he rules, and he rules with a tempered steel gauntlet encased in a glove of woven Iranian silk.

The terminal is brightly lit and carefully guarded by those police in black and soldiers in gray. Outside, throng the people, urchins swooping in to try to seize a bag and carry it to one of the cars that line up across the street—the taxis of Teheran come in squads to collect the steady stream of visitors that crowd the incoming airplanes of the night.

Waiting at the gate were people dimly seen, but I recognized the *chadur* of the Middle East on some of the women; others, I noticed even then, were dressed in European style, skirts and slacks, with blue jeans at a premium.

And then it was across the street and into the hands of a smiling cabman, lean, brown, mustachioed, a genial bandit who promised to take me to my hotel for 350 rials. I looked over the modern gray taxi. It looked familiar.

"Hillman." I said.

"Peykan," he said.

We were both right. I learned next day the cab was a local product manufactured now in Iran, except for one or two complex machined parts, but from designs of the Hillman company of England.

And that, too, I learned, was typical of the change. For as we left the airport in the bright lights of the superhighway, I saw Mercedes buses, Leyland lorries or trucks, and French cars and these, like toothpaste and television, are manufactured in Iran on license to foreign companies from many lands.

Coming into Teheran—more change. We passed the brightly lighted 45-meter high Shahyad tower, a tribute to the glory of the new regime and a sign of the hope for the future, for it stands above all in the area, a modernity silent as the camels and the fat-tailed sheep pass by.

At my hotel I learned I had *not* been cheated by my cab driver. The 350-rial price plus tip made the ride cost six dollars. But my cell of a hotel room was to cost $25 (£10) a day. Meals were to be commensurately expensive, and so was all else in this inflated city in this inflated land in this inflated world. And I was lucky to have a room, although I had a cabled reservation, so did others. For some reason, mine was kept while before me stood a man who was going to end up sleeping in a cot in the hotel's ballroom, and in the end, to feel fortunate to have a place at all.

Many were the surprises I met in those first hours. Next morning, I took a tour. It was Friday, the Moslem Holy Day, and there was literally nothing else to do; the business offices were closed, so was government, and the streets of the capital city in their quiet and bareness of traffic belied the presence of three million people and six hundred thousand vehicles.

The tour began with mosques, and the usual sights of beauty and history. The bus stopped and we went into a pleasant big park, almost overrun by young people, boys and girls of high school age. All of us, Germans, British, French, Americans, noted that these youngsters seemed to be dressed decently. It was a big change from a quarter century before when a visitor leaving one of the handful of modern hotels was immediately besieged by beggars. And these youngsters all seemed to be studying. They carried books and papers, and actually sat in the shade and worked!

Again the new and the old. Why were they there? we asked our guide.

Because their homes were so crowded he said. The poor people of Teheran did not have enough room for the children to have quiet for study. So they came to the parks. But they went to school!

And why study so hard?

Because the university entrance examinations would be held in a month's time, and the state universities would have places for only about 15 per cent of the hundred thousand youngsters who were expected to take the exams. The pressure was tremendous.

Our tour moved from one lovely tourist sight to another, Mosque, museum, rug factory, curio shop, and out to a village outside town where we saw youngsters swimming in a swimming hole, while their mothers and fathers washed the family rugs a few feet away. The old here, surely, and the new again as we came in the airport road and saw the Paykan auto factory with the hundreds of shiny new cars lined up.

Contrast. Contrast. Contrast.

The longer I remained in the land, the more contrasts showed. Coming up Takhte Jamshid avenue, one of the fine new boulevards of the northern end of the city, one day I turned a corner not a hundred yards from the huge compound of the American embassy, and encountered a Bactrian camel, "parked" in a narrow street, awaiting his master who was in a nearby shop. I supped in a village on mutton and saffron rice, and I ate in splendor in a restaurant of French cuisine from sparkling silver and crystal and gleaming china. I rode in a British Land Rover to a modern experimental farm to see fat-tailed sheep, and a quarter mile away passed a young shepherd riding on his donkey and guarding his flock, a routine he followed every day of his life.

I drove to the Teheran oil refinery to investigate the on-the-job training program for young engineers, and on the way passed through a village where the women were washing clothes in a filthy mountain stream. In contrast to so primitive a ritual were the television aerials on the roofs of their mud huts.

I had come to see the Shah and I never did. For I had made my arrangements and applications for an interview through the Ministry of Information and Tourism and that is not how one sees the Shah.

My friends in the Ministry offices in New York had set the ball a-rolling. The final arrangements were to be made in Teheran. But they did not tell me that on the day of my arrival, the Shah was packing up for a long state visit to several countries. They did not tell me, either, that one sees the Shah only by direct contact with the Ministry of Court. The Shah decides who shall see the Shah, and the protocol for a visit goes like this:

Contact the Iranian Embassy in Washington (or London or Paris).

The Embassy is in touch with the Foreign Ministry in Teheran.

The Foreign Minister is in touch with the Minister of Court.

The Minister of Court first investigates the petitioner, back through all the avenues, and then approaches the Shah.

The Shah decides.

And anywhere along the line the whole process can be stopped by any one of a dozen officials. Five years ago, any reasonably placed journalist or writer could get to see the Shah, but by 1975 he had become so much in demand, so frequently appearing on the world's television networks, that the private audiences became fewer and more selective every month.

And, I learned, when I got to Iran and not before, one could sit in Teheran and rot for years, petitioning and asking questions, and one would never get a firm refusal.

By that time I had my impressions. I had secured what I had come for, the proof that the revolution of Iran is indeed real and working, and that it has a very good chance of success. My course led to London. And so I went away without my audience.

Could I have had it had I persevered? I sometimes wondered.

In'sh Allah! It is up to God.

And the Shah.

2

Renaissance Man

One day early in the spring of 1975 a well-dressed young Japanese stopped his hired car at the entrance to the Imperial Palace high above the teeming streets of Teheran on the side of the mountain *massif* and explained his mission. He had an audience with Mohammed Reza Pahlavi, the Shahanshah, the King of Kings, the master of the Peacock Throne and the heir to all the grandeur that was ever Persia's.

Trim, snap-to, bright-eyed guards examined this young Japanese and checked their records, then waved him through. In a few minutes Mike Matoba, sculptor, of Atlanta, Georgia, and late of Japan, was inside the palace, bowing before his Imperial Majesty and Farah, the Shabanou (Empress). Then to work, for Sculptor Matoba had caught the attention of the Ministry of Court, and was commissioned to sculpt a life-size family group of the Shah, his four children and his wife, the empress.

The Shabanou was herself, all graciousness and interest in the art of the young man. He set up his complex camera equipment, as he was to do this job largely through photographs, in the manner he had done Henry Kissinger, that busy traveler. And that obviously is how the Shah had learned of Matoba's work; for it is well known in Palace circles that the way to introduce a new idea into Iran as well as people is through the Imperial Embassies in the power centers of the world.

Even the Shah was on his best behavior; at his most democratic. He talked pleasantly to the young man, and when Matoba had trouble with adapters for the 220-volt current to fit his 110-volt equipment, the Shah went scurrying about, helping the photographer find the proper outlets. The Shah on his knees behind a couch is not a sight given to many in the world to see.

That was the Shah of Iran, Renaissance Man, at play.

Less than a week later, the Shah, the Shabanou, the Minister of Court, the Foreign Minister, and all the courtiers needed to create and maintain regal comfort were off in two big jet planes, headed for Paris, Caracas, Mexico City, and Washington, on one of those trips of state that so please the Shah. He was celebrated and entertained and he wined and dined the powerful men he met, including President Gerald Ford, leader of one of the two most trenchant nations in the world. They treated him as equal, these presidents abroad, but, of course, he was not an equal in his own view—he was the King of Kings, the lord of all he surveyed, the purveyor and controller of oil, the master of energy, who had suddenly been brought into his glorious own.

Day-after-day the Shah was interviewed. Day-after-day his picture and that of his consort appeared on the front pages of Teheran's daily newspapers. There was nothing unusual in that fact; the Shah's picture, the Shah's statements, the Shah's movements are faithfully reported on those front pages day in and day out of every year.

And every day the Shah made his usual statements, helping to build the image of a powerful, growing nation that would soon take its place among the industrial powers of the world. He warned the westerners that they were lazy, which he was wont to do constantly.

He warned the world that oil was running out and must be conserved. He established, as he always did, the grounds for even further increases in oil prices to add to the stunning revolution the oil producing and exporting countries had levied on the world during the Palestinian troubles between Israel and her Arab neighbors. This was the Shah playing statesman, in his guise as rational man among irrationals. That role he loves to play. It is obvious that the Shah sees himself as an emerging force in the power politics of nations. All that he is doing in Iran—and much of it is directed toward the benefit of his people—points toward bringing the old land of the Persians into the end of the twentieth century, a task scheduled to be accomplished by a timetable that will do the job in a dozen years. The Shah reminds himself, his people, and the world, that Iran's huge oil reserves are not inexhaustible. In eighty years he expects them to be gone. But by that time, if he accomplishes his self-proclaimed mission, Iran will be more than self-sufficient, she will be the leader of the Middle East and an important industrial exporting center of the world.

So as the Shah made his gaudy and triumphal tour, few among the leaders he conferred with recalled that this 56-year old absolute monarch of Iran was the son of a peasant, an unruly army officer who was ill-paid and ill-treated by his masters, to the point that when Shah Mohammed Reza Pahlavi, the King of Kings was a little boy, he was often sent to bed hungry. The story of his success and that of his family is one of the glittering monuments to world change.

When the Shah came home from his travels later in the spring, he was met at the airport by a grave and worried Prime Minister, Abbas Hoveyda, his favorite courtier. Hoveyda had the unpleasant task of informing His Majesty that two U.S. Army officers had been killed that day in the streets of Teheran by young terrorists whose mission is to destroy the Shah and his government. The Shah's face turned dark. His black, close-set eyes gleamed as fiercely as those of any eagle as he listened, and his beak-like nose seemed to sharpen. And the Shah spoke then and decreed death to traitors, to the White Revolution of Iran, as he had done so many times before. Savak, the internal security force, so secret that Iranians whisper its name, was to be involuted and made to clear out the dissidents who would destroy the government of the Shah. There in those moments was the third side of Renaissance Man, the cruel despot protecting his own with any means at any cost, the absolute monarch showing his power.

That power has been developed by the Shah himself, and whatever the world thinks of absolute monarchy or despotism, it would be unwise to denigrate this canny and lucky ruler of Iran who has literally brought himself and his nation up by bootstrap since the years of the Second World War when Persia, now Iran, was occupied by British and Russian troops. The Shah has already come a long way. Renaissance Man may go further in the Twentieth Century.

3

Plan for Revolution

Westerners who see Shah Mohammed Reza Pahlavi of Iran disporting himself slickly on the Swiss ski slopes, or paddling about with his family in the warm waters of the Caspian sea have the idea that this monarch of all the Persians is an aging spoiled ruler worthy more of contempt than admiration.

They are making a grave mistake.

For to understand Shah Mohammed and his people, one must understand what went before, not in the ancient times of Cyrus and Darius that the Shah likes to invoke, but in the days of his father, the usurper of the throne of Persia, who established the dynasty by overthrowing the old Shah.

What the Shahanshah does today, from nationalizing resources to raising the prices of oil, is precisely what he was trained to do by his father; and were old Reza Shah still in the saddle the same results would be obtained, minus the finesse that this highly educated "ruling machine" is exerting in world affairs.

When Shah Reza took power he set out to reform the government itself, to end corruption, to make sure that tax moneys got into the treasury. He promised that he would end foreign domination of Iran. He promised to make Iran an industrial nation. He promised to educate the children. He promised to bring about huge social reforms that would make his people second to none in the world. He was, in other words, beginning a Renaissance in the grand manner, to return Persia to the position of leadership in the affairs of the world that it had not enjoyed since before the days of Alexander.

For three or four years, Shah Reza planned, and put his ideas into effect. The British military left Iran. The Russian military was forced out and the number of concessions to the Russians sharply reduced. A year later Iran obtained control of its own customs duties for the first time in years, and began making treaties with other nations to cover trade relations.

By this time the Shah was not only proclaimed, he was crowned, and he took over the absolute rule of the country. To be sure, Iran retained its Majlis (Parliament) and its constitution, but the Shah was none the less an absolute ruler, observing the forms because he truly did want to bring about reform. The problem was that he did not trust anyone else to do it, and if the Majlis would not do his bidding, in effect he ruled by decree.

One by one, Shah Reza brought the warring tribes under control. His favorite method was to send a force to seize the leader of a tribe, spirit him off to Teheran, and by holding him, unharmed, as hostage, to bring about the capitulation of the tribal head's people and put them under control of the central government.

If there was one field in which the new Shah was an acknowledged expert, it was the military. And before anything could be done, the military force had to be perfected, and established as totally loyal to the central government. In the 1970s, half the world wondered why Shah Mohammed Reza Pahlavi spent so much of his country's income and so much of his effort in creating the strongest military and naval force in the Middle East. Part of the reason, at least, is the inheritance from his father. It hasn't been long, for example, since the Kurds of the southwest were in open rebellion against Iran as well as Iraq. And Azerbaijan, to the northwest, was pacified long ago, and yet any Azerbaijani under consideration for an important government post underwent the most searching examination by the political police and authorities, before he was completely trusted.

"If only I had a thousand rifles of the same calibre,"* said the Shah one day as he reviewed his Cossacks early in the game and saw his guards in motion.

As the Crown Prince grew older under his father's reign, the boy had learned of the needs. From age ten he was in military school and learning about rifles made him understand what they might accomplish. Soon Iran had five army divisions plus a highway patrol to protect travelers from brigands, and a small navy and an air force. The Shah established officers' training schools in Teheran, and turned to the French, who did not threaten him, to permit him to send his military students to Paris for advanced training. Having eliminated the British, and the Russians, he employed French military advisors, and France soon became the European "friend" and primary influence in Iran, second only by Germany. Iranians began learning foreign languages. In the time of Shah Reza, French was the second language of educated Persians and many of them also spoke German. The German influence began later than the French, but it grew fast. (In the 1970's it is growing once more.)

So the foreigners by 1930 had been brought largely under control, and the Shah had his way in ending all signs of extraterritoriality. He was slower to pacify the tribes and unite the country. The task was almost superhuman, for Iran had virtually no transportation facilities when Shah Reza came to power. Wheeled transportation by cart could follow only the three major roads of the country. All other movement in the 1920's was by pack animals. As for construction, one can still see evidence of the primitive way

*Mission for My Country, p. 40

homes were built outside the big cities of Iran. The people used unfired mud bricks to construct the village huts with beams laid across to support mud-straw roofs. As it seldom rains in the desert and mountain country, these structures served, except that a real downpour could wipe out within minutes (and sometimes did) the living places of an entire village.

Change depended on communications and transportation, and to that end the Shah began a railroad and roadbuilding program that progressed as quickly as money and suppression of the tribes allowed. He planned a trans-Iranian railway and set to work on it. In a few years he built 17,000 miles of roads and 1700 miles of railroad.

The old Shah tried as best he could to finance his expansion at home. He wanted no more foreign influence, of that he was certain. The Germans were given the privilege of organizing a national bank but when they did not come up to the Shah's expectations he turned them out and put in knowledgeable Iranians. An American financial mission was sought to aid the country, a popular move in the 1920's when the U.S. was both determinedly neutral and growing rich, but when the Americans tried to direct the Shah too closely, he ousted them, too.

The Shah, let no one forget, was the ShahanShah—king of kings.

The best of all possible worlds would have called for Iranians to hold all the important posts, but the trouble with that in the 1920's and 1930's was that not enough Iranians could cope with modern ideas. For many hundreds of years the Mullahs had been in charge of a Koranic education system in Iran. Gradually, in the cities and larger towns, the Mullahs had been displaced, and the mosque schools gave way to institutions run by professional teachers. When Shah Reza came to power there was only one teacher's college in all Iran, and he soon set about remedying that deficiency. But what a task. First, he had to find teachers and get text books printed.

Each aspect of life in Persia posed the same voluminous problems, for one does not take a country out of the 14th century and move it to the 20th in a few years without facing a few odd tasks, here and there. A man better educated or less determined than Shah Reza could well have thrown up his hands in despair from the beginning.

Nor could the Shah have accomplished his aims alone. Such is the obsequiousness of Iranian society (and has been for thousands of years) that the Shah takes and gets surface credit for any and all progress of the country.

I saw this attitude in action on my last visit. I was interviewing an important woman member of the Shah's government, when she dropped the name of the royal family in such a manner that I knew she was an intimate.

Yes, she had gone to school with the Shah's sisters, she said. Yes, she knew the royal family very well. I was about to ask her more detailed questions about the life of the family and interrelationships when we were interrupted. Later I tried to pursue this line of questioning at a luncheon party whereupon my lady acquaintance raised her voice loudly, in a totally different and apparently artificial manner, and began singing the Shah's praises, very loudly.

It could be said she was afraid of being overheard, but the answer is not satisfactory. She could have ignored my question. She could have gone silent, on that subject. Instead she chose to grovel beneath the name of the Shah.

Yet as I sensed, there is no reality in such grovelling. The people at high levels pay lip service to the Shah's image.

It was essential that Reza convince the people and the landowners that he *was* the Shah. That could not be done by coronation alone, not among a people as wordly wise and infinitely cynical as the Persian nobility. First, he had to create personal power. He did this over a period of time by taking as his personal land most of the province of Mazanderan. This accomplished two purposes: it made him wealthy beyond normal avarice; it lulled the landowners into believing that the Shah was sympathetic to them. The avarice was perhaps understandable in the life of a man who had been a poor soldier since his teens. But there was never any question about the rest in the minds of serious observers. Indeed, Richard Frye, an historian of Persia who spent many years there, has compared Reza to Russia's Peter the Great. No one in history made a greater impact on his country than Reza Shah did on Persia in those years between the 1920s and the coming of World War II.

The Shah's advisors certainly led in much of this development, although this Shah gave precious little credit to any who served him. There were three aides of utmost importance, they stood out above others like the mountains rising out of the desert plain. One was Firuz Mirza, a Majlis deputy who had supported Reza during the days when he was war minister. He was minister of justice, and responsible for much of the codification of the system, following the French. He was minister of finance, and as such helped push out the foreign influences and replace them with Iranian power. He became too powerful to suit the Shah. He was arrested in 1929, and that was the end of him as a force in Iran. He was accused of bribery, a most unlikely charge given his character, and was murdered by the Shah's agents.

The second minister of note was Abdul Hoseyn Timurtash, who held the delicate position of Minister of Court.

Minister of Court in the Iranian government was a combination of slave, personal secretary, and court chamberlain all rolled into one. He was a brilliant man, with a knowledge of modern society the Shah would never achieve; a totally civilized person able to lead his master on a course that would serve the country. But those near the Shah began to distrust and fear Timurtash. He was primarily a civil servant. The army did not approve of him, and the secret police, who came more and more into prominence in the 1930s, did not like him either.

He was suspect because he admired foreigners, particularly westerners, and he told the Shah they had much to offer. Since the Shah's anti-foreign feelings were always just beneath the surface, such assertions were easy to misunderstand, and they were. The Shah was particularly furious about articles that appeared in the foreign press.

Unable to read any foreign language, and completely unversed in the study of other societies, the Shah had no yardstick by which to measure the kind of freedom and criticism that appeared in newspapers from Western Europe and America. There could be, in his opinion, no criticism of the Shah or the court. When it appeared, Timurtash took the lash for it, and as time went on, and the Shah became ever more suspicious of the one man who was supposed to be trustworthy and aware of all affairs within the Imperial Household. Timurtash fell from grace and one day the Shah raised his hand and Timurtash was arrested. Soon he, too, was murdered by those who said they would serve the Shah.

Last of the three servants was Ali Akbar Davar, who worked faithfully as minister of Agriculture, then as minister of Commerce and Minister of Public Works. Finally, he served his Shah as Minister of Finance until 1936 when one day he committed suicide. Teheran erupted with charges that he had killed himself one step ahead of the Secret Police. With his death came a sudden change in policy in Iran.

The Shah had set in motion all these wheels of progress, but in the middle 1930s the Shah began to change. He was a big broad man for a Persian, and he had affected a simple military uniform of brown blouse and blue riding breeches, a few simple decorations he had won as a soldier, high boots and a curved sword. He had that eagle beak of the Pahlavis, the deep set eyes of the family too, and the tight mouth of the man of action. He appeared, at least to a German minister who saw him in 1931, as a strong and forceful figure.

But not so in 1936, the year in which many political murders were committed with the Shah's connivance if not on his orders, they said in the bazaar at Teheran. The German who had been so impressed earlier was already gone. He had left the year before convinced that the Shah he saw at the end was an opium addict with very little life left to run. The Shah now affected a clay-colored uniform modelled on the Russian, his hair had gone white, his face had shrunk and he seemed physically weak where he had been strong. He was no longer the eagle leader of his people.

He had become grasping beyond belief. He kept seizing more material goods, more land for himself. He snarled at those about him, and worried about assassination and the continuation of the "dynasty" he had founded a dozen years earlier.

And yet the revolution that he had begun would not evaporate, even when he had apparently lost interest in it. It sat there, largely quiescent in the last days as corruption took over. The cities grew and prospered; the rich became richer than ever. The Shah was committed to the change and much of it continued after he had lost the old drive.

But other forces were at work as well.

4
End of an Era

The old Shah, Reza, the King of Kings, looked about him like a sick eagle in the last days of the 1930's, and surveyed suspiciously all those around him. It was said on the streets that he was totally under the influence of his secret police, and his sympathies for things German, and even Nazi, were the talk of the bazaar. The others—the Russian and British diplomats who had been so influential in the days of the Qajars—aroused nothing but contempt and anger in the breast of the Shah of Shahs.

For ten years, Reza and his ministers had struggled to gain more control of the country's resources, and to trade concessions for the tools of self-improvement. Many a selfless minister has gone to his grave, his accomplishments unsung, because of the ruler's "I-Am-The-Shah-And-All-I-Survey-Is-Mine" attitude toward the world. And, of course, there was indeed some validity in the claim that the ruler's hand was behind every measure. No minister was permitted to become so important as to endanger the Shah's position, no matter how loyal he was. Having come to power by ruthless suppression and coup himself, the Shah knew how to protect himself. It seems certain that this aspect of rule was very much on his mind late in the 1930's, for as the years wore on, the reforms lost much of their impetus.

The Shah must be given credit, however, for laying the groundwork for great changes in his country. The Trans-Iranian railroad was completed, running from the Caspian to the Persian Gulf, and Iran became a nation of the wheel, at least in part, rather than one dependent on pack animals alone.

The schools began to multiply, not quickly, for Iran was too poor a country for that, but they grew. Before Shah Reza, there were virtually no educational institutions. He built an agricultural college in the town of Karaj, some 30 miles outside Teheran. The agricultural college began to experiment with seeds and feeds, and with sheep and other animals. What had been for hundreds of years a traditional society, quickly showed some aspects of becoming modern and scientific.

Shah Reza was particularly hardheaded in forcing his country away from feudalism, but he had no intention of creating a "democratic society" along western lines. He had toyed with the idea, attracted by what Ataturk was doing not far away in Turkey, but he had realized as Minister of War that Iran was not going to be susceptible to democratic rule. Virtually none of the people could read or write. Without education and nothing but the ancient culture of tradition, what strength had they to support a democratic society with its reliance on the true will of the mass of people? Shah Reza was not sure democracy was a good idea anyhow; and at the stage of development of Iran in the 1920's he knew it could not work. All this was part of his rationale in seizing power from the ruling line of Shahs. It also served him equally well in his suppression of opposition to his own rule. There was nothing new in the despotism of Shah Reza, except perhaps that it was more vigorous and effective than Iranian despotism of the few hundreds of years just past.

Being ShahanShah, ruler of rulers, he could establish a losing industry and keep it going on the principle that eventually it would become profitable. He did that. And he did what every despot has always done, take the money from the poor and build imposing monuments to the power of the central government. In the case of Iran the monuments were big buildings, Ministry of War, National Bank, Ministry of Justice, Ministry of Finance, and Teheran began to spread northward from the ancient city centered around the bazaar down on the plain below the mountain.

In twenty years the Shah brought remarkable changes to his capital, if not so many to his country. Comparing him to rulers of the past, this was not odious. Most of the old Iranian kings had first attended themselves to the needs of their capital city, and then looked to the problems of the countryside. The Shah *intended* to better the lives of his people but he was shrewd enough to know how much groundwork must be laid before it could be done. In the meantime, he could make a show of policy and intent in the capital.

For example, one had to have education—difficult when Persian is not a common language in the world, and when less than half the people under the Shah's rule used Persian as a primary language. The others were fragmented into tribes and used the dialects of the regions. The Shah encouraged first the building of teachers colleges, and in twenty years built 35 of them. In 1935, the cornerstone of Teheran university was laid; a university founded on the French system, with the faculty of law (political science) the most popular. The Shah wanted medicine and engineering to be emphasized, but the sons of the wealthy wanted law, thus they could find their way into government employment. And then, as in the past, the Iranians showed one Oriental characteristic that would prove most difficult for either the old Shah Reza, or the new Shah to come, to eradicate: the educated Oriental did not soil his hands, thus an engineer would work with pencil and slide rule, but getting him to the field to supervise construction was something else again.

Change, in other words was not easy to accomplish in an ancient country with equally ancient traditions. The Shah brought agricultural reforms to his own farms, but the villagers objected to his orders that they work twelve months of the year. They were used to working spring, summer and fall, and starving through the winter. It took nearly superhuman effort to get them to change.

Because of this Shah's fear of the infiltration of communism from the northern provinces so close to Soviet Russia, he outlawed all political parties early in his rule. That did not prevent the Communists from operating sub rosa. It did make them fair game for the political police, who were vigilant and brutal, again in the tradition of the land and people. The Shah was quite capable of enforcing his laws and rules with his own hands, too.

By the middle 1930's, control of the palace over Iranian life in the cities and towns was nearly absolute. In the Majlis, the political processes were scarcely more than pretexts, and most members of this body were (1) residents of Teheran no matter what section they represented, and (2) elected without opposition. The Majlis did pass laws, laws dictated by the Shah and his minions. Yet the Majlis did serve one useful purpose. Theirs was the closest thing to a legislative body that Iran might have, and, in an odd way, it could be said that the representatives sometimes listened to the people and considered their plight. That was important, for the Shah's considerations were far more grandiose. He was determined to bring Iran up, but he gave very little consideration to the will or the legitimate immediate aspirations of the people. Most historians of modern Iran hold that the people were certainly no better off, at least hose in the countryside, than they had been under the Qajar kings.

Certainly there was no freedom of press or speech or action. The poor peasants who flocked to the towns and cities to seek some kind of livelihood found themselves near starving, and with no recourse. The students at the schools and universities, educated in the European tradition of university dissent, found no place to air their feelings. At one election a group of students was rounded up and sent together to a polling place to vote. At the station they were handed folded ballots and told to drop them in the ballot box.

One student began unfolding his ballot to take a look at it. He was restrained by a policeman.

He looked up, puzzled.

"Don't you understand," said the policeman, folding the ballot up firmly again, "that these are secret ballots?"

But if the political process was under control, through the Majlis, the Shah's courts, and the secret police, not so much could be said of the religious problem in the country. In a way, the religious leaders comprised the single effective voice of opposition to Shah Reza, not a liberal opposition, but quite the reverse.

The mullahs (teachers and interpeters of religious laws) were the most important element in all Islamic societies from the days of Mohammed. So powerful were they in the middle period that they stifled the growth of science and modern technology in all Islam for five hundred years. In the manner that the church of the Christians opposed dissection of human bodies (and thus the study of anatomy), so did the churchmen of Islam. But they were powerful even beyond the others, and this situation remained in effect until Shah Reza came to power. The other Shahs had quarreled with the holy men, but had never breached the old religious traditions.

But the ferment caused by the war that destroyed the Ottoman empire spread into Iran, and the Shah's decision to modernize army and country was supported by the military and the intellectual elite of the country. It was said that the Shah paid lip service to the clergy by declaring himself Shah instead of "President" of a government that would have the outward form of a Republic. Probably this overstates the case.

In any event, having achieved supreme power, the Shah used it to diminish the power of the clergy.

One would not think that so far removed a matter as reorganization of the judicial system would affect the church, but under the Qajar dynasty, the church had effective control of the courts. The law was the law as interpreted through Islam. When Shah Reza's Minister Davar brought in a system modeled on the French, the mullahs realized that the Shah was declaring war on them.

One of his early acts was to force all who would wear religious robes to show their proficiency in the study of Islam by passing examinations. No longer could personal favor control the matters of the Islamic religion. The long robe and the turban were proscribed only for the real students and authorities of the religion. The establishment of teaching hospitals and universities also struck at the power of the clergy, so did the establishment of schools in the cities and towns, as noted.

But that was only beginning. The Shah elevated Zoroastrianism, a native Iranian religion, and this infuriated the mullahs, but it also cut into their power. He began taking away some of the land of the clergy, and taxing other. He forbade the passion plays that had been held in the month of Muharram, plays in which the participants and audience both worked themselves into frenzy, plays that sealed power for the mullahs as much as any Easter service did for Christians.

Again that was not enough. He began a process that mullahs considered desecration of all Islam. He ordered them to allow non-Moslem foreigners to enter the mosques. He ordered the dervishes, or holy men, driven from the cities.

He instituted a Pahlavi cap—a sign of acceptance of western ways—and his followers adopted this headdress (much as Nehru's followers would adopt the Nehru cap in a modernizing India later). This, too, was an affront to the religious people, but not nearly so grave as putting students, boys and girls, into uniforms. Thus the girls were taken out of the veils Moslem women had worn for hundreds of years. And once the girls were out, in 1936 the Shah forbade all women to wear the veil. For the first time in their lives, some women went freely on the streets of Teheran and Isfahan.

These reforms of the old ways were brutal and punitive against the mullahs, and they responded by rousing their followers to heights of religious anger that often erupted in riots. The police and the soldiers came then, and were even more brutal, with clubs and swords, than the Shah had been with decrees.

One day on a visit to the Moslem shrine at Qum, Shah Reza

showed his contempt for the mullahs by entering with his boots on.

The Shah had the religious leader, who had criticised the Shabanou for taking off her veil as ordered by her husband, brought before him and personally flogged him.

On another occasion, when the mullahs had roused up a crowd of excited Moslems, the Shah's soldiers turned machine guns on them.

This use of naked force accomplished its aims, on the surface, but it left deep scars in Iranian society, and determination by the forces of Islam that they would not be put down. They apparently acceded to the Shah's strictures, but secretly they were active in cells and groups, opposing him in every possible way.

In this way and in one other way, the Shah Reza sowed seeds of destruction in his land, even as he spent and built and planned for a modern Iran.

The other way was his misreading of the future in foreign affairs.

Adolf Hitler was apparently a man who appealed greatly to Shah Reza. And why not? The Shah had no background in the liberties so prized in the western world, and when Hitler destroyed those liberties in Germany the Shah was not shocked. What attracted Reza was the effective use of naked power to bring Germany from a situation of virtual prostration to a growing prosperity and importance in world affairs in a matter of months. To a Shah so cognizant of the problems of power and the management of consent, this was a real accomplishment.

After Hitler's emergence, the Germans began to prosper in Iran. By the middle of the 1930's, the flow of German advisors and German specialists into Iran was so great as to arouse concern among both Russians and British, who regarded their struggle for suzerainty over Iran as a private affair. The Russians held their eye on Azerbaijan, and their fingers in the Caspian, where they and the Iranians fished together for sturgeon. The British interest was south, Abadan, where they maintained their oil refinery of the Anglo-Iranian Oil Company. But to have those Germans crowding in with trade and all the old appurtenances of peaceful infilltration was too much for the Russians and the British. By 1938, the Russians were making a formal diplomatic protest against the German economic penetration of Iran.

The Shah growled and went about his ways as he would. Shah Reza was never a man to be told what to do, and particularly not by the foreigners he detested because of their power over his economic resources. Since 1933 he had been in constant quarrel with Anglo-Iranian oil about the amount of money he received for the looting of the Iranian land's greatest natural resource. After all, except for oil, the land's only major exports were caviar and rugs. Some foodstuffs came out of Iran but not enough to create a major factor in the economy. And of his three export resources the foreigners controlled two. The Shah was ever conscious of it, and ever angry about it.

And as for Germany, the infiltration continued, in a steady stream of technicians and teachers who came to establish language schools and teach in the Iranian state schools. By 1940 the British, too, were aroused, for now war had broken out and the Shah was in effect trading with Britain's enemies. London worried ceaselessly over the future of Anglo-Iranian oil, and the lifeline at Abadan. The fleet would be in sore trouble if German saboteurs managed to destroy or cripple the refinery.

The Shah's attitude did not settle any stomachs in Whitehall—by 1940, the figures showed that half of Iran's trade was with Germany. Junkers was running an airline into Teheran. The Anglo-German cultural association was pouring forth propaganda to bring Iran into open opposition against the allies. The situation went from impossible to intolerable as German influence increased and the Shah paid no attention to the complaints of the Russian and British envoys to his country.

Then Hitler invaded Russia!

lashad gives one an idea of the old in Iran.

akil Mosque at Shiraz—reminders of the past.

A silken Persian carpet—it might take five years to make.

They still make the pottery in the old ways.

Ͻne does not think of the Persians as steel producers—bul here thoy are. . . .

ıe Shah is bringing modern ways, and modern bridges.

Teheran refinery in 1975.

Aali Qapu—one of Isfahan's great palaces.

5
Abdication

A quick look at any map of the Middle East shows what must have gone through British and Russian minds at the moment Adolf Hitler sent his *wehrmacht* charging across the Soviet Union's western borders. Could Hitler but make use of Iran in any way, he could create havoc and confusion that might affect the outcome of the war.

In the summer of 1941, Teheran was abuzz with rumors, and the Germans were as busy as anyone manufacturing tales of woe bound to drive further wedges between the Shah and his old antagonists, Russia and England.

The Germans were, in fact, planning to drive through the Caucasus to Iran so as to make use of that oil of the Persian Gulf for their war machine. These were, of course, the days of victory. Hitler had seen the war going his own way for so long that he had mesmerized himself into believing the conquest of the Soviet Union would go as had the victory over France.

Because the Germans were victimized by their own propaganda, they failed to make use of the time they had. Those teachers in Iran, or some of them, had other objectives in view as well. Yet there was no sabotage, as the Russians and British feared, and Shah Mohammed Reza later attributed this to the Nazi blindness about the course of future events.

Hitler's invasion of Russia came on June 22. The Russian interest in Iranian affairs increased immediately; the Russian ambassador called on the foreign secretary and announced that the Germans were planning a *coup d'etat,* to seize power for a thoughly pro-Nazi group of Iranians. He demanded, as had the British, that the German nationals in Iran be arrested and jailed or deported immediately.

The Shah would not listen. He was determined to maintain his independence and authority. For nearly twenty years he had done so successfully. Now, he misread the nature of the crisis and the determination of Great Britain and the USSR in these desperate weeks.

British and Russian diplomats in Teheran conferred, and agreed that the danger was worsening by the day. Russia's stake in the Abadan refinery and the oil fields was obvious; the Nazis must not get that oil for their tanks. On July 19 the two legations delivered a joint note of protest against the Shah's failure to act.

The Shah continued to be aloof.

On August 16, the Shah had still not taken action, except to step up the mobilization of his forces and stop leaves for the troops.

The British had the definite feeling that the Shah was temporizing, and this worried them. What for? The only conclusion they could reach was that his sympathies were with Hitler. Otherwise why would the Shah not recognize the urgency of the problem?

There was a reason. Shah Reza did not receive these envoys personally, but left diplomacy in the hands of his cabinet. His cabinet, understanding the Shah's megalomania and zenophobia, was afraid, to a man, to tell the Shah the truth.

The crisis deepened as the days went by.

The Shah left Teheran for a trip to Aqdassieh, the summer camp of the Iranian Military Academy, to attend to a favorite chore. Personally he would commission the senior class cadets on their graduation as sub-lieutenants in the Iranian Army. Shah Reza knew how to secure the loyalty of his officers from the start.

Two days later, August 21, the Shah held a formal reception at the Gulistan palace on the occasion of the anniversary of the Revelation of the Word to the Prophet Mohammed. The tension was electric in the foreign quarter of Teheran, but the Shah seemed unmindful of it all.

On August 25 the allies acted. Soviet and British envoys delivered notes saying they were forced to take strong measures. Already their troops were marching, and as the notes were delivered Teheran Radio was broadcasting the news that both Soviet and British troops had crossed the frontiers.

The Shah was astounded and distressed. Only now he was ready to talk to the envoys of the big powers, and he told them he would comply with the demands made in the previous notes. But it was too late. Already the Russians were engaging Iranian gunboats in the Caspian. Already the town of Khoramshar had been occupied. Russian planes were bombarding Teheran with leaflets telling the people to remain calm.

In the south, the British moved with equal speed. They sent a parachutist battalion into the oil fields to protect the installations from sabotage. They began a frontal advance in the west.

General Hasan Arfa, who had been charged with the defense of the Teheran area, proposed to the Shah that he undertake a scorched earth policy. If the allies came by force, let the Iranians destroy everything. But the Shah, wise at last, rejected the policy as destructive to Iran more than to the allies. Whatever else he might be, Shah Reza was first and always the leader of his country.

The Russians continued their advance, occupying the northern part of the country, still against Iranian resistance. But in a day or two the Shah stopped the fighting, again as destructive and useless, and granted the Allies the terms they wanted in armistice rather than see his government fall and his country destroyed by such superior force.

Prime Minister Ali Mansur resigned. He had been unacceptable to the allies who suspected his personal loyalties. And with that resignation and other changes in the cabinet, came disruption of the order the Shah had maintained by his personal power. General Ahmad Nakhchevan became the new minister of war. To placate the allies, he dissolved the regular army and sent the conscripts back to their villages. He was in effect taking into his hands the same power the Shah had seized two decades earlier when he became war minister for another Shah.

Here was the first sign of internal crisis. This Shah who had ruled with an iron hand for fifteen years was under challenge in the traditional Iranian manner. Shah Reza acted swiftly. He ordered General Nakhchevan to be arrested at once, and jailed in the most secure prison in Teheran. He put out the order that the recruits and soldiers were to be sent back to the training centers.

In the tribal areas, particularly Kurdistan and Kermanshah, the recruits abandoned arms that were gratefully seized by rebellious tribesmen. Now they had the wherewithal to create a whole new set of troubles for the central government. In the confusion that set in with the occupation of the country, the tribes began to act. From another front the rule of Shah Reza was thus threatened.

The Shah was under attack from half a dozen quarters. All his repressions of the past years were now creating repercussions. The failure of his foreign policy brought swift disaster in domestic affairs. The one-man rule was falling apart.

He declared martial law in Teheran, and he reassumed personal control of the army that was his major instrument of policy. Shah Reza called Mohammed Ali Forughi, his new prime minister, and ordered him to get statements from every member of the Majlis, denying that the Shah was a dictator of his government. He also directed that the Majlis must declare its loyalty to him once again.

But the Shah's rule had broken down. Many members of the

Majlis refused to sign the ridiculous assestions, and they told Forughi they would sign nothing. The Shah talked of "democracy" in Iran, they said, and there was no democracy at all.

In other times, Shah Reza would have dissolved the Majlis, or thrown the dissident deputies into prison. But outside pressures were descending on him.

The British and the Russians were much concerned over the breakdown of civil government in Iran, and not pleased with the martial law of Teheran. In accordance with their demands, the Shah had rounded up the Germans in the countryside, about five hundred in all. They were confined to the summer residence of the German Embassy in Shimran, put up in temporary camps erected there. Many of these Germans had devoted their lives to Iran, and felt as much or more at home here than in the Reich. Others objected to confinement. So a number of the Germans melted into the countryside. When the allies heard of the escapes, they said again that order was breaking down, and prepared to move on Teheran for a total occupation of the country.

The handwriting was there. For a month the Shah had maintained a facade of power, but each day the strength of his government eroded. His only resource by this time was the unquestioned loyalty of the army, but if the foreigners took over Teheran, then the army must either fight to exhaustion, or the army power was meaningless.

Wearily, the Shah sent the Imperial family down to the palace at Isfahan. There was one exception. He called for his oldest son, Mohammed Reza, the crown prince, and informed him that the time had come for the Crown Prince to take power.

The old hawk eye glittered as the Light of Lights spoke to his son. He detailed the events of the past month. He spoke bitterly of the refusal of the allies to deal honestly with him. He had asked, he said, that Churchill and Stalin give him their *real* plans and their *real* desires. Instead, he had been given a mixture of gibberish about a handful of German missionaries and teachers and businessmen in the country.

For years he had been planning for the day that the Crown Prince would assume the throne. They were not close, this father and son, but once or twice the Shah had spoken to the young man about the prospects of the future.

Now he spoke quickly and frankly. He could not remain as ruler of an occupied country. His policies were not acceptable to the allies, and thus he must go. The policies must be changed, but the young Crown Prince must also find his own way.

After this talk, the Shah announced his abdication, confirmed it to the ministers, and moved outside the palace to get into his Rolls Royce for the drive to Isfahan, and the long, cruel wait to see what the powerful allies would dictate for his future. It was his intention to go to South America to live out his life in the western hemisphere, far from the memories of the past.

And at 11 o'clock that morning, the major officials of the government were assembled at the hall of the Majlis, along with the generals of the army and the legislators. The legislative hall was a blaze of uniforms and formal morning dress, medals and sashes.

Outside, the troops of a guard company waited with their military band, and when the limousine and escort of the Crown Prince came in sight, the band struck up the Iranian national anthem.

Having learned from his father the sources of power, the Crown Prince was wearing an army parade uniform with medals, and he strode with dignity beyond his twenty-one years up the steps of the legislature, passing the assembled generals and civilians, looking neither to right nor left.

He marched to the rostrum of the Majlis, as provided in the constitution and laws of Iran, and he put his hand on the sacred Koran as he swore to uphold the constitution and be the rightful monarchy of his country.

And a new Shah had come to Iran, Shah Mohammed Reza Pahlavi, second in the dynasty of the Pahlavis, and now the new King of Kings, Light of Lights, and emperor of all he surveyed.

6

Shahan Shah

From the moment that Shah Mohmmed Reza Pahlavi took official position in the ceremony at the Majlis, he was pressed to a policy of survival for Persia, one his father would never have been able to stomach. Within a matter of hours, the British and the Russians would be entering Teheran. They had taken over his country, and whether or not he would get it back remained to be seen in his attitude toward these victors of the moment.

And who was this Shah who had suddenly emerged into the limelight in a matter of hours? What was his training, and what were his ideas about government and the future of his people? Was he equipped to rule with wisdom and skill so as to reduce the frictions with the occupying forces and wait for the great chance that would somehow enable him to liberate his people from foreign dominence once again?

One thing was known. He had not been born to the silver spoon, and if he could not remember the poverty of his babyhood his elder sisters could. But that was behind, for in a matter of days, his father the abdicated Shah, would be aboard a British warship, heading for a carefully controlled exile, first in Mauritius, and then in South Africa. All the thousands of hectares of farms, all the palaces in the cities of Iran, the crown jewels, all he surveyed, in fact, now belonged to this 21-year-old ruler who mounted the Peacock Throne.

From the age of six, the boy had been subjected to the strictures of royalty, for that was his age when he was made crown prince and heir apparent on the day of his father's seizure of the Peacock Throne.

Until now, the boy had lived a family life in a small brick house in one of the old districts of Teheran. With his new status came new responsibility, and the immediate sign of it was the wrenching away of the six-year-old from the bosom of the family. The Shah had two wives, and before he became Shah they had borne him several children. Half brothers and sisters were all living together in one house. But an heir apparent must have special training, and it began.

It is not often that a six-year-old has a school established just for him, but this was the case with Crown Prince Mohammed Reza. His father insisted that the boy be given a military education. A school was created, and once it was established it was populated by the Crown Prince, four brothers and half brothers, and the carefully chosen sons of favored officers and civilian officials of the Shah's government.

The Prince was a small, dark, sensitive and moody boy, not considered very strong by his brothers and sisters. It was his father's dictum that the boy be given a man's education, and made strong for the trials that would lie ahead for him. The Silver Lion of Iran must be stronger than any other man in the kingdom. Arrogance, selfishness, wastefulness, harshness—these were nothing in the life of a king. Strength to the Shah Reza was everything.

Shah Reza was a wiser man than many believed him to be. Anyone who knew the Shah could have predicted that the Crown Prince would have a military education. But not all could predict that he would also be given a civilizing influence in high degree. The Shah decreed that the boy should have a governess to take charge of him at home and that the governess would be French.

It might have been German. It might have been English and, given the Shah's background, possibly Russian. But not really. The Shah's antipathy to the invaders of his country was such that inevitably he would turn to the French, people with a long cultural background, but no apparent designs on Iranian integrity.

Prince Mohammed Reza was an active child, but sickly. Soon after being named Crown Prince he came down with typhoid fever, a common enough illness in a land where the storm sewers run on top of the land. He also contracted whooping cough, diphtheria, and several other childhood diseases and then malaria, the most serious of all. He fell from the back of a horse and was nearly killed. Yet, he survived all these misfortunes. But they did leave him with a residue: he had visions of Islamic saints and holy men during this period. He spoke tentatively about them, and his father, totally irreligious, scoffed so loudly that the Crown Prince had sense enough to keep his visions to himself. But his feeling for the religion of his people, come upon him at so early an age, was to prove an important factor in the future of Islam in Iran.

The prince was an apt student of the foreign ways to which he was exposed. He was good at languages, and took easily to French. Soon he was absorbing French culture at a rapid rate, learning of art and literature, and above all, of cuisine. The old Shah Reza cared nothing for such. He slept on a mattress on the floor of his room in the palace and never would use a bedstead for he believed in being hard and tough. He ate sparingly, tea for breakfast, seldom with fruit or any other food; boiled chicken and rice for the big midday meal, and more rice and meat or chicken for the evening meal. He had neither appetite nor small talk, nor much interest in matters cultural. Rule, and military force were the matters of importance to him, Let his women and children adopt the living styles of the high caste Persians in the capital.

But the luxury around him began to affect the boy prince early.

For he lived in one palace in Teheran in the winter and in another palace at Shimran in the hills above the capital in the summer. He had beautiful horses, and riding instructors, and later polo ponies. Any pursuit was granted him by his father if it involved exercise. He learned wrestling and boxing, all from experts who made sure that their young charge gained both proficiency and confidence. He lived, in short, the life of a prince in an absolute monarchy.

The father was absolute in his training of the son for the post at hand. The Shah made it a practice of spending an hour a day with the boy when official duties permitted. The purpose was to instruct the Crown Prince in the programs the Shah was bringing to the country. For a simple soldier, Shah Reza had a stronger sense of dynasty than his predecessors of the Qajar kingdom. If he wanted his policies to be followed in the future, the time to lay the groundwork was with the child, and that is what he did.

The burden of these meetings, and later of almost daily luncheons with the Shah was not personal father and son talk, but the business of the realm. And while the boy was to be educated as broadly as possible, the Shah made sure that Crown Prince Mohammed Reza learned his Persian history, and the culture of his people, and became proficient in the reading and writing of his own language as well as those of the foreigners.

The boy responded and gained a sense of destiny. "From the time I was six or seven," he wrote in his autobiography, "I have felt that perhaps there is a supreme being who is guiding me . . ."

In 1931 the Crown Prince at 15 completed study at the elementary school in the palace. He had a good command of French, the language of culture and diplomacy. English was to be his next linguistic conquest, even though French dominated the Arab world of those days. The Shah was bent on westernizing Iran, and he wanted his son to lead the van by having the finest of western educations. He considered long and hard, and eventually he opted to send the Crown Prince to Switzerland, where there were no political implications.

So the Crown Prince went there along with his brother, Prince Ali Reza. Two other boys went with them at the suggestion of the royal family. One was Hussein Fardoust, boyhood friend of the Crown Prince and son of a loyal army officer. The other was Mehrpour Timurtash, the son of the Minister of Court, whose family was close to the Shah at that point.

The Crown Prince and his brother were sent to board with a Swiss family named Mercier, for the prince was still a sickly child, and the doctor felt that for health and security reasons he would be best off living in the heart of a family and not among rough and knockabout teen-age boys.

In 1932 the boys all transferred to Le Rosey boarding school. The Crown Prince's improvement in health and physique by then was nothing short of remarkable. He had always been a studious and introspective child, getting good marks in the Palace school, and at this preparatory day school in Lausanne he had continued to show academic proficiency in most subjects. Further, he began to participate in athletic competition with a real fervor and soon excelled in track and field events and was captain of the football and tennis teams.

At Le Rosey, the Crown Prince was more or less treated as an equal among equals. He soon developed a reputation as a good mixer among the other boys. The Royal Family was satisfied with the school and the progress of the two princes and would send four half brothers to Le Rosey a year or so later.

But the Crown Prince was never allowed to forget who he was. He professed to be much intrigued by the "democratic" institutions of Switzerland, at least as much as he was by French literature. Yet, in the winter of 1933, Minister of Court Timurtash was arrested in Teheran and charged with treason. Mohammed Reza's friend, Mehrpour Timurtash, was hustled away from the school, and back to Teheran to share the family disgrace and downfall. And the Crown Prince learned a bitter lesson in the sociology of Imperial Rule: you must never get close to anyone.

The loneliness was not helped by the special regimen followed at Le Rosey. The Shah was not an ordinary student. He *had to* excel. His father was very positive about what he expected. He had a special tutor sent from Teheran to coach him in Persian. After all, the future Light of Lights of Persia must have a thorough understanding of every facet of his country's national history, the literature, the geography, the resources and the tribal customs of the fringe peoples. Indeed, young Mohammed was pursuing two separate educations at one time.

In spite of this restriction, the Crown Prince got on well with the Europeans in his classes, and he would have liked to have the free and easy life they enjoyed. But except for mixing within the school yard, the prince was kept out of it. Part of the reason was the family physician's concern for the continued good health and safety of the royal charge who was his protege. Part of it was on orders from the Shah back in Teheran. The Crown Prince was past puberty now, and the Shah wanted no complications of any sort in his son's life. Indeed, that was one of the reasons LeRosey became the *royal* school. This was a boy's school. The school the Prince first attended had girl students as well. There was to be no temptation set before the Crown Prince that would in any way endanger the future of the Peacock Throne. So while the other boys mingled in the towns near the school and were invited to visit the homes of girls and to attend parties, Dr. Moadeb Nafici kept a careful watch on the Crown Prince and never allowed him outside the school, unless he, the Doctor, was along.

Loneliness begat work and philosophic introspection. Coming from a land of absolute power, the growing prince was able to compare his country's situation with that of Switzerland, and through his studies, with that of the more powerful western democracies.

Next door to the Swiss was Hitler's developing National Socialist state, neither national nor socialist. Back in Teheran the Shah showed his admiration for the strength of Hitler. Off to the west, by contrast, was France, deep in depression and strikes with the problems of a corrupt society and a quiescent Third Republic. On the southern border lay Mussolini's Fascist state with some of the trappings of democracy but none of the freedoms. To the north was England, the home of Empire, whose politicians insisted on freedom at home, but were not so eager to grant it in the spheres of influence they enjoyed abroad. To a sharp and inquiring mind, the lessons of the Europe of the 1930's were very plain. The Crown Prince saw the need for certain liberties, particularly economic opportunity, to persuade the people that life was worth the struggle of improvement. But he developed no great attachment for the democratic process he saw about him, for much of what he observed appeared to him to be license.

The Crown Prince grew ever more conscientious in his approach to his studies. Kept restricted, even sequestered, he accepted the virtual imprisonment and used his time in study. Except for reading and athletics, his amusements were a radio and a gramophone. It was not hard to convince himself that his task was to prepare now. In the last two years at Le Rosey he redoubled his efforts to acquire information and skills. And the enforced isolation had another effect on him: it increased his sense of the religious. Without prompting, certainly none came in the weekly letter from his father in Teheran, the Crown Prince turned to the Koran for solace. He began reciting his prayers morning, noon, and night as prescribed by the Prophet.

He also studied the procedures of rule of his father and the purposes his father laid down to him in the weekly letters.

For example, consider the plight of the Iranian peasant. His father was probably the largest land owner in all Persia yet his treatment of the peasant left much to be desired. Since 1928 the peasant had been proscribed in his dress, first he had had to wear the Pahlavi cap and then the European type of hat. He had been taxed on tea and sugar, certainly two necessities, to build the Trans-Iranian railroad.

The peasants loved their Shah, even so. They were pleased because the Shah had put an end to the activities of bandits for the most part. He had pacified many of the tribes in the outlying districts. Mohammed Reza saw all this and learned of it from his tutors and his father.

And what about the towns people? In these years the cities and towns were growing as poor peasants left the land, lured by success stories of the few. And some did prosper in the cities. But many were reduced to beggary and final return to the countryside, for they could neither read nor write, and had no place in the few commercial institutions that did exist in Iran's larger cities.

As for the tribesmen, who made up such a great proportion of the Iranian population, they had their own languages, their own customs, and their own way of life. For the most part they were nomads, and as such many of them preyed on the peasants and the town and village people. The Shah's repression and confinement of the tribesmen led to pitched battles and much bloodshed. Martial law was often in effect in one part of the country or another. The tribal problem was not settled, and the young Crown Prince knew there was particular unrest in Azerbaijan in the north and the Kurdish areas along the Iraqi border on the west. The Shah's repressive measures had not solved the problems; in the north, in particular, the Russian Soviet forces were propagandizing and waiting for a chance to create havoc.

Education brought the Crown Prince a kind of idealism of his own, one that would have shocked his father in the last years, when the Shah appeared to have an increased concern over his personal wealth. The prince decided that when he assumed power one of his first acts would be to declare a moratorium on rent and produce collections from the thousands of peasants who worked the royal lands. This experiment would give him a chance to assess the prospects of the peasantry.

He had other idealistic plans: he would establish a public complaint box, and then the people would feel free to drop in complaints about the unfair tax collector or the official seeking a bribe, or the avaricious landlord. The Crown Prince, in his innocence, actually believed these complaints would actually reach him, untouched, and that no one would take action against the people who might make complaints against them.

Those were the dreams of youth.

He dreamed and worked and studied until the spring of 1936 when he was graduated from Le Rosey. The Shah now wanted to see what five years at school had done for the Prince. He was now 20 years old and time that he assumed some princely responsibilities after all that education. He must now be trained in the military and be prepared to lead his country when the time came.

He spent the summer with the royal family in the mountains above Teheran and in the pleasant breezes of the Caspian. Then it was back to school, in uniform, at the Teheran Military college, where the Shah made officers for his growing army. For two years the Crown Prince would train with other young men and would learn under French officers, for the school, like so much else in Iran, was modeled along French lines.

While the Crown Prince was studying military science and tactics, he was also being groomed for other new responsibilities. The Shah laid out a program: the young man was to become familiar with every aspect of life in Iran and he was to visit every nook of the land so he might understand the problems of government. Each day the Prince came to the palace half an hour before lunch, and the Shah spent that time and the luncheon period lecturing his son about his duties and the problems as the Shah saw them.

These were lectures, indeed, not discussions. The Shah was so forceful a man, so used to being obeyed, he was unable to carry on a two-way discussion. So the Crown Prince listened, and observed, and spoke at the proper times and learned about his country in the way that his father wished him to learn.

As the months went on, he gained courage to speak up occasionally. If he saw something that needed changing he said so. And, wonder of wonders, the old Shah sometimes listened to him. On one occasion, the Crown Prince suggested that some of the political leaders the Shah had imprisoned be freed. Among these was Dr. Mohammed Mossadegh, long-time governor of Shiraz, and member of the Majlis, who represented the opposition to the crown and had for years been fighting the Shah in one way or another. Mossadegh had been jailed for his activities. The Shah had never forgotten that when he seized power from the Qajar kings, one of the handful to resist him openly had been this same troublesome Mossadegh.

But just now he was trying to show his gentleness toward his son, and reluctantly he agreed to free Mossadegh and other enemies in order to pacify the people. Mossadegh praised the young prince for he was certain, he said, that he was marked for extermination by the Shah as had been so many hundreds of other opponents of the old man's iron rule. He had been held in a dungeon in an isolated prison, charged with high treason as a tool of the British, whom the old Shah still regarded as his enemies.

The Shah was fretful these days. He read, quite correctly, the signs of unrest in Europe and his personal sympathies lay with the Germans who had supplied so much in material and skilled training to his modernization program. The internal politics meant nothing in a Persia that had never known any more freedom than the Germans possessed. Had Hitler established himself as king and had he a daughter, the Shah might well have tried to marry her off to the Crown Prince.

For in 1938, the Shah was feeling mortal. One day while up country with his son, he paced back and forth in their tent and fretted because he had not perfected the administrative controls of the outlying provinces. If something were to happen to him just then, he said, it would be unfortunate for Mohammed Reza and for the nation.

This same concern set the Shah to thinking about the marriage of his heir. It was time that Mohammed Reza did marry and produce a successor, to be sure that the line of Pahlavi would continue. That much the Shah could promise himself.

One day while leafing through a magazine, the Shah saw photos of the Royal Egyptian family. He stopped suddenly when he saw a picture of the Princess Fawzia, for she was a beauty, a brunette whose facial characteristics and form bore a striking resemblance to Marilyn Monroe.

For months the Shah had been concerned about his son's future. Whom could he marry? Whom should he marry? There were a handful of kingdoms in the Middle East, and it was to these the search must be confined, for nowhere else could a suitable Moslem girl be found. The Shah had no sense of religion at all now, but he knew it would offend the people of Iran were Mohammed Reza to marry a Christian of one of the European kingdoms. He considered a number of families, including those of neighboring Saudi Arabia, but he couldn't forget the photo of the beautiful Fawzia, and through his ambassadors he began to make inquiries.

King Farouk of Egypt had four sisters in the palace, Fawzia, Faiza, Faika, and Fathia, and of them all Fawzia, with her raven hair and even features was the ripest and most beautiful. Yes, said the Ambassadors, such a marriage might be arranged to the advantage of both kingdoms and the happiness of all concerned.

So the negotiations continued in the fall and winter of 1938 until it was agreed that Fawzia would come to Teheran and live as the Princess and later as the Empress of the Persians.

In the western world it would be seemly for a Crown Prince to go to the court of his intended bride and pay a few calls. But this was not the way of Eastern royalty. From time immemorial such marriages were arranged to the convenience of the ruling monarchs and their ideas of the needs of the nation. The marriage of Fawzia of Egypt and Mohammed Reza of Iran was no exception. Mohammed never set eyes on his intended bride before he left Persia in February to travel to Baghdad, thence to Cairo where he would be married.

On March 2 he left for Cairo. He went to the coast and met the Egyptian Royal Yacht *Maroussa,* which had been detailed to pick up the bridegroom. The Minister of Foreign Affairs, Yehia Pasha, was aboard to meet the royal Iranian party, along with Prince Mohammed Ali of the royal family.

They sailed across the Mediterranean until they reached Alexandria. There in the harbor they received a twenty-one gun salute from the Egyptian coast guard ships, the fort, and HMS *Penelope,* a British warship docked at the moment. Down to the shore this day came Mohammed Pasha Mahmoud, Egypt's prime minister, to represent the government and King Farouk, who was waiting for them in Cairo.

They went ashore and into limousines, and thus to the railroads station through streets arched with flowers, crowds along the curbings and in the gutters, waiting for a view of the man who had come to spirit away their princess.

The prime minister went on the special train with them. En route from Alexandria to Cairo, they were met at stations by cheering people who waved Iranian red white and green flags, and the colors of Egypt. It was a day of wild festivity.

On reaching Cairo, the party headed for the Abdin Palace in a procession of state, and there Crown Prince Mohammed Reza met for the first time his bride to be, the elegant and beautiful Fawzia. He was presented to his future brother-in-law, King Farouk, who was all smiling grace. Even the Queen Mother, who secretly had her doubts about this new line of Pahlavis (second generation only), was kind this day. It was not for nothing that the Shah, back in Teheran, had spoken of the riches of Iran, and the palaces and his fortune and the Peacock Throne, with all that it meant in terms of history. The Shah's might be stolen history and grandeur, but the existence of his magnificent crown jewels and the huge land holdings made it all very real.

The press that day was given a glimpse of part of the dowry Fawzia would carry with her to Persia. Her brother provided her with a glittering diamond pendant worth 15,000 pounds (60,000 dollars) and a pair of earrings of like value, plus a crown valued at 25,000 pounds (100,000 dollars), a suitable gift for a girl who would become empress of all the Persians.

There were some political and social problems to be worked out. The Crown Prince of Iran, even in his shining military uniform with all its medals, was not regarded as a first class catch by the Egyptian family, but they too were suffering these days from a paucity of royal Moslem suitors of the proper rank. And as for the attitude of the Shah—he had the temerity to "check out" the pedigree of Fawzia.

Now, as the two young people met awkwardly for the first time, they summed up one another. Fawzia was undoubtedly beautiful, but she did show signs that one day she would do as Farouk was doing, for it was the curse of the line to put on weight in the wrong places. The prince, by all odds, would not have that problem. His father was as slender as he had been in youth, and the prince was a stalwart, energetic young man who took exercise as part of his regular daily routine and had no trouble with his glands. Aside from those narrow, beady eyes, he could be regarded as a handsome man, erect, trim, curly haired and even of features, with the hawknose of the Persians.

As they worked toward agreement, the Shah back in Teheran unveiled his naked power once again. Persian law said that a ruler must be a Persian citizen, whose father and mother were both also Persian citizens. The measure was written down in the constitution of Iran.

So there was nothing to be done but change the constitution, or make special provision. The latter was easier. As Mohammed Reza courted Fawzia in the gardens of Abdin palace, the Majlis in Teheran made Fawzia a Persian citizen.

The marriage was planned for March 15. Perhaps one or the other of the parties *could* back out, if he or she took a violent dislike to the other. But from early childhood, royalty is taught not to expect of marriage what the average citizen would want. It was a matter of *noblesse oblige.* The purpose of this marriage, as with all such affairs, was to produce a suitable consort who would reflect properly on the image of Iran in the world, and, even more important in the long run, to produce a male heir. Other kings in other countries might satisfy themselves if their children were happy, and be prepared to accept for the kingdom eventual rule by a female, but not Shah Reza of Persia. He had been lucky enough to have several male children by his wives, and if the Crown Prince were to sicken and die as it once seemed he must, his brother or one of his half brothers would succeed. That is why they were all educated together at Le Rosey, although, of course, only the Crown Prince was educated to rule.

The date of the wedding was set for two reasons, neither of which had anything to do with bride or bridegroom. First, March 15, 1939, was the anniversary of modern Egyptian independence. Second, by one of those fortunate accidents of fate, it was also the Shah of Iran's birthday. Such gifts from heaven could not be overlooked. The mullahs and the seers agreed that these signs gave forth most propitious vibrations for the future. In Iran, where the evil eye and the evil djinn were a part of daily peasant life, the holy men agreed that the signs were indeed good.

On the morning of March 15, then, the Shah's son, Crown Prince Mohammed Reza, was up early, saying his prayers at dawn, making his ablutions, and putting on the special clothing of his wedding day.

The royal Iranian party had much to do, and there were religious conflicts to be resolved or politely ignored, for the Pahlavis came from the Shia Muslim line that is dominant in Iran, while the family of Farouk were Sunni Moslems, as were most Egyptians. It was much like a marriage of Greek Orthodox and Roman Catholic, except for one salient fact: only the groom and his party and male representatives of the bride appeared at the actual wedding ceremony. Princess Fawzia waited in her mother's apartments in her wedding finery, including a gown from a couturier in France.

The Crown Prince went to the grand reception hall of the Abdin palace, and made his obeisances to the Sheikh El Marighi, an eminent Sunni holy man of Cairo. King Farouk, in his splendid costume, was at his side as they participated in the brief ceremony and signed the wedding papers.

That was all. The whole party then moved to other rooms where the Crown Prince saw Fawzia as his wife. Then they went onto the balcony to appear before the cheering crowds of Cairo. This wedding day of their princess was a national feast, and thousands came to see the couple. The Crown Prince stood in his gray and blue and silver uniform, smiling and waving. The new Crown Princess and future empress, stood at his side in her white silver lamé gown, the diadem upon her pretty head, and she smiled the happy smile of youth. In her arms she carried a huge bouquet of white flowers that had been flown in especially from Holland. This was 1939, and the flying of flowers was regarded as a particularly unusual luxury of the kind for which Farouk and his family were famous for indulging themselves.

In an hour the wedding party was moving into the courtyard of the palace, and into Rolls-Royces, Mercedes, and Cadillacs for the royal procession through the city. The cars were decorated with more of the Dutch flowers and blooms from the palace gardens. The streets were lined with joyous people, and the police and soldiers of the guard kept a careful vigil as the parade moved to the palace the young couple would occupy on their brief Egyptian honeymoon. An airplane dropped flowers on the crowds below and did stunts to amuse them.

Never had there appeared to be a happier couple, as they smiled and chatted in French.

The Egyptian honeymoon lasted until April 3, when the bride's trousseau was pronounced ready for travel, and the Queen Mother announced that she would accompany the couple along with Princess Faiza, Princess Faika, and Princess Fathia to make of the triumphal entry into Teheran a visit of state. They took the train to Alexandria in great pomp, and then boarded a special chartered steamship that was given entirely over to the royal group. There were special menus, a picked crew, including a royal guard, and not a single expense spared. With toots and salutes and much waving and shouting, the royal party was seen off in Alexandria. They sailed through the Suez canal, the Red Sea, the Indian Ocean, into the Persian Gulf, and to the port of Shahpour, which was reached on April 14, at the height of the beauty of spring, before the dreaded heat descended on the region in May.

The wedding party now boarded a festooned train of the Trans-Iranian railroad, for the long journey to Teheran. Meanwhile, from across the world wedding telegrams and gifts were dispatched to the couple. The King of England and the President of the United States sent gifts. The Japanese sent an airplane with five dignitaries and a crew of three, which would stop off in Siam, India, Iran, and finally in Iraq, thus using the festive moment for two purposes: to deliver the Emperor's wedding gifts, and to show the world how much Japan had improved in air power in the past few years.

The train travelled north for two days and was met at Teheran's new railroad station by a guard of honor which carried the party in open cars through the streets of the Iranian capital. The streets were lined with happy people as had been Cairo's, and the Shah had caused to be erected for this day, triumphal floral arches bearing the rich blooms of the Caucasus and of Iran's northern spring.

The couple were taken to the royal palace, for another wedding festivity. The Egyptian Queen mother was given use of the Gulistan palace, along with her royal daughters, for their stay.

The Germans (this was the spring of 1939), made a great show for themselves. Count von der Schulenberg, the German ambassador to the U.S.S.R., brought a party from Moscow in a special plane just to join his colleagues, and the round of receptions, parties, and parades, that kept Teheran excited for two weeks. From Isfahan and Tabriz came silver and rugs and precious silks for the bride and groom. From the tribes came gifts of sheep and camels and all that the tribe might possess. From the royal family came gold and jewels and the promise of a new palace to be built for the couple in the hills that lead up to the snowcapped Elburz mountain range where the great peak, Demavand, towers 18,600 feet above the city.

Into the city crowded generals and kings and queens and princes from more than a dozen lands to join the festivities. Farouk had sent his family and half a dozen important personages. Others came from Oman and from Saudi Arabia, and the other Arab kingdoms and sheikdoms. From Britain came Princess Alice, the

Countess Athlone, the Earl of Athlone and the Duke of Spoleto. Italy sent its royal representatives and so did Luxembourg and Belgium.

The Shah staged a magnificient reception in the Hall of Brilliants at the Palace, and a military review on the first day, which featured the crack guards now goosestepping in the German fashion the Shah admired so much. At night he sponsored a huge and lengthy fireworks display.

There were many parties going on almost everywhere. For the drinkers, there was every kind of whiskey and vodka and gin, sherries and cordials and fine wines, capped of course with case upon case of vintage champagne. For all there were mounds of the famous beluga caviar from the Caspian. Only the finest for the royal family and its friends. There was mutton and beef, and Sturgeon a la Russe; every conceivable delicacy that could be bought, created, or imported was loaded on the tables of the dining rooms and reception halls.

For ten days the whole capital was given over to feasting, and down by the bazaar the poor had never before been bestowed so lavishly with gifts by their Shah.

The night of April 26 capped it all. From the Peacock Throne in the Hall of Brilliants, the Shah appeared in all his finery, something quite unusual for a ruler whose ordinary costume was a shirt and Cossack cut trousers stuffed deep into battered riding boots. He and the mother of the Crown Prince held forth, along with the princesses and princes—children of all his marriages. When guests and hosts were replete with the delicacies of the kingdom, the smiling Shah led them all outside the palace for another military review. This display would be one for history to remember well. Outside on the stands, Shah Reza announced a signal honor for his new daughter-in-law—a crack cavalry regiment named for her. This was akin to giving her the old Cossacks in which he had served for so long and so well.

For four hours in the coolness, they watched as troop after troop of cavalry, regiment after regiment of infantry, tanks other armored vehicles and trucks passed by the reviewing stands. And seventy planes made a flyby, a most impressive air force for a Middle Eastern kingdom in 1939. The Egyptian cavalry in scarlet and blue paraded for for the Shah, along with troops from France, Britain, and Russia. And again, as darkness fell, the whole was ended by a fireworks display even more impressive than the one earlier, all dedicated to Queen Mother Nazli, of Egypt, as representative of King Farouk.

So the marriage party ended, and the visiting dignitaries began making their way homeward, while the Crown Prince and his bride settled in at the Marble Palace built by the Shah for royal use. All seemed serene in that spring of 1939. Then came summer, and the European war, with its irritating troubles for the Middle East countries. But even this was overshadowed in the Marble Palace by great news: Princess Fawzia was pregnant. The Crown Prince would soon have an heir, and the Shah a grandchild.

When the baby was born—what a disapointment. It was a girl. They must try again to have an heir, for under Iranian law and custom the crown must pass by direct line of descent to a male heir. It was conceivable, if the Crown Prince did not produce a male heir, his father could disinherit him or reduce him to the rank of Prince, and make brother Ali the heir, if he produced a male child.

They named the baby Shahnaz, and began to hope for an heir again. But nothing happened. The worry was only ended by the exigencies of the war in Europe, and fresh worries about the future of a kingdom threatened on several sides by opposing interests.

Then came that day in September, when Crown Prince Mohammed Reza was called to the Imperial Palace for that last talk with his father who announced he was going to abdicate in the Crown Prince's favor, Suddenly, in a matter of hours, the Crown Prince became the ruler of his country. He was the ShahanShah, King of Kings, and all was his—the Peacock Throne and everything it signified.

7

Divided Kingdom

Seldom has so young a king inherited so much trouble so quickly. The question the new Shah's ministers and advisors were asking themselves was: would the Shah be allowed to rule?

And the answer was yes and no. Shah Mohammed Reza would be allowed to keep his throne. Indeed the British, and even the Russians, wanted as much stability as they could get at this time. Out the window for the moment were the Soviet imperial designs on Azerbaijan. Britain was pleased if she could protect the flow of oil from Abadan. For the rest, they wanted order in the country.

The way to maintain order was to occupy, and so in 1941 the British and Russian occupations extended even to Teheran. Hardly had the young Shah participated in the official ceremony at the Majlis that made him ruler, than he was back at the palace, issuing orders relative to the imminent occupation of Teheran by British and Russian commands. One of his first acts was to appoint men he trusted as liaison officers with the commands.

For many months the Shah had steeped his son in the politics of neutrality, for Iran on the outbreak of war had declared for armed and ready neutrality, and no longer ago than June 22 had done the same. Four months later, the new Shah was forced to welcome men he regarded as invaders, and to accomodate his country to their heavy demands.

But the real worry was internal security. Old Shah Reza, pacing in his tent a few years before, had known his pacification of the tribes and his control of the provinces was only nominal that without daily show of force from the military the control might end.

And end it did. Once more the roads were attacked and patrolled by brigands and highwayman. No lone traveler was safe from robbery, and many a time robbery also meant murder, for the tribesmen operated on the ages-old theory that dead men tell no tales.

Were that not enough trouble, the army was on the verge of open rebellion. Most of the officers were pro-German. There was no secret about that. They openly questioned the ability of the 22-year-old Shah to rule. Some called him a puppet of the British and the Russians, and as much as they could, the younger officers showed their dislike of the occupiers to the point of open contempt.

The young Shah possessed more acumen than many gave him credit for. He recognized immediately his major problems which were to placate the foreigners without losing absolute control, and most important, to keep the forces of power united enough so that when the occupation eventually ended he would not be forced out.

That meant compromise.

The presence of the allies was an embarassment politically, for the old Shah had outlawed parties, and particularly the Communist party. The young Shah handled that problem by declaring a political amnesty. Some 50 Communist leaders were released from prison and immediately began the organization of the *Tudeh* party which in Persian means "the masses." From then until the end of the war Tudeh had a free hand at organization.

But the Shah simultaneously took action that set free an even stronger element within the nation. The old Shah had stepped hard on the Muslim clergy, now the new Shah for several reasons eliminated many of the old restrictions. Almost immediately after Shah Mohammed Reza took over, he had made peace with the Shiite leaders who had been kept under restraint, and who, in turn had come to regard Shah Reza as an usurper of power and a dictator. One of the earliest manifestations of this change was the removal of restrictions against wearing of the *chadur* or veil by Moslem women. The Shah so ordered, and within a matter of hours the *chadur* was again being worn by thousands of young and old.

Also in a matter of hours, the new Shah realized that if he hoped to keep his throne his foreign policy must be tailored to the demands of the British and the Russians, for the allies were not about to stand on international law or honor. They demanded the establishment and continuation of a government friendly and even subservient to their needs.

With the help of Mohammed Ali Faroughi, the Prime Minister he had inherited from his father's regime, the young Shah managed to convince the British and Russians he could help secure their position and the safety of the materials that were to pass through Iran into Russia, and out of Iran to support the British fighting forces.

The trouble was that the Germans were marching and moving very quickly. The German plan called for a drive to the Persian gulf, and obviously for the German occupation of Iran with its fine railroad and valuable oil resources. The Germans even envisaged a future drive on India to link up with the Japanese and thus control the world.

Wild pipe dreams? Perhaps they seem so from the vantage point of thirty years and more, but the speed with which German armor moved, and the later surprise attack of Japan both had the allies worrying and wondering in the winter of 1942.

The Shah already had his hands full. Outside Teheran, except where the occupying forces maintained troops, there was little chance for the central government to keep order. The tribal chiefs, who had been kept in virtual house arrest under Shah Reza, were released and quickly made their way homeward, there to do as they pleased. And what they pleased was usually troublesome.

In the west, Hama Rashid, a Kurdish chief occupied half a dozen towns and cut the Sanandaj-Tabriz road. He was in effective power for months, forcing the government to send a full-fledged expedition to control the area. He defeated the first expedition and killed one Iranian general. He spent months dodging the authorities, who spent millions of rials to control the area.

On the Turkoman steppe, the Turkomans went back to their old tribal ways, denying the rule of the central government to the point that the government civil servants left the area. And off to the east on the frontier, the tribes of Zafaranlu rebelled, which meant more troops must be dispatched from Teheran.

Finally, one of the two largest and most powerful tribes in all Iran, the Qashqai, began to seek redress for many wrongs. Years earlier, the old Shah had imprisoned the tribe's great Khan, Sohlat-ad-Dovleh, and so evil were the conditions of his life that he died on the Shah's hands. The four sons of Sohlat never forgave, especially Mansur, who went to Germany to study and nurse his hatred, and Khosro, the youngest and strongest of them. When the central government announced a pro-allied policy, they defied the new Shah. Openly they let it be known that they were sheltering German agents, and that they would continue to do so. They harried and worried the government forces in their area, and not even the power of Russia and Britain could dislodge them in this fight against their personal enemies.

The Japanese attack on Pearl Harbor was greeted with cheers by many in Teheran. However, in the army, whatever their feelings, the officers were soon persuaded their allegiance lay with the new Shah. The old Shah's methods and his training of his son in the military tradition undoubtedly saved the throne for Shah Mohammed Reza. He had, after all, served as a junior officer in the field with many of these young officers, and they remembered it. He had attended their academy, and acted as much as an equal with them as anyone could expect. He had shown himself in his military contacts to be cool and objective. He was a man to whom they could turn with respect.

But elsewhere in Iran, the man on the street was vigorously pro-German and pro-Japanese. The intellectuals were divided among the pro-Germans, many of whom had either studied in Germany or at German schools in Iran, and those who had lived in France and England, who were pro-Allied.

Oddly enough, except for those who had been conditioned by the old Shah Reza, few were anti-Russian as such. The Russians kept low in Iran. They did not visit the cafes and restaurants, and there were very few incidents involving roughness between Russians and Iranians, whereas there were many fracases between British Tommies and Iranians and often over girls.

It was inevitable that a treaty would be negotiated to give the British and Russians what they demanded and had in fact seized. One thing they demanded was the discharge of Prime Minister Mohammed Ali Faroughi, who was replaced by Ali Soheili, who would go down as one of the strong prime ministers of Iran—notably pro-allied as he must be in these times.

Many a problem arose. The Russians brought into Iran an army of 120,000 Poles who wanted to fight for the liberation of Poland from Germany. Quartered near Teheran, they were another foreign element that created friction plus a strain on the Iranian economy.

The rich—the city dweller merchants and the country dweller landowners—did everything possible to subvert the Shah's regime. These privileged people had stung under the lash of Shah Reza, who had, in his way, attempted to level out the mountains and chasms in the matter of national wealth. They did everything they could to subvert the rule of the young Shah. What they hoped for was a return to the Qajar dynasty. They had long memories, these rich ones; twenty years meant nothing; they still hoped for the return of the privileges of another century.

For all his difficulties, and for all his personal problems, the young Shah represented a threat to them. They encouraged his personal dilettantism, and indeed there was much of that in the over-privileged young king. Sadly, his marriage to Fawzia was not going well. She had a penchant for strong young men of Arab countenance. He had an equal yen for attractive, slender women with large busts and coal black hair. A succession of both her lovers and his mistresses passed through their several palaces to become a public scandal in Teheran.

But politically, the young Shah was intelligent and adroit if not powerful. The allies wanted a treaty: he gave them one guided by Prime Minister Soheili. The allies would have the oil, and the transportation, and the use of Iran as a staging ground. But they would also respect the political independence, territorial integrity, and sovereignty of Iran's government. Six months after the war, they would withdraw their troops. And they would promise to assist Iran after the war to pay for the damages they were causing in the orderly growth of the nation because of their military demands.

This treaty was shrewd bargaining from Iran's point of view. The allies were going to have their way after the war, anyhow. And already the young Shah could see that the Russians had never lost the old Czarist interest in biting off Azerbaijan. So Britain and Russia were committed. They would *not* try to seize Iranian territory, and they would get out and pay for what they had used.

The British in particular were not pleased with the Persian government. Shah Reza's particular bete noire had been England always, and they felt the young Shah was following in his father's footsteps, that the Pahlavi dynasty was anathema to England.

So they put on pressure for drastic changes.

The most significant of these was to force the resignation of Prime Minister Soheili and replace him with Ahmad Qavam, a man the British knew to be openly antagonistic to the Pahlavi dynasty because he had been mistreated and imprisoned by the Shah's father in the 1920s.

It was the old colonial policy of divide and rule, and the Shah was infuriated by it. He resented the interference but being virtually powerless, he affected a blasé naiveté that enhanced his reputation as playboy, and perhaps averted the destruction of the Pahlavi dynasty.

Even so, both he and the land suffered sorely in the war.

He had come to power with a strong feeling for change and a hope that he could guide his country to a constitutional freedom that his father had long since abandoned in favor of dictatorial practices. He had, in other words, the exuberance and idealism of youth.

But before he was 25 years old, this young king had experienced practical international politics at their shoddiest.

The most serious of these were the plans to inflate the economy, which was British policy, and the preparations for severance of portions of the country from the central government, which was Russian policy.

Once Ahmad Qavam had succeeded to the Prime Minister's post the British began pressing for an inflation of the currency. They wanted plenty of money in circulation for the use of their troops. But Qavam was an Iranian nationalist primarily, and he refused, saying the Iranian constitution prevented this kind of inflation. The British then put pressure on the young Shah to get rid of the man they had gotten appointed. They also tried to get the Shah to dissolve Parliament because the Parliament would not accede to British demands.

The Shah held out. He stood up, one of the few times he was able to do so, and categorically refused to dissolve the Parliament.

This brave stand proved of little consequence. Power prevailed, and a few weeks later British troops were in Teheran, ostensibly to quell unquellable riots (which the Shah suspected to be fomented). It was made very clear that unless the Shah and the Majlis met the British demands, the troops would remain in control of the capital. So the currency was inflated.

The result was horror for the people, as they saw the cost of living soar upwards of 400 per cent.

The Russians did not help. Iran's rice and wheat came from the northern provinces near the Caspian, and usually these were shipped south to feed the rest of the country. But the Russians kept the wheat and rice either there, or sent it to feed their own people, and the Persians went hungry. Rationing of rice and sugar and wheat were instituted, and then the black market came, with tribal chiefs and even government administrators selling ration coupons to line their pockets or support insurrectory movements in the countryside.

But it was the Russians who used Prime Minister Qavam to do a bit of work that was to cause the young Shah untold difficulty in months and years to come.

Since the allies were claiming to police most of the country, the Russians said the Iranian government should help supply arms for the purpose, and they demanded 100,000 rifles 3,000 light machine guns, and 1000 heavy machine guns for the policing. The Iranians had the weapons to spare because one result of the occupation was the reduction of the Iranian army from more than 100,000 men to some 15,000. So the arms were delivered. And where did they go? Straight to Azerbaijan, to arm the people the Soviets wanted armed there.

The Shah, with his agents in all parts of the land, learned of these depradations, but when one is too weak to stop them it is sometimes best to ignore them. So that is what he did. These first two seasons of occupation were a serious trial to him. The Russians wanted to dismantle the Iranian munitions factories and cast them away as they later did the Manchurian factories. The British wanted to take off all the Iranian government's stands of artillery. Only by playing one against the other was the Shah able to dissuade the two reluctant allies from dismembering his nation. Later, in 1942, when the Americans arrived with their Persian gulf command to aid Russia, the Shah had a third force to play against the other two.

Riot, food demonstration, and riot again. At one point, Prime Minister Qavam gave an order to fire on civilians demonstrating for bread outside the Majlis, and was with difficulty persuaded to revoke it. The British sent food and the Americans sent food, just enough to avert chaos, but not so much as to overwhelm the Persians with gratitude. The Persians, and particularly their young Shah, would remember for a long time what it means to be weak and occupied by foreign powers during a major war.

Prime Minister Qavam's measures failed, and Prime Minister Soheili returned to power. It was a good change for the troubled young Shah. For in the beginning months of 1942 the tribes were on the move, and the communications within the non-occupied areas of Iran were much in danger. The Shah had virtually no military forces with which to maintain the authority of the central government. He had to resort to cajolery, bribery, and whatever power he could exert from the tarnished Peacock Throne.

Each day of this shoddy existence, each affront to the sovereignty of Iran and the authority of his rule, was etched on his mind. He would never forget.

The Shah personally supervised the movement of his senior military officers. The Qashqai revolted in the south, and he moved his officers around to get the best to go to that front. He kept to his father's old precept of instilling the loyalty of the army in the throne.

It was good that he did so. For as if the young Shah did not have enough trouble, in the summer of 1942 there appeared on the scene in Teheran again Sayyid Zia ad Din, the man who had encouraged Reza Khan to stage the original rebellion against the Qajar regime in 1921. After the coup by Reza, Sayyid had settled in Palestine, and he had been there all these years. What ghost of politics the British unearthed to bring Sayyid back, the Shah could not fathom, but he knew there would be trouble, for already he had heard of attempts being made to bring a Qajar prince back to the throne of Persia.

So in 1942 the young ruler was faced with growing unrest of his people, hunger in the streets, detestation by the people of the occupying powers, tribal rebellion, Soviet scheming in Azerbaijan,

British power play in the south, and an incipient palace revolution in behalf of the Qajars. They called him playboy, even so!

But what the outside world failed to understand about this young ruler was that he was the creature of his country, his times, and his heritage.

No one could expect to understand what he faced unless one knew the recent history of Iran, the history of the Pahlavis, and the relationships of the Pahlavis with a number of important politicians—and especially this Sayyid Zia ad Din. For in the modern history of Iran two men of high rank have threatened the Pahlavis. Sayyid was the first, and the second was Mohammed Mossadegh who very nearly unseated the present Shah in a long struggle. If one would understand the Shah-Mossadegh struggle, then one must know what the young Shah knew—the history of his father's quarrel with Sayyid.

8

The Coming of Reza Khan

The story of modern Iran begins with the Shah's father, Reza Shah Pahlavi, who overthrew the decadent monarchy early in this century and created his own new dynasty after the manner of the ancient kings. One tends to forget, in the passage of millienia, that many of the celebrated rulers of the past were regarded by their neighbors and by the people they conquered as upstart robber barons at best. So the fact that the Pahlavi dynasty stems from humble root should not obscure accomplishment either. Farouk of Egypt, who claimed a much longer and nobler line, observed gloomily one time that soon there would be but five monarchs on the thrones of the world, the king of Spades, the King of Hearts, the King of Diamonds, the King of Clubs and the King of England. In Farouk's case it was true; he and his family despised the Iranians, but Farouk is long gone from the royal scene, while the Pahlavis live on in the greatest imperial splendor to be found in all the world.

The Imperial Peacock Throne itself was taken from the once-powerful Mogul Empire of Persia and India. And if the Shah cannot personally claim a long line of descent, his country's history is grand enough for all to see, at the temples of Persepolis, at Isfahan, and in the north where the independent-minded Azerbaijani live.

The ancient history of Persia is a compendium of war and magnificence whose artifacts abound around the land, but the modern history really begins, as does the story of the present Shah, in the 19th Century with Shah Nasr ad Din who in 1879 formed a brigade of troops called the Cossacks, because they were modelled after the fierce Russian horse shock troops of the Czar. The force was Persian, but the officers were Russians in the beginning and for many years the chief officers continued to be Russians, on the principle that it was easier to buy foreign loyalty than to trust the uncertainties of Persian temper.

Nasr ad Din switched the country's foreign allegiances; the British had been powerful. They lost out under him, while the Russians secured many concessions, from fisheries along the Caspian to banking concessions in Teheran.

Intellectuals and tribesmen objected to the Russian influence over their Shah, but by this time the Cossacks were the mainstay of the army, paid by the Russians' Banque d'escompte, and the commanding officer was a Russian general who reported directly to the Russian general staff. Small wonder, then, that Nasr ad Din was assassinated in May 1896.

It was at this time the Shah's father, young Reza Pahlavi, went from a village to Teheran at the age of 20 and joined a Cossack regiment. This was to shape his life and eventually influence deeply the life and behavior of the present Shah.

Reza Pahlavi had connections; his uncle was Nasrat Ullah Khan, who rose to be a brigadier general in the Persian forces, and in that position helped Pahlavi join the crack Cossack guards.

From a point of vantage then, the present Shah's father saw how the Russians influenced the Persians, how the rulers gave and then took away the rights of the people. Reza Pahlavi was there, he saw it all; the leader of the troops was Colonel Liakhoff and the Cossack Brigade did the work.

In 1909; the tribesmen stormed down on Teheran and deposed another Shah. He fled into the Russian legation, and then to Russia and to exile. Again, young Pahlavi observed.

All this while, young Pahlavi, known as Reza Khan (Khan being a hereditary title of rank) was making his way upward through the ranks of the Cossack brigade. He was a fierce fighter, charging about on a white horse, exposing himself recklessly to the long rifles of the tribesmen in their frequent clashes. He marched steadily upward.

He married a woman of strong character, and she began to bear him children. First came the girl Shams, and then the girl Ashraf, and finally, on October 26, 1919, an heir was born, the boy Mohammed—the present Shah.

During these formative years, as the father was moving upward, he was also doing the bidding of his military masters. The Cossack division—as it now was constituted—protected Russian interests in the north, until the Bolshevik revolution caused confusion.

By this time the influences that would shape modern Iran were working. In the north was Russian control. In the south Sir Percy Sykes had organized a force of South Persian Rifles, which defended British interests and stood against the Cossacks in time of trouble.

As the young Cossack guard learned by candlelight to read and write in the barracks, he observed the politics that flowed about him. He was subservient to the Russian arm as long as it lasted. But he was aware of the other currents. Among the Persian nationalists there was considerable fear that if the allies won the war, Persia would be divided between Britain and Russia. So a pro-German element crept into local politics, and was to remain there. As early as 1915 there was talk of a rebellion and establishment of a government with close ties to Germany.

But the Majlis was dissolved about then, that cut down the propaganda, and soon the Germans began suffering reverses in the battlefields of France and on the sea. The end of the war in 1918 saw Persia in a state of tremendous confusion, with Pro-

Russian, Pro-German, and Pro-British elements all vying for attention, while around the perimeters sulked the tribesmen, so intense in their local nationalism.

By this time there were definite interests to be served. The full importance of petroleum was only beginning to be appreciated in the world, but it was known that Persia, or Iran, contained huge reserves of oil. Out of all those early concessions emerged the Anglo-Persian Oil Company, and during the war, the Royal Navy in particular recognized the tremendous importance of the installations and the Persian Gulf to Britain's lifeline that extended into India.

A few months before the birth of the boy Mohammed to Reza, the officer of the Cossack guard, the British had been approached by ministers of the Iranian government with a proposition that would give Britain more influence than ever. From the Persian point of view, the need was intense, for so ineffective was the government of the Qajar shahs that the governors could not pay their bills. Reza Khan was on hand one day at the Foreign Ministry when the foreign minister himself had to arrange for a loan in the bazaar, so he could pay for a dinner of state.

The Cossack guards were often reduced to accepting their pay in kind, whatever the government might have on hand, from construction bricks to yard goods.

Obviously a military man would feel constricted by the need to be also merchant and contriver, and Reza Khan, stormy in character at best, brooded over the injustices of military life. Worse, as Princess Ashraf was later to recall about her childhood, the children of the regiment often went hungry because of the incongruities of Persian military life.

So much confusion assailed Iran!

The Azerbaijani, a proud race of Turkish language and sometime customs in Persia, had broken away in the Bolshevik revolt and formed their own Republic. Then in 1920, the Soviet Army marched into Azerbaijan.

The whole of the north was in turmoil. White Russians were

fighting Reds and all around the perimeter of the land the tribesmen were in open rebellion.

In all this upheaval, one of the most prominent men was Sayyad Zia ad Din Tabtabai and, in 1920, he was trying to establish a Persian republic. His scheming was constant. One day he would show up in the guise of a journalist, his one time profession. Next time he was seen he would be a mullah, a Moslem holy man. Then he would appear as a frock-coated dignitary in Teheran. Sayyad Zia was a man of many parts. He moved from Russian occupation zones to British occupation areas as freely as any man in the country.

Reza Khan, now the colonel of the Cossack regiment, was strengthening his own hand and watching in dismay as the foreign powers gobbled up his country.

The Anglo-Persian treaty was signed, but the reestablished Majlis stalled in ratifying it. The British began sending in missions, a financial mission to reorganize the treasury, a military mission to reorganize the army.

Many Persians disagreed so violently that they committed suicide.

Reza Khan was considering all this action and reaction. The Qajar line of Shahs obviously had come to the end, worn out by corruption and inbreeding. Persia seemed likely to be lost entirely as a country.

Reza Khan was promoted to Brigadier General, and given full command of the Cossacks Guard infantry regiment. That made him a powerful figure beyond compare. He saw the confusion and dissatisfaction all about him. He did not like the Bolsheviks who were trying to gain control of large segments of his country.

To supply the needs of his military men, Reza Khan sought assistance where he could find it, and he was befriended by General Dickson, a British military officer brought from London to reorganize the Persian army. Dickson saw in Reza Khan the best type of fighting man, brave, bold, and decisive.

In the fall of 1920 Teheran seemed calm; the appearance was

totally deceptive. For in the north the Soviets were making a tremendous drive for power.

Reza Khan led a detachment to Azerbaijan just then to stop tribesmen from disrupting the nation's communications and seizing power.

Soon Reza Khan was meeting with the politician Sayyad Zia ad Din Tabatabai, talking about the need for a seizure of power before all was lost with the restless movement of so many elements. The Shah, at his hunting lodge in Farakhabad, sensed the crisis, and shut himself up, surrounded by loyal guards, to await the events of the next few days.

It was February, 1921, the snows lay heavily in the mountains, and the cold of winter permeated the land; they met, the politician and the soldier. And the politician asked the soldier to seize control of the major towns, arrest the principal officials of the Qajar dynasty, and create a new temporary government with Sayyad ad Din at the head.

And what was in it for Reza Khan?

He would become commander in chief of the army.

To a man whose whole life had been the military, it should be prize enough. It was agreed, and next day on February 21, 1921 the coup was completed. Sayyad became the new chief of state. Reza Khan received the title of Sardar Sepah, command of the army, and a golden sword studded with jewels.

Soon, however, Reza Khan was dissatisfied with his bargain. He had not known much about Sayyad Zia ad Din, and what he learned about Sayyad's ties to the British did not please him. The officers that Reza Khan had suborned for the plot were also unhappy. What is a jewelled sword as compared to all power?

Reza Khan marched into Teheran a conqueror, and for the first time since his boyhood of discipline he could show the foreigners what he thought of them. Hassan Arfa, a young officer in command of a squadron of cavalry, stood in the courtyard of the Marble Throne, before the Gulistan palace, while the Shah acceded to the seizure of his power. In came Reza Khan, a powerful figure in the kingdom, wearing a black Cossack uniform with the ribbon and the jeweled sword he had been given. Reza, tall and dignified, slender and agile, passed before the line of the Shah's old officers, most of them red faced and overweight. He paused before the Chief of Police, General Westdahl, a Swede, who was the biggest and fattest of them all. The General saluted the new commander in chief, but so long had it been since he had shown proper discipline that his fingers did not reach his fur cap as they ought to have done.

Reza Khan seized the offender's hand, and forced it upward with such vehemence that the sheepskin cap tumbled off onto the ground, while the red faced Swede stuttered and stumbled.

That gesture showed how Reza Khan would behave in the new role of commander.

In the beginning, Reza Khan agreed with all the moves the new prime minister and virtual dictator wanted to make. They had agreed on independence, nationalism, non-alignment with either Britain or Russia, and many reforms, including regular pay for the army. The cabinet was totally filled with new faces; hopes were high.

But Sayyad Zia was a strange, mystical man (a type not uncommon in Moslem politics). He claimed divine guidance and descent from the Prophet. He was not willing to listen to advice. He was a slender man, of medium height, and deemed handsome by some. But he demanded the rights and perquisites of a son of the Prophet, and in matters that concerned the army, Reza Khan could not but disagree from time to time. Soon as Minister of War, the canny Reza Khan spent his time consolidating his power. It did not take long to realize that Sayyad ad Din did not have the sensibility to compromise that was necessary for a leader.

The insistence on the descent from the Prophet by his prime minister alienated the Shah, for his alliance with God and his power were thus threatened. The insistence on bringing British officers into command positions in the army, alienated Reza Khan.

Matters began to come to a climax. Sayyad Zia insisted that the South Persian Rifles be disbanded. In the way it was handled, the

British simply took it all away, moving some equipment to India and destroying the rest.

And having promised a bloodless revolution, Sayyad Zia found it necessary to call for the arrest of more and more people, including some from the provinces whose detainment or death could have brought about civil war. The Shah found Sayyad Zia a liability; he did not know how to govern. Reza Khan's officers, and the new friends among whom he moved were particularly infuriated.

As the weeks rolled by, Reza Khan consolidated his personal power until he had undisputable allegiance from the army. He then announced to the Shah his agreement that Sayyad Zia had become a liability. On May 25, 1921, Reza Khan told Sayyad Zia. What was left unsaid was enormous in its import, for the soldiers of the realm were ready to march at one word from Reza Khan.

And so Sayyad Zia ceased to be prime minister of Iran. Suddenly, all the old faces returned to Teheran, but with them one new face, the face of the general, the grizzled countenance of Reza Khan. And to anyone who looked closely, it was the most important face of all.

From his father's lips young Mohammed had heard these tales, and his studies of modern Iran had confirmed the dangers to him, so that even when he came, in his inexperience, to the throne, he had some background in the nuances of the politics of his country. In a way, he was lucky, because the first challenges to his authority came from outside the country; from Winston Churchill's Britain and Stalin's Soviet Union. Such challenge could not help but unite all Iranian patriots around their Shah, and that is what happened. Faced with this background; faced with a future of uncertainty in the cockpit of World War II, the Shah was yet to be tried. He was still too young and too unsure in the ways of intrigue to begin using the power that was his.

9
Seeds of Power

Young and inexperienced, still Shah Mohammed Reza Pahlavi was privileged to be onlooker, and sometimes party to the major events of an era, and to know the giant figures of our time more or less intimately.

In the summer of 1942, Winston Churchill stopped off in Teheran and had the courtesy to accept the Shah's invitation to luncheon. They talked of war and strategy, and while Churchill was never one to reveal his state secrets to a king he considered scarcely better than a puppet, the young Shah came away with the impression that here in Teheran had been born the seeds of Churchill's later "soft underbelly of Europe" policy. Perhaps. Perhaps not. But what is illustrated here is the cameraderie that existed between the monarch in his early twenties and perhaps the greatest war leader in the world.

The next encounter was in 1943, and it proved several important truths about these leaders, and much about Iran. The meeting was the Teheran Conference of the Grand Alliance, with Churchill,

Stalin, and President Franklin Roosevelt at that historic meeting.

In early November, two weeks before the conference, a flood of Muscovite agents rolled into Teheran to check out security. Concurrently there began a rumor that a plot was afoot to kill at least one of the Big Three statesmen. If, as many Iranians believed, the plot was part of a Soviet ploy, it all worked so well that the Americans and the British agreed to hold all the meetings inside the Soviet Embassy. The Shah invited President Roosevelt to be a guest at the palace. There was also the American Embassy for the President's use. But he was persuaded to take residence in the Soviet compound because of the ease of it all, it was said, with obvious reference to his crippled legs. Perhaps. It was odd, however, that the area of the Soviet Embassy to which the President was assigned was the communications compound. One might assume the Russians, with their most sophisticated bugging devices, had made proper preparations for the American arrival.

The architects of American policy in this period seemed to be Patrick J. Hurley, a retired general, and Herbert Hoover, Jr., a State Department professional. Many blamed them for the failure of the U.S. to seize a diplomatic initiative just then with the Iranians. Indeed, the young Shah was looking for a friend, surrounded as he was by "allies" who yearned for his territory and his oil, and by countrymen who wanted his throne.

The Shah invited President Roosevelt to the palace, but Roosevelt would not leave the Soviet compound, and the Shah was in the delicate position of having to go there, a supplicant in his own country, to pay an official call. He did it, but he did not forget it. The foreigners who snubbed him would pay for these snubs a thousand times in the future in meeting the protocol demands an unforgiving Shah would place on them when he became a truly important international figure.

Of them all, only Stalin, whose political leanings were as far from the Shah's as any human's could be, stayed behind after all the other leaders had left Teheran and spent four hours talking with the Shah about world problems.

The Shah did have one vital conversation with a group of American officials about the time of the Teheran Conferences. While the Big Three were discussing the fate of the world, the Shah was concerned with the fate of his country overwhelmed by events and occupied by two of the leading powers. He wanted economic help.

The Russians had offered him tanks and fighter planes, but he was leery of the Russian advisors who would come with them. How right he was as Egypt was to learn later when it accepted military aid from the Soviet Union under similar conditions.

The Shah told the Americans the fundamental needs of Iran after the war were both economic and social, First, Iran had to reinstitute a unity that had been established, at least on the surface, by Shah Reza and which had been fragmented and lost in the cutback of the military and the occupation by the foreign troops. All that had been done to unite and pacify the outlying tribes must be done over again. The Shah did not put it quite as he saw it, but he regarded the Kurdish and other tribal leaders as little short of brigands to be tamed.

Once order was established, the young monarch expected to take drastic action to bring about social reform. Most of Iran's land was held by a handful of landlords. This must be changed; these landholders must be cut down to size, and poverty must be stamped out of the country. The wealth must be redistributed.

These advanced views, coming from the son of Shah Reza, one of the most rapacious men in the history of Persia, were a little startling to the Americans.

Each man, said the young Shah earnestly, is entitled to:

1. Get food at a reasonable price.
2. Be educated.
3. Live under sanitary conditions.
4. Be able to maintain a decent, civilized home.

For a Middle East monarch, these were truly revolutionary ideas. They went far beyond his father's pacification and land plans. These ideas were the result of all those lonely hours he had spent behind the walls of Le Rosey school in Switzerland, studying the works of Thomas Jefferson and other liberal spirits of the past two centuries.

To achieve all this, said the Shah, would require outside economic support, which he hoped to get from the allies, and Draconian measures at home. It was a plan quite unlike anything that had ever before been proposed for Iran.

The Shah then laid out for the Americans his program:

He would achieve security by disarming the tribes. He was going to get the backing for that through a strong cabinet, representing disparate forces, and a powerful Majlis. He wanted American advisors to assist with his serious financial problems because Iran was a poor country. The biggest single revenue factor in terms of export was the revenue from the oil fields, and that did not amount to $20,000,000 a year.

But money would not alone do the job; it must be spent properly, and among the first steps must be the revival of old Shah Reza's once strong military establishment. "Otherwise Iranian blood will flow", the Shah told the Americans.

They talked for several hours, and were impressed with the social ideas of a young man so steeped in luxury; a king with the reputation of a playboy. Yet in all seriousness he was advocating a program that was nothing short of revolutionary.

The American officials left that meeting so impressed that they recommended in effect to take over Iran on a "big brother" basis. Finally, these proposals reached President Roosevelt, who said he was "rather thrilled" with the idea of using Iran as an example of what American policy could do. Thus was planted the seed of a long term commitment between the Shah and the Americans.

The immediate result of the Teheran Conference was a promise by the Big Three of help for Iran. But the confusion and anarchy continued to grow during the years of occupation. The British, quite understandably, were concerned with their war effort. The Soviets were a little more devious. Even as Stalin carried on the titanic struggle for the salvation of his country, he planned ahead for the postwar years, and his planning definitely called for the dismemberment of Iran.

The immediate problem was local. The people rioted in the streets of Teheran for bread and against inflation. Murder for political and religious reasons became an almost daily occurrence. And as the war drew to a close, Tudeh gained strength from Soviet infusions of money and material.

When it became apparent that the Axis powers were going to be defeated, several nations had Iran in their postwar planning. In the fall of 1943 representatives of Royal Dutch Shell came to Iran to seek oil concessions. The next spring two American companies sent representatives. The Soviets sent their own people.

What a dilemma! To achieve his national aims, the young Shah needed money, and the granting of oil concessions with their future royalties would bring the money. But he also recognized the danger of permitting foreign influence to become dominant. His intelligence agents and his secret police knew, too, that the situation in Azerbaijan was building to a crisis. He could expect the Soviets to exert every influence possible to first detach Azerbaijan, and then to communize his country.

So the Shah refused to deal with any of the foreigners. Not until the last foreign soldier had left Persian soil would there be any more talk about concessions. He made it even more positive: the Majlis passed a law forbidding government officials to even *discuss* oil concessions until the occupation ended.

The end of occupation was to occur six months after the cessation of hostilities. Meanwhile, during the last two years of war, the Shah, seeing what was happening around him, made himself as strong as his inexperience and youth would allow. He was nominally Commander in chief of the armed forces. With the help of several old cronies of his father's, the he became effectively chief of the forces, and such men as General Hassan Arfa reported dutifully on the events they observed.

The Majlis was virtually uncontrolled, the 136 deputies moving from one coalition to another for some temporary purpose. Sometimes the 12 Teheran deputies would vote together as Teheran men; sometimes they would split into Shiite Moslems and other factions. The Imperial Court, the army, the clergy, the merchants, the landholders all had their representatives in the Majlis, not in parties but in factions.

The country was also burdened with many newspapers. Not that freedom of the press was always maintained. The papers were sometimes suppressed by military authority or the court. But these papers almost all represented special interests, and some existed to blackmail the court and politicians. The young Shah's enthusiasm for the freedom processes, and particularly the press, was much diminished by what he observed between 1942 and 1945, and he participated in suppression of elements of the press.

But he was afraid, and there was no question that he had reason to be, particularly after the burning of the Prime Minister's house by an angry mob in 1942, when the bread of Teheran became a major national issue. For several nights an uncontrolled mob ran through the streets of the city burning shops, looting, and robbing. Mohammed Reza saw then what could happen in anarchy, and he determined that when he had the power restored, he would never permit return to such disgrace.

All this was happening while one Prime Minister was succeeding another, and members of the Majlis were playing musical chairs with the cabinet offices. Of the 136, some 70 of the members of the Parliament held cabinet offices from time to time. The young Shah, inexperienced as he might be, could see that the constant changes in government, forced by coalitions could not help but weaken all the processes. Further, such temporary government does not instil any deep loyalties. And with the shortages of war, and the opportunities for black marketeering and profiteering, corruption became an established fact or in the Iranian political process. Vast fortunes were made out of the occupation and the shortages. The Shah saw, but he was silent. He was having enough trouble holding together the forces loyal to him, for in the last three years of the war he was beset by enemies who wanted the

Qajars returned; others who sympathized with the Soviet demands and desires, and still others who hoped to profit from the establishment of the trappings of a republic.

The confusion lasted for months, but Shah Mohammed Reza sat in the Palace, went through the imperial forms every day, and waited. He had the one instrument of power that had brought his father to rule; he had the loyalty of the army.

At the end of December, 1944, the Shah was fortunate when the moderate deputies of the Majlis got together long enough to force a vital change in the government. Theoretically it was to ease relations with the Soviets, who were currently angry about their failure to get the oil concessions. So General Hassan Arfa succeeded to command of the army. The Russians applauded, for Arfa had always behaved impeccably toward them, and they believed him to be Pro-Soviet. But down deep, Arfa's loyalty was to the memory of Shah Reza, and to the person of the son, Shah Mohammed Reza. This factor was to be of limitless importance in the coming developments in Iran.

10

The First Coup

In the winter of 1945–46, the optimists of Teheran watched as the American and British troops left the country as they had promised to do in the treaty of alliance signed during the war. The Soviet army forces should be next, and they all should be evacuated, under the treaty, by March 2, 1946.

But March 2 came, and the Soviet troops remained.

From his intelligence, and from his shrewd chief of staff, General Arfa, the Shah knew in advance that the Soviets intended to stay on. And he knew why.

During the August before the Tudeh party had seized a number of government buildings in Tabriz, the capital city of Azerbaijan. The Russians had prevented the Shah from reinforcing the garrison. The Shah knew what was coming next—an attempt to tear Azerbaijan away from Iran and make of it a Soviet satellite.

Soon it happened. The Tudeh changed its name and organized an autonomous Republic of Azerbaijan, choosing its own prime minister. The Russians gave the new government complete support.

Meanwhile, in Teheran, the King was nearly checkmated by a combination of opponents—domestic and foreign. The Kurdish tribesmen, who had armed themselves during the war years, saw the removal of the occupation troops as a signal for their rebellion to achieve a national status in the lands to the west and south. In the capital city, Prime Minister Ahmad Qavam counselled compromise and adjustment to the demands of the Russians. He proposed to establish a joint Soviet-Iranian oil company to exploit the resources of northern Iran as Anglo-Iranian was doing in the south. He would give three cabinet ministries to members of the Tudeh party, knowing they were Communist dominated. He would recognize the independent Azerbaijan government that was so closely linked to Soviet Russia.

But the Shah was adamant, and he still had the single most potent force in Iran: the army. Further, he had the goodwill and backing of the United States and Britain in standing up against the Russian demands.

Qavam came to the palace counselling compromise. The Shah refused. The Western powers were not very helpful; it would be nearly two years before they would be ready for confrontation with Russian expansionism. But the westerners and the United Nations and the army were the only weapons the Iranian crown had at its disposal.

The Shah decided to use them all.

He made a formal complaint against the Russians in the Security Council of the United Nations. This was more effective than such complaints would become later. The U.N. was a new instrumentality and all nations professed to take its deliberations more seriously in 1946 than they would a dozen years later. The Soviets had quite enough commitment in Eastern Europe and in Asia, and the complaint to the Security Council, coming when it did, caught the Soviets unprepared. They agreed to move their troops out of Iran and did so in May.

With the Russians gone and the complaint made, Prime Minister Qavam was in a delicate position. He had arrested the Shah's friend, General Arfa and other officers; he had, in other words, tipped his hand that he was willing to let the Russians and the Communists take control of Iran.

The Shah knew only his own actions could save the situation.

For the first time he became a hard, stern figure, quite surprising to those who had suggested that he was nothing but playboy and puppet.

The internal politics became vicious and unrestrained, as the Communists, the religious leaders, and the Shah's adherents fought for control, with various other special interests taking and changing roles to suit themselves. The Tudeh, still very strong in the Teheran area, curtesy of the Russian occupation, hoped to dominate the elections proposed for that summer of 1946. They had a plan that would give them control of the Majlis, and that would mean the end of the Shah's rule.

The Shah sensed all this. He called in Qavam, ordered the new elections and ordered the Prime Minister to set up a new cabinet immediately without any Tudeh participation. This blow struck home; it deprived the Tudeh of much of its basis of support in Teheran.

The machinations these days were constant and complicated involving all the pressure groups in Iran, from tribal leaders to landholders.

Down south, the Russians fomented a strike of the workers in the Anglo-Iranian Oil Company fields, and three British warships came sailing into these waters and put troops ashore at Basra. If, as the Iranians said the Russians rigged the strike, it backfired, because the British and the Americans suddenly realize that Soviet aspirations toward Iran threatened their interests. It was at this point, the summer of 1946, that saw the end of acquiescence by the Western Powers to Russia's expansionism in Iran.

That change was vital to the Shah. Even with control of the army he could barely sustain himself. Also, he was beset by a succession of prime ministers who tried to bully him. But he was holding on—after July, 1946, he began to gain in the power struggle when he was backed by Britain and the U.S.

In September, the Shah's men moved against the tribes. At Isfahan, the Bakhtiari leaders were planning a rise of the tribes. However, they were arrested before they could move. But in the southeast the tribes did rebel. Coming as it did, this revolt, plus the trouble in Azerbaijan, could have been fatal to Iran. The Tudeh in control there seemed ready to declare total independence.

So the Shah was in the most serious crisis of his brief career. But in a way, the tribal upheaval strengthened his hand. The tribesmen demanded that Tudeh be outlawed and all Tudeh politicians be dismissed from the government. And this demand became more serious when a confederation of western tribes threatened to march on Kermanshah if the Tudeh were not disbanded.

Prime Minister Qavam shuffled his cabinet around in October and carefully refrained from appointing any Tudeh leaders to it.

Then came one of those breaks in the political picture that was so typical of the tangled state of Iranian affairs. General Ali Razmara had been playing all sides. He was first of all a general of the army and pretended to be—and perhaps he was—generally aligned with the Tudeh faction. At least he so convinced Minister Mozaffar Firuz, who *was* pro-Tudeh and ambitious beyond belief. But, looking at the situation in the fall of 1946, General Razmara decided to cast his lot firmly with the Shah. In a matter of weeks he had gained a tremendous backing in Teheran. The tribesmen were brought to the capital and declared their loyalty, because they trusted Razmara's ability to clear up the Tudeh mess in Azerbaijan.

With the change about on the part of Razmara, the Shah had the strength he needed to move, and his first move was into Khamseh province, near Azerbaijan. The government sent a strong force into the town of Zanjan, and the Azerbaijani insurgents then retreated along the rail line.

At one point the rebel forces had shown so much strength the Shah's men had feared Tudeh would try to occupy Teheran itself. Now the insurgents evacuated Zanjan and moved along the rail line towards Mianeh on the border of Azerbaijan.

In Teheran, the Shah's police uncovered a "plot" by Tudeh to seize power. It may have been real, but it may have been fabricated as were many plots in Iran over the years. In any event, it marked the end of Tudeh as originally constituted. The Russians stood by quietly while their party fell apart and went underground. A number of Tudeh party members were arrested and flung into the Shah's jails. Others disappeared—murdered or in deep hiding.

The Shah now put on the pressure. On December 3, 1946, Prime Minister Qavam was told to issue a new decree; the Shah had a plan for reoccupying Azerbaijan. The new elections to Parliament would cover every single area of Iran, and the Shah had never officially recognized the Tudeh takeover of Azerbaijan. So now he proposed to bring his troops into that province, maintain order (and suppress the Tudeh government) and then hold new elections.

At the palace, the Shah called a war council. He wanted to move the troops that day. Some political leaders and some generals demurred. They feared such a move would bring the power of the Soviet Army down on them.

The Shah did not think so. The Russians were swallowing and digesting territory in eastern Europe; they were bemused in Korea; they were attempting to support rebellions in the Balkans. The Shah did not believe the Russians would seek a confrontation with Britain and the U.S. in Iran. He overruled his supporters and officials and ordered the army to march.

Here for the first time since assuming the throne, the Shah took decisive action. It might have been the end of him, but the Soviets were bemused, as he had calculated. The troops marched, three columns of them, heading for Tabriz, the Azerbaijan capital, and the lesser cities that were occupied by Tudeh.

The Shah, committed, was the Shah aroused. For several years he had been a skilful airplane pilot, and now he went to the airport and flew his own plane over the rebel positions at Tabriz to ascertain their strength. He was not frightened by what he saw.

Back he came to put on more pressure.

He ordered Prime Minister Qavam to proclaim the Azerbaijan government a rebel organization because of its resistance to the troops. The leaders of Tudeh would be punished, he said.

This move served two purposes. First, it would smoke out the Russians in case they might be prepared for military action in Iran. In that event, the Shah could always stop his troops, turn back, and take his case to the United Nations. The second purpose was to discredit Tudeh and the leaders of the Azerbaijan separatist movement. The declaration made them outlaws and paved the way for the arrests and imprisonments that would follow.

On December 10 the central column crossed the Qezel Owzan river. The rebels had blown up the bridge and the troops had to ford the stream. Then there were skirmishes, as the retreating Tudeh moved back into the heart of Azerbaijan. No military intervention from the Russians materialized—the rebels had been deserted by their friends.

The insurgents were fighting and fleeing. Some escaped. Some were killed. Some were arrested.

The Russians did act, but in so doing they told the Shah precisely what he wanted to know. The Soviet Ambassador sent a message to the Shah urgently requesting an audience. It was granted and he came to the Palace, where the Shah greeted him and waited to hear what he had to say. Would it be the dreaded threat of the Red Army?

It was December 15.

The Ambassador began to threaten.

In the name of the Soviet government he demanded the immediate withdrawal of all Central Government forces from within the borders of independent Azerbaijan. He said the move was a violation of the United Nations charter, it was naked aggression, and the Iranian government was threatening world peace by its unilateral action.

So—it would not be war. The Shah knew his Russians, and had the Ambassador instructions to move armies, he would never have bothered to bluster.

So the Shah was cool. He said it was the Tudeh in Azerbaijan that had threatened the peace of the world, and that he was engaged in restoring territorial integrity and order to his own country. He then produced a telegram just received from the rebels. Ghazi Mohammed, Ghazi Sadr, and Molla Mostafa were the leaders of the rebellion and the government. They had just given up and accepted the power of the Central Government over Azerbaijan.

The Russian Ambassador was stunned. He mumbled out more in pleasantry, and then he made a quick exit from the palace.

The Central government troops marched into Tabriz. They occupied all the cities and the border posts. The lucky Tudeh soldiers and politicians escaped across the border into the U.S.S.R. The unlucky were hunted down and killed or thrown into prison. Retribution in the Middle East was always swift.

And the first great coup of Shah Mohammed Reza was won.

He had watched and waited, considered and schemed, and when the opportunity came, he proved himself an apt son and student of old Shah Reza.

11

Years of Crisis

Royalty, especially in time of crisis, has to appear in public, and once the rebels were put down in Azerbaijan, Iran's royal family presented a high profile for the first time since the wedding of the Shah and Princess Fawzia.

Fawzia, alas, was not involved. The marriage had been a failure in every way. No male heir, too many mistresses for the Shah, and too many lovers for Fawzia made the palace a center of scandal. Fawzia had taken to making excursions back to her native Egypt, and finally, the trusted General Hassan Arfa had seen her home for good. Rumors were floated that the health of the princess was uncertain, and that she could not bear the climate of Teheran. She did not come back, but from Egypt there were reports that Fawzia came storming back to her brother's palace speaking in loud tones of "those vagabonds and Persian sheep thieves," the Pahlavis.

But Princess Ashraf, the Shah's sister, went swiftly to Zanjan and Mianeh to supervise the distribution of relief supplies through the Red Lion and Sun, the royal equivalent to the Red Cross. Her appearance made it clear that the royal family was showing its interest in the people, and, if as was likely to happen in Iran, much of the substance of relief was diverted from the people, still the common folk appreciated the signs of interest in their welfare. The Pahlavi dynasty's position became a little better entrenched.

The Shah was still sitting on a powderkeg as 1947 began. He had barely overcome the first vital threat to his rule, and he knew that was only because the Russians had been unwilling to act in the winter of 1946 to save the Azerbaijan revolution. He also knew well that the Russians might step in at any time, and for one particular reason: during the period when Tudeh was strongest and the Shah was wondering if he could stave off their drive for national power, the Central Government and the Majlis had been bullied into creating a Soviet oil concession in the north. But in all the confusion of recent months the Majlis had not ratified it. The Soviets now pressed for ratification, and Ambassador Sadchikov threatened Prime Minister Qavam with the might of Russia if he did not yield.

Mozaffar Firuz, the Iranian Ambassador in Moscow, reported home that he was sure if the Majlis did not ratify the concession the Red Army would march on Azerbaijan and perhaps even on Teheran. How was that to be interpreted? Mozaffar Firuz was already suspected of having Russian proclivities. That was one basic problem of Iranian politics in modern times: it was difficult to tell what side a politician was on from one month to the next. Old Shah Reza knew the reason. Iran was corrupt from top to bottom. In his day he had paid his officials very little, and once he was asked by an outsider why he did this. He paid them half of what they worth, he said, because he knew very well that they were stealing the other half.

So was Firuz to be believed or not?

Luckily the United States had a canny Ambassador in Iran in 1947—and President Harry Truman was seriously concerned about Soviet imperialism around the world. For the Russians had shown in Poland, Korea, Bulgaria, Hungary and Rumania, that the old Czarist imperialist ideas had not been shelved by the Soviets. In Manchuria they had stripped the factories and storehouses of materials the Chinese Communists could have used. In addition to these old Czarist practices, one had to contend with the realities of the international revolution, as the Shah had discovered. The Americans also had discovered these facts by the beginning of 1947 and Ambassador George Allen made an important speech, defending the right of Iran to give or refuse various concessions to anyone in the world.

To the Shah, this meant the United States would support Iran if she had the courage to stand up to the U.S.S.R.

The Persians did stand up, and the Majlis voted overwhelmingly against granting any concession to the Russians. The Soviets, of course, took the position this was a move fostered by the United States and one that inimical to Soviet interests. But the Iranian point of view was quite different. The Shah and his supporters were simply tired of foreign exploitation and for once they had a chance to do something about it.

The Russians protested. The Americans began to send arms and supplies to Iran under the various programs begun under President Truman and Secretary of State George C. Marshall. And the Shah began to consider those old boyhood dreams of his.

Internally, the kingdom was in almost as much of a state of flux as it had been during the war years. The old Shah had been careful and close handed in his use of power. It could not be said that the young Shah had the same degree of control that his father had exerted before the weakening influence of the war. All the old privileged classes, the landholders and the clergy among them, had come back to positions of strength in these years and it was not going to be easy to dislodge them. Further, the Shah was in a weak position because he had no heir and by then it was common knowledge that the royal marriage was collapsing.

Prime Minister Qavam did not last long after the war. He was replaced by Ebrahim Hakimi as chief minister. He, too, only remained a short time. He was replaced by Abdul Hosein Hazhir, a vital younger man. He shared the Shah's feeling that the nation needed reforms to bring it into the 20th century, and that in fact Iran's survival depended on it becoming part of the modern world.

But the country was not yet ready for these reforms, and the Shah was not yet fully in control of the political forces to have his way in the forthright and sometimes brutal fashion of his father.

So one prime minister followed another, remaining in office only so long as he could manipulate the various forces. Out of this came little progress—that was the point of the special interests, to maintain confusion and prevent the kind of social legislation the old Shah had begun, and that the landholders knew the young Shah favored. And the Shah knew that he could never carry out his program until he had the resources in his power. Examining the problem coldly, he could see what those resources were. First and foremost was the resource of the people, proud of their heritage, ill-educated, not even united as to customs and languages. That resource would last and serve Iran well, but it was almost latent in its usefulness. The people would have to be educated, trained, taught even to read and write in a common language, and early on, the Shah decided that the tongue for all within the borders must be Persian or Farci.

The second resource was oil, an estimated 35 billion barrels beneath the ground. The trouble here, however, was that Iran was not in control of her own oil resources. For nearly fifty years the British had held the oil concession in the south, and although Anglo-Iranian Oil Company had a fine-sounding name, it was a British company, operated by the British for British interests. And it would remain that way until the Shah could effect a basic change.

After the revolution in Azerbaijan and the bringing of Central Government control back to the Palace, the Shah began planning to push the foreigners out of his country. He was told by his experts that the oil resources could scarcely last a hundred years. How long would the Pahlavis last then? If the dynasty was to survive, the Shah would have to create a new source of wealth in a dry and mountainous clime whose historic use had been as grazing land and with small areas in the north suitable for crop raising and orchards.

These were questions he pondered—not as a Thomas Jefferson might have pondered them. He proposed to be, as his father was, the ruler of the country. He would bring reforms, he was already a good enough reader to see that the grand appeal of Marxism was land and labor reform; and he was egotist enough to believe that he could capture that kind of revolution and turn it to the path of monarchy. He had one basic weapon (two, if you count the army): the people were used to monarchy and the peasants seemed rather to wish their monarch to live in as God-like fashion as possible.

So the Shah's direction, in the middle 1940s, was to put together an Iranian Oil Company which was to explore the countryside outside the 100,000 square miles still granted Anglo-Iranian under the oil concession as revitalized in 1933. The British were taking 19 million tons of oil out of Iran then (1947) and the Shah and his oilmen were resenting every ton of it.

True, the Shah was planning, but as far as results were concerned he had not shown himself in any way to be his father's equal. During the elections of 1947 the disturbances in Teheran were so severe that for several days the Shah took refuge in the palace grounds in what amounted to an armed camp. After the elections were safely won and the Majlis installed in non-revolutionary hands, the Shah felt it possible to move about more, and he made some public appearances, even going to Azerbaijan again.

The year 1948 marked the Shah's emergence on the world scene. He began with a trip to Malta, where he was received with pomp by the Governor General and the Prime Minister. He went on then to Britain that spring to be received by King George VI and the Queen, to get medals and visit warships, visit the House of Commons, be guest at a grand garden party at Buckingham Palace, be lunched by the Lord Mayor of London, to visit Anglo-Iranian Oil Company (not without malice in his heart and plans for the future) and to fly a jet plane. It marked his growing love affair with jets. For a king, he was a remarkably good pilot.

He was restless this year, and with good reason—in the fall came a dual divorce: Farouk of Egypt divorced his queen Farida and on the same day the Shah divorced Fawzia, who had pleaded malaria and never come back to Teheran after her departure more than two years earlier. For a while the press tried to pretend the reason was illness, but the Ministry of Court finally had to admit at least some information about the erotic scandale that had been going on in the palace.

The Shah, on his trips abroad and his stays at home, continued to live in magnificent sin with a number of black-haired beauties. For a time, it might even appear that a raven-tressed motion picture star was going to be the new Empress of all the Iranians. Of course, the law still said the Empress had to be a Persian citizen, but the law had been changed for Fawzia and the law could obviously be changed for another.

Shah Mohammed Reza, however, was enough master of his loins not to make the fatal mistake of marrying the wrong woman for the wrong reasons. He was master in another way, too. The Shah and the people around him have never had a feeling for freedom. The press was always an instrumentality to be used to promote the purposes of the regime. True, during the period of weakness, from 1941–46, literally hundreds of publications mushroomed but they didn't last long. These newspapers, and magazines and news letters represented every shade of opinion. They were protected by the military authorities of the U.S.S.R. and Britain, and by the general confusion that set in during the dual occupation. But with the troops gone, the regime was not inclined to accept journalistic license. The Shah was also tremendously sensitive to the foreign press' views of his country; he wanted a good deal from Britain and America, and he did not want bad publicity. Thus, came many a suppression; dozens of arrests of journalists in 1948 and 1949. That winter the correspondent of the London *Times* was expelled for revealing facts inimical to the Shah's regime.

That winter also occurred a new crisis in the life of Shah Mohammed Reza—something entirely new to him. On February 5, under the most apparently innocent of circumstances, the Shah was nearly killed.

He had gone to Teheran University to distribute prizes and by his presence indicate his support for higher education. He was on the platform of the auditorium of the school his father had founded, shaking hands with the rector and officers of the University.

As the Shah in his splendid uniform bowed and smiled, the photographers for the newspapers gathered round to get his picture. Even in those days the Shah appeared regularly on the front pages of the papers.

One photographer stepped forth out of the mass, as if to get a better picture. He was Fakhre Rai, an ardent young man who did not believe the Shah was serving the interests of his country. He aimed not a camera but a pistol at the Shah, and he fired in rapid succession.

On stage the Shah was hit. One bullet struck him in the lip and one in the back. Police jumped on the photographer as he got off the last of his five shots. He was nearly killed in the melee.

The Shah was only grazed in the back, and the bullet that struck him in the lip came out his cheek without doing serious damage. He was rushed to the military hospital nearby, where he could have adequate treatment, and protection. For who knew what forces were abroad this wintry day?

But in a matter of hours, the Shah was back at the palace, safe and under heavy guard. He broadcast to the nation that day, calling for order and unity.

He got the order, but the hard way. The assassination attempt was certainly an indication that certain forces in the land wanted the Shah out of the way, and the kingdom destroyed.

What forces?

Tudeh's Communists had gone underground and to Russia. But among the students of Teheran University there was a definite radical group, or groups. Some of the radicals were certainly Marxist. Some were anarchist, but the Marxist leftovers of Tudeh, the Shah decided, were the dangerous force, the organized group who would act in such a fashion. The political police began arresting suspected radicals throughout the city, and in the university communities of other towns.

The Shah and his secret police then instituted a reign of terror. Five newspaper editors were arrested, tried, and swiftly sentenced to a year in jail for "vilifying" the royal family. Their criticisms of the wild parties and rich entertainments of the Pahlavis and their friends were taken by the authorities to be treason. They were accessories before the fact of the assassination attempt.

Meanwhile, any old leaders of Tudeh who could be found were rounded up. Fourteen of them were tried for treason. At the universities the students kept their heads down if they wished to be safe. For from that time on the universities, and Teheran university in particular, would be the hotbed of rebellion against the absolute rule of the Pahlavis, and they would be infiltrated and watched year after year.

The planners of the assassination were sought and the gunman was sentenced to death, but as a public relations gesture the Shah commuted his sentence.

But the unrest continued that year. On November 4 the Shah's "Young Turk" supporter and one-time prime minister, Abdul Hosain Hazhir, was shot and seriously wounded by a religious fanatic. It was not just the Marxists, not just the agents of Soviet imperialism, whom the Shah had to fear. All Iran was in turmoil still.

12

Soraya

Since the day Fawzia left the palace for Egypt, the Shah's mother and his sisters had been insisting that he needed a queen. So much was evident to the man on the street, and one way to lessen the danger of the times would be to install in Teheran a queen of great popularity who would help take the peopel's minds off their troubles. And then, there was always the question of an heir and of succession. It had become of more importance in recent years.

The question of succession was particularly emphasized in 1950 with the return to Iran of the remains of Old Shah Reza, who had died in exile in South Africa. The Shah staged a state funeral for his father. There was no better way of showing that the Pahlavi dynasty was in Iran to stay.

The coffin was brought from Johannesburg to Alexandria and then by ship to Teheran. The Shah invited the neighboring Moslem nations to send representatives and units to participate in the grand ceremony. The Iranian forces were there in their dress uniforms, the generals and admirals with all their medals and members of the diplomatic corps in formal dress. There were representatives and military units from Pakistan, Turkey, and Iraq. The Shah's body was placed on a catafalque and as the military marched past, the bands played the funeral music, and planes flew overhead.

Altogether it was a sad and impressive moment, as the Shah had hoped it would be. It was an honor to his father, it emphasized establishment of the dynasty's continuation, and was a grave warning to enemies internal or external that the Shah was vigilant.

Under the watchful eye of Hussein Ala and the royal family, then, the search for a queen was redoubled.

Hussein Ala had the major responsibility. He was even then an old man, one who had served the Pahlavis well. What he was now called upon to do, of course, also meant serving himself well at the same time. He had been educated at a private boarding school (public school) in England; he had served as Foreign Secretary and Prime Minister. He was, indeed, the first to stand up against the Russians in the U.N. Security Council at Lake Success.

And he was immensely rich. If he had not been rich before, the Ministry of Court position would have assured his fortune. He was in charge of some 400 court employees, whose appointments must be renewed every year. He renewed them or not as he pleased. He also had authority over the jobs of hundreds of other officials, and it was deemed wise of these to come to Hussein Ala at the end of the year bearing gifts. The most suitable gift was money.

By Iranian standards Hussein Ala was not corrupt. He seemed to be an effective bastion, standing between the royal family and the world. For at that time only ten of the 400 employees of the palace and the family residences, had access to the Shah, and that access was controlled by Hussein Ala. He managed a half dozen palaces from his office, which was inside a doorway guarded by a pair of large stone lions and just within the palace grounds. From there would go orders to the Queen mother's summer palace near Kajar, or to the residences of Princess Sham and Princess Ashraf, or to the second wife of old Shah Reza, or her children, the half brothers of the Shah.

He was in charge of dispensing pay and allowances, and when Princess Fatima married and went to live in San Francisco, the Ministry of Court took care of all the problems involved in such a move.

After the interment of the old Shah, a sort of hysteria struck the nobility of Persia. It manifested itself in strange ways. Scores of letters came to the palace from fathers offering their daughters as the new Queen consort of the Shah. One nobleman even ran his daughter's picture in a Teheran newspaper, advertising her beauties for the Shah and his ministers to see. For a time, it was rumored that the Shah would marry the daughter of Hussein Ala himself, but that proved untrue.

The search was conducted near and far. But finally, as it was narrowed, it came within the purview of a handful of influential people—the people around the Peacock Throne.

In May, the Queen Mother took over the search herself, and she was assisted by one of her ladies in waiting, Mme. Furuzafar from Isfahan. Ladies and nobles from all over the kingdom submitted the names of beautiful young women with proper lineage to be queen of all the Persians.

The Queen Mother was now doing what her late husband once did. He had selected the spouses of all his children. She would find her son a queen, and in so doing would strengthen her own position at the court. She sorted through a hundred biographies and examined photographs of more than a score of young women until she narrowed the choices to two. One of them, it just so happened, was the niece of her lady in waiting, Mme. Furuzafar.

This girl was eighteen years old that year, and she was the daughter of a khan (leader) of the Bakhtiari tribe, which lived in and south of Isfahan. An alliance with the Bakhtiari was much to be desired because this was one of the most powerful tribal factions in the kingdom. So when Mme. Furuzafar suggested her niece, she was heard, and when she produced the lovely girl's photograph, the Queen Mother was half convinced, for Soraya Esfandiary was a slender, black-haired beauty with rich full lips, dark brows and mysterious almond eyes.

Her mother was Eva Karl of Berlin. The marriage was a part of the cultural alliance of the Persians with the Germans under the old Shah. Esfandiary had spent much of his youth in Berlin, and Soraya had grown up there. She spoke German and Russian before she spoke Persian.

Soraya was enrolled at the Froebel school in Berlin, where she was a good enough student. She also had her first taste of acclaim, playing the Princess in the play "Sleeping Beauty." But when the Esfandiary family came home in 1937 from Germany there was absolutely no thought that Soraya would be marrying into the Pahlavi dynasty. She was, after all, only five years old.

The next ten years were spent in Isfahan, where Soraya attended a school kept by a matronly German woman and learned Persian as well.

In 1947, when Soraya was 15, the family took her to Switzerland. They lived in Zurich and she was enrolled in a finishing school in Montreux.

She was as happy as a girl could be. She was much in demand in the social life of the school. She went dancing at Hotel le Cocu on Lake Geneva, skiing in the mountains in the winter, sometimes at St. Moritz and sometimes at Gstaad.

When the word reached Switzerland in 1947 that "the Persian climate did not agree with Empress Fawzia" and that she was going back to Egypt, Soraya scarcely remembered it. She was too involved in the social life of a wealthy young woman of Switzerland. Nor did Soraya have any reaction when the shock of the Shah's divorce struck Iran. She was not looking for lightning to strike, although even as a girl she had ominous feelings about her own life. She fully expected Kismet to catch up with her at some point because she was so absolutely happy in Switzerland. But she did not read the court biography of Fawzia with its ominous implications as that lady passed out of the life of Iran:

"They have nothing with which to reproach each other," wrote the Minister of Court about the divorce of the Shah, "since neither adhered strictly to matrimonial etiquette."

So the girl in Montreux went dancing again in Lausanne, and kept to herself her feelings of guilt about the future, with no thought of the ominous message. There was no reason to believe it was meant for her.

But Soraya did not reckon with the ambition of her aunt, or the determination of the Queen Mother to find a suitable wife for the Shah. And when the Queen Mother had narrowed the field to two girls, she dispatched Princess Shams, eldest child of the Pahlavis and two years older than the Shah, to visit Soraya. By this time Soraya had been taken out of the finishing school in Switzerland and was sent to St. James School in London. It was a sign of the times: the postwar world was dominated by Russia and America and Britain. Germany was ruined. So it behooved a well-bred young Iranian girl to master English and the Anglo-Saxon ways. Thus, the school in London.

So Princess Shams and her entourage flew there in a private plane, bringing some members of Soraya's family along to make the girl feel a little more at home. Soraya was summoned from her school one day to a formal tea in a private room at Claridge's, and there Shams took a good look at the candidate for her country's throne. The awesome princess kissed the young girl on the cheek and tried to make her feel comfortable, but every moment she was observing and making mental notes.

Shams had been given a great responsibility—the right to decide whether the girl was equal to the task of becoming Empress of the Persians. It would mean a cram course in the ways of royalty, and even more hard work in the study of Persian royal ways.

On the second day of Shams' visit, the Persian ambassador was in attendance when Shams nodded and announced she was convinced: the girl would do nicely.

Suddenly, as with the kiss in "Sleeping Beauty," the whole world of Soraya Esfandiary was turned about. She was ordered to pack for she would not be returning to the English finishing school. Two days later, Shams and her entourage took Soraya to Paris for a rush course in queenly culture and a suitable wardrobe for a young woman who was to marry the Shah.

They put up at Le Crillon hotel, on the Champs Elyssees, and they dined at the fashionable restaurants. In the daytime they went to Fath-Dior for the showings, and to other couturier establishments, where Shams' servants explained what would be needed, and seamstresses began to work at double speed.

Mornings were spent by Soraya in a "training" program. She was given books on Persian history and culture to read. She was tested on her knowledge of Persian literature. Shams watched her walk across the room, and determined that Soraya's walk was much too serpentine for the palace.

She would have to learn how to walk regally.

She would have to lose her Isfahan accent and acquire the speech of Teheran and the court circle.

She would have to learn the etiquette of the palace.

The rigors of training continued. One small ceremony occupied hours of exercise:

Soraya's cousin, Malechior Baktear, was her partner in this exercise, the purpose of which was to train her how to greet the Queen Mother when she met her. For the old woman was a virago, and the whole project might come to a sudden end if in Teheran Soraya made some slip of etiquette that convinced the lady that the girl was unfit to occupy the Peacock Throne.

So Malechior Baktear dressed up in his best, to create the proper atmosphere, and played the part of the Shah, while Soraya played herself, the aspiring princess.

Baktear stood in one room, looking Shahlike. Soraya approached the doors and equerries threw them open. Coming forward in her long voluminous gown, she curtsied deeply as the doors opened, then advanced five yards, and curtsied once more, bowing her head to her sovereign.

There, that was the way she would meet the Queen Mother on that first day.

They practiced the exercise, and they did it again, and a third time, and more until Soraya was ready to drop with exhaustion.

But she would be queen, and so she continued her efforts, reading, writing, learning, trying on clothing, practicing courtly ways and courtly accents.

The days went by, and then the weeks. The bills mounted, for hotels, for clothes, for cars and for all the luxuries that Paris could offer in these relatively lean times.

Summer passed, and Soraya struggled with the problems of courtliness. Then autumun came, and Shams began to grow restive. She had word from the Queen Mother, who wondered if they were ever coming home.

So then began the final examinations. Shams listened as Soraya proved how well she had conquered the Isfahan accent when she spoke Persian. Shams examined the wardrobe and her way of wearing it critically. Shams checked to be sure the future queen walked regally.

And then the examination was over. She had passed and they were flying back to Teheran for the supreme test. Soraya would be presented to the royal family.

In the palace, the Queen Mother had assembled the royal family for the inspection of the prospective bride. The Queen Mother was sitting in a yellow silk chair that had the aspect of a throne—cold, forbidding, making no concessions—as she prepared to inspect the girl. Around her were clustered the princes and princesses, Ashraf, Fatima, Ali, Abdur, Sholam, and a few yards away, standing by himself in his uniform and medals, was the Shah.

Soraya came in, in her long court gown, curtsied flawlessly, advanced, and curtsied again, while the Shah came to her and took her by the arm. Even the old Queen Mother unbent a little, for here indeed was a personage who could be considered regal.

The room relaxed. Soraya had passed all tests.

Three days later the Court Calender announced the betrothal of the Shah to Soraya Esfandiary. The wedding was set for December 27, 1950.

Princess Ashraf—the Shah's twin.

Soraya—once she was Queen.

Teheran University's school of fine arts gives an idea of the new in Iran.

Universities like Iran National have sprung up all over the land.

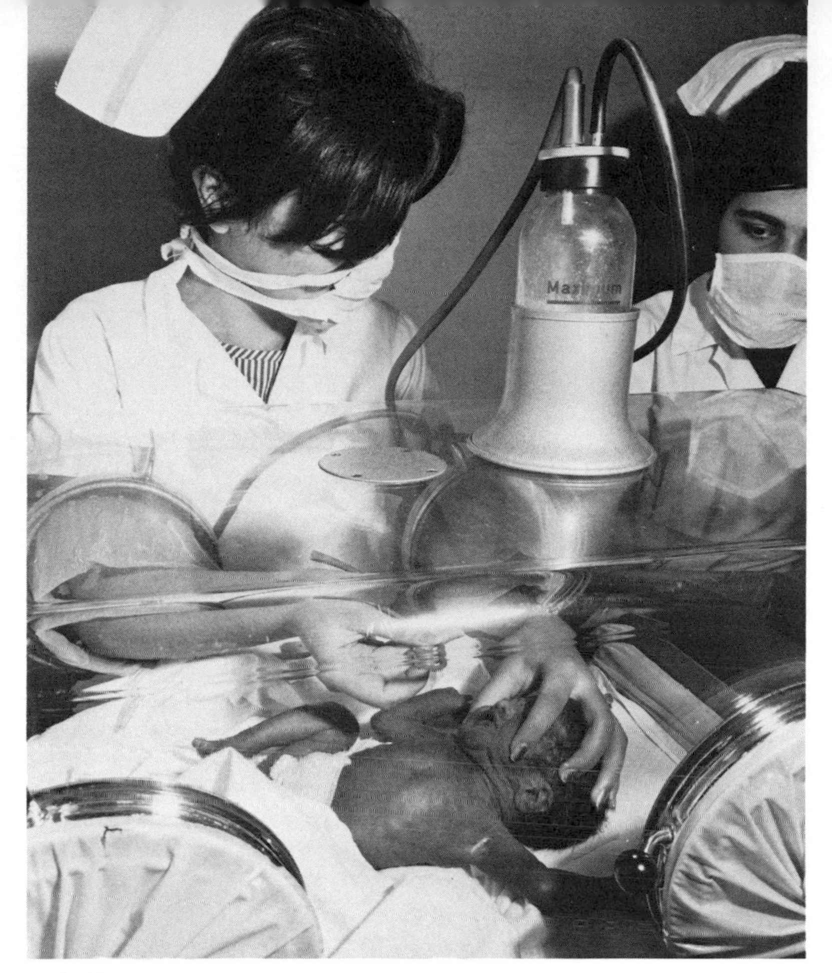

ledical care in Iran.

The quickness with which Iran acts to prevent the spread of epidemics from neighboring nd other countries, and the results it gets, indicate the extensiveness and efficiency of public ealth programs in Iran, especially on the preventive side. This has been partly due to the rowing economy. An immediate impact has been felt on the rate of mortality which has been duced considerably, only to swell further the population growth, now at 2.5 per cent per annum.

Generally speaking, the number of physicians, hospital beds, and outpatient clinics has oubled since 1963. The increase has been most remarkable in the number of nurses, about 00 per cent in the same period. In 1965 no more than three per cent of Iranian physicians erved in rural areas; today, over 23 per cent of them are in villages. The ratio, however, is not tisfactory, considering that still about 60 per cent of the population is rural. Also, the ratios doctors and hopital beds against the number of people — one to each 4,000 and 940 people, spectively — are far from satisfactory even if they are much better than those in many other ountries.

The creation of the Health Corps in 1964, under which young graduates from medical and lied schools extend, in lieu of military service, basic medical care and facilities to the remote eas of rural Iran, has been instrumental to health development in Iran. As a result of their rvice, a substantial part of the resources normally spent by the public sector for general health evelopment has been released for more concentrated efforts on more demanding areas. Thus, *ter alia*, the number of hospitals has increased from 351 in 1964 to 502 in 1970, and that of spital beds from about 24,120 to just under 35,800.

Graduation ceremony at Teheran School of Medicine.

Education and medicine are two fields which attract more female students in Iran. While the number of Iranian students is on the constant rise, the ratio of female to male students is improving to even each other out.

Educating its young and rapidly increasing population has put a heavy burden on Iran; however, education becomes both a means and an end for rapidly developing countries. As part of Iran's educational revolution or reorganization, increasing attention has been paid to research, curricular improvements, book production and distribution, etc.

A Literacy Corps soldier and his villagers. The goal is 100 percent literacy.

The young men of the Literacy Corps also help build.

Literacy Corps—a new method to promote education.

In a vast country like Iran, with a principally young population — over 50 per cent of the population is under 18 — and with a birth rate of about three per cent, despite a receding illiteracy problem, the extension of universal education is a tremendous task and calls for new solutions and unorthodox methods. These have included the use of mass communication such as educational television and radio, and the creation of the "new-frontier" Education Corps (Literacy Corps); the latter, a purely Persian initiative, has set a world precedent and example.

The Education Corps was created by drafting high-school graduates who were surplus to the current army requirements and by sending them to villages as teachers after some induction training. So far, nearly 85,000 young people (about 9,500 of them girls) have served a period of 14 to 18 months in villages throughout the country, giving primary education to about five million children, literacy courses to nearly half-a-million adults and teaching them basic health, home economics, modern agricultural techniques, co-operative methods, etc. However, still about seven per cent of school-age children in urban areas and around 45 per cent in rural areas go without adequate schooling.

For a rapidly developing country, education becomes both a means and an end. The development apparatus of the nation needs increasing number of skilled workers and experts. Higher education, vocational and technical training, and now permanent education are the order of the day. Next to the site of the 2000-year-old Gondi Shapur University in Khuzestan, a new one has sprung up to bring the total up to seven throughout the country. The eighth one is to be set up in Kerman with a $10 million donation of an Iranian entrepreneur.

13
The Queen

The Persian people are both suspicious and superstitious as are most primitive peoples, and the coming marriage of the Shah to Soraya was regarded with deep concern by those who addressed themselves to divining the future through signs. Some did not approve of the mixture of her parentage although, unlike Fawzia, she was a native born Persian citizen. Some did not approve of her foreign education. And some, harking back to the Qajars, took the position that this marriage would be disastrous for Iran.

The Iranian Constitution had been so drawn that without a major change no person of Qajar blood could ever again sit on the Peacock Throne. That ruled out the succession of all but one of the Shah's brothers. The old Shah Reza finally had four wives and two of them were Qajars princesses. So many of the 11 children of the old Shah did have Qajar blood.

All the more reason for the Shah to marry quickly, and present the nation with an heir.

The Mullahs were consulted, and the most propitious times

were mentioned for the marriage, and that is how the date was set. But it was not to be.

Each day that fall when his official duties were done, the Shah came to visit Soraya at the Queen Mother's palace, driving his white sports car. Even after the assassination attempt of 1949, he still liked to drive out in the country alone or with a friend to escape his cares. The Savak—his secret police—dreaded these excursions and were forever trying to frustrate him. But occasionally he did get away. A few times that fall, the Shah and Soraya escaped for drives. After one of them, she came down a few days later with an illness.

"Gastric flu," said the court physicians.

"Poisoning," said the penny press. Dark forces were at work in Teheran, they predicted, and the omens were wrong for the happiness and success of this marriage.

The illness turned out to be neither gastric upset nor poisoning. It was a severe case of typhoid fever, and the empress-designate was confined to her bed with the doctors worrying whether or not she would survive.

The crisis came, and she surmounted it, but she was far too weak to undergo the stress of a court wedding in December.

That situation did pose a quandary. By Persian myth and custom, any marriage of royal personages between February 15 and August 15 was likely to turn out badly. (Had not the Shah's marriage to Fawzia been a disaster?) The mullahs and the seers counselled against such waiting; it could not but bring bad luck. And as for waiting an entire year, it was impossible; the court structure was simply not geared to keeping an extra unemployed empress about without title or task.

So the Shah chose almost the last possible lucky day, February 12, 1951, for the wedding ceremony.

Meanwhile, in December and January, as the court servants prepared for the ceremony, Soraya spent most of her time in bed or resting on a chaise. She also became accustomed to the unbelievable luxury which was lavished on her in true Persian royal style. If she wanted truffles, a plane went to Zurich and flew them in. If she wanted sweets, a plane was flown from London with the finest toffees and chocolates. From Montreux she retrieved her record collection. Whatever whim she expressed was immediately indulged. The Shah, that absolute monarch, spared no expense to make his sick fiancee as happy as he could.

And while Soraya rested, the court prepared for the royal wedding. A stand-in was found to wear her gown and take her part in the wedding rehearsals so the other members of the court would be sure to know their roles.

So came the great day, February 12.

Hamdullillah—God is Great and God Be Praised—shouted the mullahs in the mosques on the day, and so said the Court Calendar.

Pale, and still very weak, Soraya dressed in her Christian Dior gown of silver brocade, tulle, with a thousand sequins sewn on, and a train ten yards long.

When the appointed hour arrived, up came a unit of Persian lancers on their splendid horses, their silver and steel glittering in the cold air of winter Teheran, and riding with them in a golden Rolls Royce limousine that belonged to the Shah was the Mayor of Teheran, who would escort the bride to the Marble Palace for the wedding.

At five o'clock in the afternoon, the empress to be arrived in the hall of Mirrors of the grand palace, and there she was met by the Queen Mother, and Shams, and Ashraf and Fatima, and all the princes, and the cousins and the nobility, and the minister and major members of the Parliament, and the Ambassadors of the diplomatic colony and their wives. There were generals and admirals and dignitaries from all the world around.

The palace was decorated in all the splendor that the Ministry of Court could lavish upon the sovereign. Twelve hundred branches of white lilac had been flown in from Holland along with a thousand red carnations, for these latter were Soraya's favorite flower.

Queen Juliana of the Netherlands sent as her tribute a plane load of tulips and orchids and a florist to care for them; other flowers had come from the Caspian.

Soraya was prepared for her ordeal of the next few hours, and, given her condition, it was bound to be difficult. To begin with, she and her six bridesmaids must now ascend the 630 steps to the Hall of Mirrors, where she would meet the Shah. He, in turn, would step out of his nearby study, in his powder blue uniform.

So it began, Soraya and her six bridesmaids coming up the stairs, the heavy train behind her, and the strain showing on her delicate face.

Already assembled in the hall were the important persons of the wedding, including the High Mullah of Teheran, who would perform the simple service of Persia. The guests were gathered around, including the Aga Khan and the Begum who were the guests of honor this day.

On the table before the High Mullah lay an ornate gold-leafed Koran, and on a prayer rug before him were the symbols of the moment—silver, sugar, cake, and a two-yard-long loaf of bread which symbolized the hopes for a full and happy life. Lighted candles suggested a bright future, even though in the bazaar that evening old crones were reading tea leaves and predicting dire happenings at the palace.

To ward off such evil, and the spirits of djinns long dead, incense was burning in the room, near a silver carafe of water.

Soraya and the Shah met and he took her hand and escorted her to a throne, next to the Peacock Throne. She passed a golden mirror which reflected "beauty". She sat down and laid a copy of the Koran on her lap.

The Shah's secretary brought a diamond ring on a pillow and the new Empress put it on her finger. Then she rubbed her hands in sugar, to symbolize plenty. The official part of the ceremony, the simple signing of the marriage contract, had already been accomplished.

Now came the glory of celebration.

The first act was for the Shah to throw handfuls of pearls and golden coins to the watchers, and beribboned ambassadors and daintily clad ladies groveled on the floor for them. They were the prizes of the wedding, intrinsically valuable, but even of greater worth for their symbolism, for one who had a coin or a pearl stood out as having *been* at the royal wedding.

The guests then gathered to examine the gifts that had come from the leaders of the world for the royal pair, and Soviet Ambassador Sutschikov presented on behalf of Stalin a black onyx writing set studded with diamonds for the Shah, plus a white mink coat of flawless skins for the new Empress.

There were presents from dozens of nations. President Harry Truman, anything but a rich man before the publication of his memoirs, gave a crystal bowl from the famous Steuben glass works of America. King George VI sent a fine set of Georgian candlesticks. The President of the Republic of France sent French vines for the northern vineyards, where the Shah's lands and other produced respectable red, white, and rose wines.

The Austrian government sent a fine grand piano for Soraya to play in her leisure time. Pakistan sent a set of Himalayan costumes.

And so it went, each government contributing some remembrance that was indigenous to the gift-giver—but none so grand as Stalin's.

As the reception continued, the Shah saw how tired his bride had become, lugging that heavy train about in the warm room, and he cut short the reception at the palace.

Soraya went into a retiring room, and there her bridesmaids cut most of the train away so she could manage the weight better.

Now the 1500 guests assembled in the grand dining hall of the Gulistan palace, where plush carpets had been laid for the cars of the royal family, and where thousands of flowers brought in by plane from the Caspian had been planted in the snow for the single day's showing. They brought a touch of springtime to the palace in the midst of winter.

Here for the banquet the famous crown jewels of Iran were

displayed, emeralds as large as pigeons' eggs, a flawless emerald ring for the empress, a platinum jewel encrusted tiara, and the high, jewelled crown of the Shah.

At 9 o'clock they entered the hall, beneath the crystal chandeliers and mosaics that marked this beautiful room with all its promise of plenty. It was altogether a resplendent and courtly crowd, assembled to pay homage to one of the last of the absolute monarchs, in his palace, on his terms.

The Teheran symphony Orchestra played that evening for the feasters, mostly Beethoven for Beethoven was the favorite of the new Empress's western composers.

That night it was announced that the Anglo-Iranian Oil Company was giving £ 500,000 for a hospital to be erected in Teheran in honor of the wedding. The fine hands of the international oil politicians were seen even here. Anglo-Iranian was beginning to feel the pressure of the Shah's and Iran's displeasure over the siphoning off of national resources by foreigners.

The tables were laden with all that one could wish, including caviar by the quart and served with golden ladles from blocks of solid ice. Silver champagne goblets were at each place where 135 were to be seated at the horseshoe table with the Shah and his party, the lesser dignitaries at long adjoining tables. But for the true Moslem who did not drink champagne, there were several varieties of Iranian grape juice. There also was whiskey, vodka and gin and imported beers from Europe.

The menu consisted of French and Iranian specialties, for the Shah had long ago acquired a taste for French cooking that was completely shared by his Swiss-educated wife. Still wines accompanied the dishes as they came: soupe imperiale, baked salmon, saddle of lamb, pheasant on rice, asparagus with hollandaise sauce —a grand undertaking for a chef when done for 1500 people—and finally, ice cream and fruit, then brandies and cordials.

The meal lasted for three hours, the Shah and his party then left, but the revellers continued longer. It was, as they said in Teheran, a wedding party fit for a king.

14
The Coming of Mossadegh

On the night of the wedding, Queen Soraya was exhausted and the Shah knew it. So next day the pair flew to a country palace at Ramsar, the Shah flying the plane himself to this castle on the Caspian. They would have at least a brief honeymoon away from the cares of state.

The parade of Prime Ministers had continued in Teheran during these past few months. One could almost call it government by assassination, for feeling was running high against foreigners, against the Anglo-Iranian Oil Company, against events and life as it was lived in this country.

The Shah, at this point in reign, was willing to begin a liberalization policy in order to protect the throne and carry out some of the plans he had developed in his youth. This idea was not totally elymosynary—he saw since the end of World War II, the gradual beginning of a middle class as Teheran grew. He wished to encourage this, though it would have come about anyhow with the intrusion of foreign goods and salesmen into the market. He could profit by it personally. He would sell land and engage in business enterprise, thus helping the farmers secure a landhold of their own, setting an example that could later be used to unseat the powerful landlord class, and profiting for himself.

The Shah owned some nine hundred thousand hectares of land, about two million acres. These had, of course, been acquired by his father under what westerners would call questionable circumstances. They included hundreds of villages. By proper use of power in these trying times the Shah could strengthen his own position, which had never yet equalled his father's.

He established this year an organization called Amlag which was dedicated to the Imperial Distribution of Land. He wanted to make it a general policy, but he met opposition from the landlord class in the Majlis, among them Dr. Mohammed Mossadegh, the Azerbaijan leader. Mossadegh had acquired considerable power since the Shah persuaded his father to release him from prison.

The Shah's plan was to convert his wealth from land to industrial holdings as his country changed over from an agricultural country to a nation of industry. He sold the land to farmers on a 25-year contract, and soon had some thirty of his villages in the scheme. The moneys he invested in hotels, the cement industry and half a dozen other enterprises. In one way it could be said that this form of investment was assurance to all other capital in Iran that the Shah was 100 per cent behind the industrialization of his country.

The salient feature of internal Iranian politics in 1950 and 1951 was the agitation against the Anglo-Iranian Oil Company. One might say it was a sign of national maturity. It was also a reflection of the general anti-colonialism that was sweeping the "Third World" in these postwar years. The Communists had popularized the idea that Iran should own its own resources. With Tudeh gone underground, the concept of ownership lived on and grew stronger.

Politically, the Shah had been gaining ground since 1949. In that year he made a trip to the United States, seeking assistance from the Americans for his industrialization program. He did not get far. The Americans were so busy putting out Communist brush fires that they assessed the Iranian situation as not immediately dangerous, and gave the Shah a low priority. Later, that was amended by grants under Point Four and similar programs, but the massive infusion of U.S. capital the Shah hoped to obtain was not forthcoming in those delicate years.

The Shah, nonetheless, called a Constituent Assembly in 1949 and obtained from it new powers. He was able to veto bills. He also secured the establishment of a two-house Parliament, with the right of appointing one half the members of the upper house—the Senate.

Still, the Shah was not the strong figure that his father had been. He did not act with the same ruthlessness. He was much more inclined to follow the dictates of conscience, One reason for the "musical chairs" changes in the Iranian cabinet over these years was the Shah's willingness to let the dominant political group of the moment run Iranian affairs. Since the nation was so fragmented by power politics, the dominant group could never remain so for more than a few months—thus the change of prime ministers year after year.

The Shah's major contribution to Iranian political life so far had been the establishment of a Seven-Year Plan for Economic Development. Under this plan, all efforts would be coordinated to bring about the rapid industrialization of Persia, including improved transportation and communications, electric power, irrigation, public health, education, and organization of new industries. Most important was the Iranian exploitation of the nation's mineral resources.

Because funds were short, the plan was suspended at the end of 1950, but the concepts of home ownership and national pride were not. At that time they became the dominant factor in Iranian political life.

That year, the British noted Oil-Rich Saudi Arabia had made a new arrangement with Aramco, the U.S. dominated oil company, which provided for the first time in history that the owners of the oil were to have a fair share of the profits. It would be fifty-fifty from then on, said Aramco.

Then early in the spring of 1951, Anglo-Iranian Oil made a similar proposal. By this time the Majlis was in real fever of excitement over nationalization of oil. The Shah and his ministers had drawn up their long-range program for take-over. Mossadegh was leading one of the factions of the Majlis and was most fervent in his denunciations of the system. Mossadegh now drew his power from the intellectual community of students and professors, writers and artists, the most voluble group in Iran. He was also supported more or less by the remnants of Tudeh and the Tudeh hangers on. Without power, without responsibility, Mossadegh was able to rouse these legions to real frenzy in his xenophobia.

In March, 1951, the Shah had scarcely embarked on his honeymoon, when events began to hurry the nation. General Razmara was the prime minister at the moment, chosen by the Shah the year before in the hope that he could bring order and unity to the country because of his high standing with the army and landowner class. He was also looked upon with favor by the Americans and the British, and since the Shah wanted favors from the Americans, and must negotiate with Britain, Razmara would have appeared to be the right man.

But Razmara, like the old Shah, was much hated by the mystical and radical religious elements of the nation. He was also hated by Tudeh, since he had been instrumental in putting down that rebellion, and the intellectuals inherently distrusted an agent of the army. Soon he was hated for another reason: he opposed the nationalization of the oil industry.

Mossadegh had formed a united political front on the basis of electoral reform, press law reform, and revision of the strict regulations under which martial law could be invoked. But the nationalization of oil was the keystone of it. And as Razmara's antipathy to nationalization became well known, he became hated.

One day Prime Minister Razmara received a proposal from the

British offering a fifty-fifty split in profits from Anglo-Iranian. Razmara kept it to himself, even as passions were rising in Teheran. And the reason for the passion was that he had just declared in the Majlis that nationalization of oil was *not* in the national interest.

The confusion became complete. Razmara's aim was clear: he would hold up the British offer in secret until the point of crisis; he would then unveil the British offer, and the Majlis would be stunned into acceptance.

But the Prime Minister had not read the signals. Colonialism was under such severe attack that the followers of Mossadegh took heart and printed the most stringent criticisms of the royal attitude, of the military, of the Prime Minister. Seldom had such strong criticism surfaced before; even the word traitor was flung about in the papers.

On March 2, Razmara was in the Shah Mosque in the bazaar in the center of the capital, and there he was murdered by an assassin who had been stirred to his deed by the excitement of the past few weeks.

In the crisis that followed, the Shah appointed a new prime minister. He chose a man known to be a friend of the throne—Court Minister Hussein Ala. How he felt about nationalization of oil was unimportant. The issue was now like a juggernaut, it could not be stopped in Teheran. Two weeks after the assassination of Razmara the Majlis acted and took over Anglo-Iranian.

Still the streets of Teheran buzzed with rumor. There were riots in outlying districts and unrest at the universities. Mossadegh and his followers were not satisfied with the nationalization law. They wanted something more powerful. In fact, they wanted to "spit in the eye" of the foreigners. On the other hand, the army and the conservatives felt the government had gone too far. Hussein Ala had very little support from anywhere except the throne.

His ministry was brought down and he resigned when he was caught between the intransigeance of the British (who were fighting nationalization) and the equal stubbornness of Dr. Mossadegh.

At this point, Persia was in a dangerous situation. The army and its conservative allies feared Mossadegh, and the leaders were sure he wished to destroy army control of the government, and the throne itself, which lent itself to army control. The Tudeh, pro-Russian to the last, opposed nationalization of the oil industry for its own reasons. (It stood for the Soviet Union's right to have concessions.) And Mossadegh was leader of a broad coalition that favored brutal nationalization of oil immediately.

The Shah knew Mossadegh from of old and was wise enough to know that no other man could stand in the Prime Minister's place at this time in Iran's history. The issue was nationalization of oil. The Shah favored nationalization himself, because the British had refused to deal quickly enough. And so, the Shah, to the disgust of the army, appointed Mossadegh to be the new prime minister.

Who was Mossadegh—this man who would soon enough be called by such names as "the grey eminence of Persia" and "the hysterical spider"?

He was a typical Iranian politician with a high intellect, a rich man, a landowner with dozens of villages under his control, who turned to the public sphere.

Mossadegh was born in 1881 of a landowner family, and in the days when Britain and Russia were vying for influence in this Middle East country, he was studying in France and Switzerland, learning the ways of politics and public affairs. He returned to Persia, a friend of Britain, and as such was elected to Parliament in 1915. Later he became governor of the province of Fars, and still later, he was governor of Azerbaijan.

What distinguished Mossadegh most was his histrionic ability. He was able to unite dissimilar factions time after time on issues of emotional importance in Iran. He could, through his appeals to the instincts of the crowd, turn a meeting into a prayer session or a crowd into a monster. He had done both in his day, and this spring of 1951 he was engaged in this rabble rousing daily. He was the complete demagogue with the Iranian propensity for exaggeration and wild claim. He was excitable, often reduced to hysteria and had the ability of dragging his listeners into the abyss with him and then out again. He was a crowd pleaser and almost a hypnotist in his ability to persuade, no matter how loose the argument might appear in cold, hard print.

The young Shah was not a fool. From the beginning, Mohammed Reza sensed he was in a titanic struggle for power with Mossadegh—and yet it was somehow foreordained (Moslem theory) that the two of them should be thrown together—so the Shah said later.

The Shah was bemused by Mossadegh, and had been for a number of years. At one point during the difficulties of the war years, he had felt that Mossadegh had the popular support to take over the leadership of the country, and had offered to back him then. But at that point, Mossadegh wanted British approval of anything that was done, and that was precisely what the Shah was trying to avoid.

Now the Shah's role was to accept Mossadegh. There was no reasonable alternative for his national front movement had swept the country. He had already caused the closure of the oil fields and the Abadan refinery. His agitation had caused the Tudeh to rise up, and in riots down south many people were killed.

Mossadegh fulminated against the British and promised a new era of prosperity, and he had to be given his chance to secure it.

So the Shah made the appointment. And the Shah waited.

15
Mossadegh

The Shah was not so sure of himself that he opposed Mossadegh in the beginning. On the contrary, he was nationalist enough to feel that the time had come for the British to give up those rights, and when the new Prime Minister declared in his ringing, patriotic tones that he could achieve wonders, the Shah was half convinced.

The British responded with a move that indicated possible force. They sent troops to Cyprus with much fanfare. The cruiser HMS *Mauritius* lay in Abadan harbor. There was good reason for this activity, several British nationals had been killed in the rioting fomented by Mossadegh and carried out by the Tudeh supporters. But the Shah looked at the matter in another light. He met with the British Ambassador and warned him that if there were any violations of Persian sovereignty, the Shah himself would lead his troops out to resist. Here was the shadow of the Old Shah! For the first time the young Shah was showing evidence of the spirit that had ennobled the Pahlavis. It was high time—he had devoted himself to the perquisites of royalty quite long enough. In 1951, as anyone could see, Iran faced a crisis, and the Peacock Throne was threatened.

However, Prime Minister Mossadegh made one vital miscalculation in the very beginning of his rise to power. He convinced himself that Iran was in a position to take over its own resources. But it soon became apparent Iran was in no such position.

In the spring of 1951, when the Iranians became obdurate, the British took their case to the International Court at the Hague, but the court refused to intervene. In Iran Mossadegh's government took over, and then—only then—tried to make arrangements with the British employees to continue to work in the refineries and in the fields under the direction of National Iranian Oil Company.

But the British refused, and so in June, under the protection of the cruiser *Mauritius,* some 2500 British employees were evacuated and the Abadan refinery became a ghost institution. The Iranians had never given themselves time to learn the technical operations of the oil business, so they were in trouble. Production had risen to an all-time high of 31.8 million tons in 1950. By the end of 1951 it would be down to 16.7 million tons and much of that was put into the lines before the British moved out.

The United States stepped in then to try to help resolve the international crisis that Iran had precipitated. President Truman sent Ambassador Averill Harriman to Teheran to seek a way to reopen the refinery and get the fields to producing.

But it was to be government by riot and confusion, not by disinterested men. On the day that Harriman arrived, the Tudeh staged a noisy demonstration, and were set upon by a right wing (Monarchy and Mosque) group, led by General Hassan Arfa. The police kept hands off, and the disparate believers clashed openly, until the Tudeh demonstrators backed off, overwhelmed by the superior numbers that Arfa could field that day.

Buoyed by the general rebellion against colonialism that was occurring in the world, Mossadegh apparently confused sympathy with action and misjudged world opinion. He forgot that the Third World, which would sympathize with him completely, was not a large consumer of oil although some nations were large producers.

Ambassador Harriman attempted to find a compromise, and the British government accepted that approach. Not Mossadegh. Then the western powers refused to accept the nationalization of the oil resources of Iran by the Iranians.

Perhaps it took disaster to prove the point. In any event, disaster came immediately to the Iranian economy. From that all-time high of 31 million tons of oil extracted and processed in 1950, the figure fell to a million tons the following year. The reason: no technicians, no market. The world powers stuck together and boycotted Iranian oil, even if the Persian workers had been able to produce it without a hitch. But there were also many hitches. Some Iranians had gone into the petroleum industry, of course, but the ancient ways of Iran hampered them. Those who were technicians were insufficiently trained, for the most part, to do more important jobs. Those who were engineers were disinclined to get their hands dirty. The result was chaos.

By this time, Mossadegh and the Shah were not getting on well. All the court knew, and all the court was saying "I told you so." For when the Shah had appointed the 74-year-old premier, the Queen Mother and Princess Ashraf had come to protest. "This will cost you your throne," said the princess grimly, and the Queen Mother agreed. She remembered Mossadegh from the old days, and how her husband, Shah Reza, had been willing to deal with him.

But the Shah had been bemused in the beginning, as much a victim of Mossadegh's artful personality as anyone. The old man was impressive: he was fragile in body and looked as though a high wind would blow him off his feet. When not in the Majlis fulminating, he spent most of his time in his bedroom, lying on a simple iron bedstead in pajamas. This was how he greeted politicians, statesmen, soldiers and even diplomats who came to call on him. The impression he gave, at rest, was of a tired old man doing his all for his country. He was so wealthy in lands and virtual serfs that he gave no further thought to ambition. In that personal sense he was incorruptible. But in another sense, his ambitions were without peer, for he yearned to dictate the course of Iran even as old Shah Reza had done.

In the Parliament he was a spellbinder. He could summon forth all the ghosts of Great Persia past, and he spoke of Cyrus and Darius as though they were in the next room waiting to come on the political scene. He summoned for those who heard him a sense of accomplishment and glory, even as the Persian economy came crashing down about them.

In the beginning, Shah Mohammed Reza undoubtedly leaned on Mossadegh, for the old man was enormously experienced in the ways of court and politics, and the Shah was as yet still trying his imperial wings.

But as the months wore on, and they met together, the Shah began to pierce beneath the veneer of the old man's polished exterior. He was at first benign, then concerned, then worried, and finally at the end he became thoroughly aroused.

Mossadegh's intransigeance seemed fine at first. When the old man denied the right of the court at the Hague to judge the oil case, the Shah approved of the vigor of the act.

Remembering the British actions of times past, and the pain of the occupation days, the Shah approved when Mossadegh took so firm a line that the British closed down their consulates on order from Mossadegh. Well and good. The Shah was with him all the way.

But small doubts began to arise.

In their conversations, the Shah discovered that although his Prime Minister had studied in Europe, Mossadegh seemed to have almost no sense of history and no feeling for international economics. The prime minister was unable to cope with a simple discussion of production and trade. These matters were completely outside his experience and interest.

The Shah approved of Mossadegh's policy of "negative equilibrium" in foreign affairs, for to him it meant a rejection of colonialism; Iran was to stand alone. But as the two grew closer, the Shah learned that Mossadegh did not want the obverse, the independence of Iran and the buildup of the economy so the nation could stand on its own feet. At one point, the Prime Minister railed against Shah Reza for building the Trans-Iranian railroad. It had changed the whole face of the country, he complained. True as this was, the young Shah could not understand what Mossadegh wanted. Then Mossadegh stopped the Shah's own land distribution program. This was more understandable; the Prime Minister was serving his own interests as a landlord in this action.

What Mossadegh was driving at, it seemed, was an independence that was unthinkable in the 1950s—a return to the Iran of the nineteenth century, proud but poverty stricken. In the interdependence of the nations of the world, it could never work out that way.

Most disturbing to the Shah was the other face of Mossadegh, for after the oil business collapsed in 1951 the Prime Minister attempted to put all the blame for the worsening economy of Iran at the feet of an irresponsible and wasteful imperial court and nobility. There was, of course, a tremendous contrast between the mud huts and community wells of the villages and the imperial palaces of mosaic and marble where even the servants dressed in satins. A villager in the south near Karaj could look out across the fields he tilled by hand, and see the walls of the Queen Mother's vast summer estate, but never could he enter.

Mossadegh had a peculiar attitude toward the political entities of Iran. As leader of the National Front, his major enemies were the conservatives and particularly the religious parties. He allied himself, at least by his usual negation, with the Tudeh, the Communist-led underground, and allowed Tudeh to grow strong although still operating below the surface. Tudeh was adept at government by assassination and intimidation, by riot and rumor, using all the tricks of the international Communist revolution. Tudeh would not have hesitated to have used Mossadegh, and then thrown him aside like a dirty rag. Mossadegh either did not realize the danger of his flirtation with the Communists, or his ego was so great that he felt he could use Tudeh and then control it when the crisis came.

It was on this point, in 1952 that Mossadegh and the Shah began to diverge.

Mossadegh wanted to isolate Iran from the western powers. The Shah wanted western technology. This was a period when the United States was beginning to counter the Soviet expansion in the world by civil and military aid, offering supplies and military advisors around the world. The Shah was interested and was prepared to have the United States mediate the oil dispute in exchange for U.S. help.

Mossadegh turned thumbs down. The court, he cried, was interfering in the government of the nation. And like England's king, the court should reign, not rule.

There was something for the young Shah to consider. He had never thought of himself in terms of his father, who reigned *and* ruled. But to become a figurehead—that was something else again.

By the middle of 1952, Mossadegh was conducting a campaign against the Peacock Throne, and Princess Ashraf in particular was outspoken in her criticism, so much so that one day Mossadegh insisted that she be exiled because she was creating trouble in the land. It was an indication of the power of the Prime Minister and of the weakness of the throne that Mossadegh's demand had to be met. He controlled most of the press, and the Majlis was under his hypnotic influence.

By the middle of 1952, the Shah could see that Ashraf had been right in her prediction, the seeds of republicanism were sown deep in Iranian soil by Mossadegh. If the old man intended to be dictator, still that would not save the throne, and the Shah would go the way of so many other monarchs in the twentieth century.

The Shah moved to his palace at Sadabad, and there went into virtual exile in his own land. Mossadegh was feeling his power and consulted with the Shah only as a matter of show. He had won absolute control of the Majlis in the elections of the winter of 1952. His power was indeed great. The foreigners had less influence than ever before. Mossadegh this year turned down a mediation attempt in the oil dispute by the International Bank for Reconstruction and Development. And as the oil stayed in the ground, the economy grew worse, the Tudeh fomented riots, and Mossadegh looked on benignly as his power grew even greater.

In the spring when the parliament assembled, Mossadegh was elected easily as Prime Minister. Consultation with the Shah was only nominal, the reins were in the old man's hands.

But within a month there was grumbling. The roads were falling apart. The inflation of the country's currency was growing apace, and consumer goods were in short supply. Even the middle class was beginning to feel the pinch, and the bazaar of Teheran, ever sensitive to changes, was wild with rumor.

Mossadegh now demanded the powers of dictator for the coming six months so, he said, that he might deal firmly with the economic problems of the land. In the Majlis the demand was met with a sudden recoil by the lesser parties.

And then Mossadegh played his hole card. He also wanted the post of Minister of War, he said. Looking back on the history of Iran, one can see why the Prime Minister wanted that job. It was the key to power absolutely; it was the one element in Iran capable of taking control in time of crisis.

The Shah had been compromising right and left for two years. This time he rebelled, for although he was not the image of his father, he understood well enough the sources of his country's power. The army was personally loyal to him, for he had inherited a military caste loyal to his father, and he had worked at this aspect of his kingmanship.

He rejected Mossadegh's demand, and his rejection was supported in the parliament.

But who could take over the country?

There was the rub.

The Shah appointed Ahmad Qavam, former Prime Minister, in the hope that he could bring together the religious parties and the center and landlord parties to form a government. But the conservatives were outnumbered; the left was growing stronger daily because of the worsening economy.

The forces of Tudeh came out in all their might. Student riots were staged in Teheran and other cities. Mobs roamed the streets, and instead of putting them down with a strong hand, Qavam temporized, and spoke up to say that perhaps they had been on the wrong tack; that nationalization of oil had been a mistake.

He could have said nothing that would damage his cause more. The riots grew worse, and in four days the Shah had to intervene and ask the old man to resign in favor of the other old man. Mossadegh came back. He seemed to be the only figure in the country who could control.

Again the Shah found himself impelled to go back into the history of his country and his family to evaluate the positive and negative sides of the Mossadegh problem. What had his father done in times like these? There had been just such a time. During the summer of 1921, and for many months thereafter, Reza Khan, before he had become Shah, had faced just such troubles with the old Shah, the last of the line of Qajars. Reza, the father, had then played his cards coolly, and had been content to let others shoulder the burdens of civil reorganization, while he continued to build the power of the army.

In those days, the Pahlavis had lived poorly, but Reza suddenly moved them all into a home of opulence. He began educating Mohammed and the other children in the manner of the well-to-do of Persia. But he had waited to strike. The reason for it all was not unlike the problem the young Shah now faced: military weakness, for so slender were the resources at Reza Khan's beck at this time, that a single officer, six hundred miles away, was able to defy the central government.

The officer, a colonel, was recalled to Teheran one day. He refused to go. Instead, he began organizing troops until he had some 4,000 irregulars marching under his banner. It would take a major military effort to conquer them and settle the issue. Reza Khan in Teheran knew he did not have the power to strike swiftly, and if he went afield himself, he might well find his head rolling on his return. So he did nothing, but consolidated and waited and learned. As minister of war, he held one of the cords of power, the army. But he must discover how to secure the other needful cord —money. In the years after World War I, the wealth of Iran had never rushed forward to pay taxes, and since 1914 very few had paid any taxes at all. Consequently, by 1921 the land was in financial chaos. Reza Khan could see the impending crisis: before long he would be unable to pay his 12,000 troops and 7,000 Cossacks *at all,* and that would be the end of organized government in Persia.

All these years, Russia and Britain vied for influence and control in Iran. Troops either belonging to one nation or the other, or paid by them, moved in and out of the country until public opinion in 1920 forced evacuation, at least for the moment. The British forces in the south were moving out by January, 1921, and the British embassy advised all British citizens that Iran would soon be unsafe.

Slowly, as Minister of War, Reza Khan exerted his influence for stability. The provinces on the fringes of the land began to pay some taxes. And as conditions stabilized, so did Reza Khan's prestige grow, until he was the most powerful figure in the land, standing even above the Shah in public opinion. So much did the Shah fear Reza Khan's growing influence that in February, 1923 an attempt was made to assassinate the Minister of War. It failed.

The confusion continued. No government could stay in power without Reza Khan's army behind him. The Shah continued in his old weak-willed way, and in October, 1923, Reza Khan, the strong man, moved. He went to the palace and insisted that he be made Prime Minister. He would bring order out of the chaos, he said. The Shah Ahmad had no real recourse. Who else could manage the failing affairs of the land? He acceded and Reza Khan became the head of the government.

Shah Ahmad soon enough saw the end of his reign and headed for Paris. He was never to return.

A year after assuming the prime ministry, Reza Khan had consolidated his power. At this point, many political forces in Iran were demanding the establishment of a Republic. The smell of republicanism was heavy in the air; Turkey had just overthrown its regal system and established Kemal Ataturk under the trappings of Republicanism.

The agitation grew stronger. Reza Khan professed himself opposed to the whole idea of change; he quit dramatically as Premier, and retired, but only to a village a few miles from Teheran. He knew well that his supporters in and out of the Majlis would force his return; no other figure had appeared on the scene who could unite the nation.

Reza and his family, including the son who would become the Shahansha, lived quietly in the village, and continued to wait.

Affairs worsened. From the provinces came grumbles and more. It was apparent that unless order were soon restored by a firm hand, the nation would disintegrate.

As the confusion mounted in Teheran, so did the demand for the return of Reza Khan to power. One day in February, 1925, a deputation of sixty deputies of the Majlis appeared at Reza Khan's villa, demanding to see him, then asking his pardon for the wrongs they had committed by resisting his leadership in the past. They importuned him to return to Teheran and the prime ministry, and he allowed himself to be persuaded, since this was an absolute majority of the Parliament. He went back in glory, and was granted dictatorial power by a vote of 93 to 7.

If one would understand his son, the Shahanshah, Light of Lights of Iran, then one must understand the father and how he came to power, what was on his mind, and what he did about it when he achieved the total power over his government. Reza Khan would have to deal swiftly, and at the same time carefully with the elements of power in his country. And especially powerful were the landlords. One of these, for example, was a nobleman named Sardar Akram, a highly placed figure who was related to many political leaders. He had inherited an estate of *500 square miles* which included 96 separate villages. The people living in those villages, thousands of them, were little better than Sardar Akram's slaves. Perhaps they were worse off, for under slavery in the Koran a man had a specific responsibility for the welfare of his slaves, which a landowner did not have to his villagers. He owed hundreds of thousands of dollars in back taxes. Another landlord owed *five million dollars.*

This problem represented the kind of issue Reza Khan must face and solve (and onc that would also face his son). The serfs had no education. Their villages often had no water but the *jubs,* or streams that ran through them, or a single village well. The word sanitation was unknown. The concept of social welfare was not understood. Beggary and poverty were the rule for the masses, while the minority of super-rich lived like princes in the cities and behind the walls of their estates.

With the army solidly behind him, Reza Khan pondered his next moves. He had to keep the landlords under control, and this he could accomplish by a combination of veiled threat through the soldiery, and cautious negotiation and offering of plums, through his own wile. He took, he gave away, he took again, but always he promised and indicated that he was willing to listen.

The clergy liked him little better, for they saw in him a threat to the Qajar dynasty that had been so easy for the mullahs to manipulate over the years. And the clergy were also huge landholders in Iran.

In his planning, Reza Khan showed a patience and a guile worthy of a Machiavelli, for his personal resources were still slight, his education for the tasks ahead was slighter, and he was forced to manipulate a half dozen disparate segments of the body politic all at once.

Yet on October 31, 1925, Reza Khan had the forces well enough in hand to order the Parliament to depose Shah Ahmad before he had a chance to return. Reza, even with his public popularity and growing power, might not have been able to withstand the return of the Shah. In spite of the cries of the landowners and the clergy, no eruption was forthcoming. A month went by and then six weeks—Reza Khan watching carefully for the signs of rebellion he half expected.

Then, on December 13, Reza acted to consolidate his power. Keeping his senior army commanders close at hand, he had the Parliament proclaim that Ahmad was a traitor to the principles of the monarchy, and that Reza was to be the new Shahanshah, ruler of rulers, of the Empire of Persia. He was returning to the lore of the ancients and the pomp of the great kings of the past.

This usurpation of power went down well enough. And Shah Reza was lucky enough to have around him several men of considerable knowledge and skill, men whose powers either approached or supplemented his own strengths. He moved into a palace in Teheran, he crowned himself Emperor in the spring of 1926, and he made his ten-year-old son, Mohammed, the official crown prince of the realm.

All this past history began to come back to the young Shah as he contemplated his difficulties with the old Azerbaijani leader. For in truth, the young Shah was possessed of mixed emotions about Mossadegh. There was much in what the old man did that was unexceptionable to any patriot who knew Iranian history.

16

The Crisis

Mossadegh marched on. On the day that he was reappointed Prime Minister, the International Court handed down its final judgment—it had no jurisdiction in the oil dispute. When word reached Teheran, the crowds erupted noisily in support of the Prime Minister. Had he not brought them to this glorious day when their independent claims were upheld?

Summer faded into fall, still the oil dispute was unresolved and still the works at Abadan were virtually closed down. But the economy was improving. Mosadegh had his emergency powers; he was the dictator of the land, and with his limited vision, he was certain that soon the Western Powers must fall on their knees and plead for Iranian oil. Instead, they were scouring the globe for alternate sources, and Britain was achieving this end, although at high cost.

In Teheran, Mossadegh set about his self-appointed task of taking over the army. He fired several officers and dismissed Chief of Staff Baharmast. But the army did not flock to his side as he had expected. Instead, some bright young officer coined a slogan:

Premiers come and Premiers go, but the Shah lives on Forever

In the tense atmosphere of Teheran the slogan caught on. A pilot dropped leaflets bearing the slogan all across the city, with especial attention to the Bazaar. The words spread from Isfahan and Tabriz down to Bandar e Abbas. And the common people cheered and cried, for from out of the depths of the past welled a great love for their Shah, a feeling that transcended the troubles of the moment.

In his villa in Teheran, Mohammed Mossadegh fumed. He accused the Shah of fomenting this attitude, and of disrupting Iranian life to secure power for the throne. In truth, almost all power at the moment lay in Mossadegh's hands except the power of the army. But the Shah did not yet fully realize the source of his own strength. With Mossadegh in control of the War Ministry, his position was serious.

Mossadegh, now more dictatorial than ever, harried the British. He tried to sell Iranian oil to various companies if they would come in and process it. The British warned the world that any company that dealt in Iranian oil would face suits by Anglo-Iranian Oil Company, and so the oil companies refused to do business with Mossadegh. Abadan refinery lay quiet. Mossadegh broke off diplomatic relations with Britain. And the crowds cheered.

With the coming of the new year 1953, a new administration took over in Washington, one with a different approach to the Communist problem that distressed Americas everywhere. The new President, Dwight D. Eisenhower, virtually gave complete authority over foreign affairs to Secretary of State John Foster Dulles. The latter, a complete pragmatist, would use any means to fight the Communist menace, and proposed to do so everywhere in the world simultaneously. Mossadegh immediately became a constant irratant to Mr. Dulles. He began to pay close attention to Iran and to Dr. Mossadegh's behavior.

Mossadegh arrested his opponents and jailed and tortured them. Many, in the old Iranian tradition of government by assassination, simply disappeared. He declared martial law when the religious elements began demonstrating against him. In so doing, Mossadegh lost the support of one very influential religious leader, Abu L Qassem Kashani, the head of the most fanatic Muslim organization of all.

In the winter of 1953, the arrests continued. Newspapers were shut down for criticizing the government. The Shah opened a session of the Senate which he controlled through his power of appointment. Two weeks passed and Mossadegh dissolved the Senate.

These measures and his constant criticism of the Shah brought a certain revulsion among members of the Majlis. Mossadegh had a way of dealing with that: he ordered his supporters to stay away from the sessions of the lower house. Thus there was no quorum, and the house could not do business.

Puzzled by his failure to dominate the army as he had planned, Mossadegh set up a special parliamentary committee whose purpose was to destroy the Shah's powers as commander in chief of the army. He wanted the power destroyed. But this time, he went too far: the legislators refused to back him, and he had to abandon this route to power.

The last elections had sent to Teheran an overwhelmingly pro-Mossadegh group of legislators. But as he abused his power they dropped away. He declared martial law again and suspended the Supreme Court when it handed down decisions he did not like.

Criticism began to increase, and Mossadegh was psychologically unable to stand any criticism of his actions. The more dictatorial he became, the more he insisted that the Majlis approve of his every move. By midyear he had alienated so many of his former followers that his base of power was eroded.

He then declared that the legislators he had praised when they followed him unhesitatingly, had somehow become tainted. He indicated that the National Assembly, or Parliament, should be dissolved and new elections held.

But Mossadegh could not do that under the Constitution without a referendum. So a referendum was held—a typical Iranian election. In one town of 3,000 people, 18,000 votes were cast, the Shah said. And true to the old tradition of "secret ballot" the booths were separated and plainly marked. Those who voted against Mossadegh could be spotted easily, and his henchmen and the Tudeh followers threatened any number of them.

No one was surprised when the votes were counted and ninety-nine percent of them favored dissolution of the Parliament.

It appeared at this point in Iranian history that Mossadegh was in complete control. Only one institution now stood between him and absolute power as a dictator. The Shah alone was as yet undefeated.

In later years, writing in retrospect, the Shah claimed that he understood Mossadegh's motivations almost from the beginning. That seems doubtful, but certainly by 1953, coached by Princess Ashraf, the young Shah did understand. For one thing, Mossadegh was related to the Qajar kings, and even had old Shah Reza never threatened Mossadegh's life, or thrown him into prison, or deprived him of honors, he would have hated the Pahlavis.

It was then a fight to the finish, and that much was plain to the Shah in the winter of 1953. As always, he thought his single weapon was the army, which remained loyal to him in spite of Tudeh infiltration and Mossadegh manipulation.

That January, journalists were reporting life in Iran was virtually paralyzed. The middle class was shrinking and keeping low. The Imperial Court was watched from afar by agents. The Shah was as thoroughly isolated from his people as any ruler has ever been.

As the economy of the nation worsened, Mossadegh took the demagogue's way out: he ordered the printing of millions of rials in new paper currency and without in any way altering the financial backing of the currency. This scandal was not common knowledge only because of the Prime Minister's iron control of the press and other agencies of information. But the Bazaar always knew what was going on even if the rumors could not be substantiated.

The Shah says that it was at this point that the people of Iran began to understand that Mossadegh was leading the nation to ruin.

February, at least, brought a new development that surprised the world.

Mossadegh had been bedeviling the Shah constantly for support of his schemes, even as he undermined the throne. Following the apparently spectacular success of his election campaign, Mossadegh apparently believed he now had only to take the next step —drive the Shah from the country and then in time depose the Pahlavi dynasty. What he would substitute would remain to be seen. Perhaps the Qajars would be reimposed on the land. Perhaps a republic would be declared with Mossadegh in power as dictator.

He suggested one day that the Shah leave the country for a time, to enable Mossadegh to carry out his plans unhindered.

The Shah was sick at heart. He believed he had lost everything, and he readied himself to bow to the will of the new master of Iran.

Mossadegh put a tight control on all news emanating from the palace. Foreign Minister Fatemi prepared passports for the Shah, Empress Soraya, and the courtiers who would accompany them into exile.

The Shah wanted to leave by air, flying his own plane. Mossadegh vetoed that move. He said that the Shah's passage through Teheran, and his arrival at the airport would be noted by thousands and they might interfere with the plan. No, the royal party would travel by auto to the Iraqi border, and then to Lebanon.

All the arrangements were made, and the motorcade set out for the Iraqi border on schedule, the Shah wondering whether or not he would ever return to his native land. The motorcade ran into a storm and found the road through the pass to Iraq was blocked by heavy snow. The party turned back, to await the coming of more clement weather.

When the weather did not turn quickly, the Shah reserved seats for the royal party on a commercial airliner bound for Geneva. And when that happened the word was out, not even Dr. Mossadegh's orders of secrecy could conceal it.

One of the first to learn of the plan was the Mullah Kashani, once Mossadegh's supporter, who had turned against the excesses and the closeness of the regime to the Communist Tudeh. Kashani at this time believed Mossadegh was the enemy of Islam and of the Persian people, and that the Shah alone would be able to rally the people to throw off the yoke.

Kashani prepared a leaflet telling the facts, and his supporters distributed it in the Bazaar and in the streets. He and General Bebahani conferred, and they sent the representatives of the officer corps and the religious leaders into the streets to drum up support for the Shah. Kashani was wise, he knew that the only demonstration that would change the course of events would be a tremendous appearance in public that would give even Mossadegh pause in his actions.

The crowd was aroused and dispatched toward the royal palace. Outside they shouted their defiance of Mossadegh and Tudeh, and called upon the Shah to stay on in Teheran and guide his people.

Gangs of the religious thugs roamed the streets that night. The rumor was common in the Bazaar that they would invade Mossadegh's villa and murder him. He was sufficiently frightened by the story to leave his house secretly and take refuge in an American installation.

So for the first time in many a month, Mossadegh had lost a round in his battle to control Persia and eliminate the Pahlavis.

The Shah learned from this demonstration outside the palace, that he had more power with the people than he had ever believed was the case.

The Shah would stay. He sent Soraya off on a long trip to Spain and Italy so that she might be out of the way when confrontation came. For the Shah finally recognized that there must be a confrontation, and that he must win it if he was to retain his throne. How it would come out remained to be seen. But it would come. There was no longer any question about that.

17
Coup d'Etat

As spring came the snowcaps on the mountains above Teheran began to melt and the cool water rushed down the mountainside and into the jubs to bathe the warming town. Soraya remained abroad, worrying about her husband, and calling him daily for reports on the political situation.

There was no change. The Shah and Prime Minister Mossadegh were like wrestlers locked in struggle, neither wished to make the move that would bring the confrontation.

A new element was added. Iran now became one of the cockpits for the struggle between the United States and the U.S.S.R. for world power. The Russians sent in as their ambassador, Anatol Lavrentiev, one of their most skilled diplomats, who was often charged with responsibility or credited with staging the Communist coup in Czechoslovakia in 1948. Soon the Soviets were wooing the Iranians with promises of loans and grants of hard cash, plus a half dozen technical programs of assistance.

The U.S. Ambassador was Loy Henderson, also a skilled and practiced diplomat. He was promoting various technical assistance programs and doing what he could to keep Mossadegh's government from falling into the Soviet orbit. U.S. assistance to Iran began with half a million dollars in 1950 under the Point Four program, but by 1953 it had risen to $23 million and was a mainstay of the faltering Iranian economy.

Henderson warned Washington that Mossadegh's supine policy toward the Tudeh was pushing the country closer to the Communists. Washington remonstrated with Mossadegh, but he was either too weak, or too gullible or too arrogant to realize that what had happened elsewhere could happen in Iran: a small faction led and tightly controlled by professional revolutionaries *could* take over the government.

So Washington sent in emissaries of the Central Intelligence Agency to watch and to conduct a little covert activity of their own. The head of the unit in Iran was Kermit Roosevelt, grandson of President Theodore Roosevelt. He had at his disposal about three quarters of a million dollars with which to arrange that affairs would come out the American way.

The king had been living in his summer palace at Saadabad until Prime Minister Mossadegh cut down his protection there. Perhaps the armored units were needed elsewhere, for in the summer of 1953 the force was reduced from twelve tanks to four. The Tudeh might well stage an attack on the summer palace, said the Shah, and he moved the royal family to the country, staying part of the time in a palace on the Caspian and part of the time at a hunting lodge in the mountains. Tudeh was unlikely to be able to mount an attack at either place.

In the middle of July, Mossadegh grew nervous once again, in the face of proof that his enemies were growing in numbers and power. The army, in particular, was grumbling so noticeably that it came to his attention. He had fired nearly a hundred officers known to be opposed to him, but how many more were there?

Mossadegh decided he would get rid of Parliament, and rule by decree, only thus could he stop the erosion of his position by constant opposition in small matters.

The Prime Minister had come to the point where he refused to go to the Majlis. He said he was afraid of assassination. And while the bodyguard of the Shah was reduced, that of the Prime Minister was increased. His villa became his fortress.

He laid plans for a new referendum, even though the Shah said it was unconstitutional and as ruler he could not authorize it. Mossadegh hinted darkly that forces were at work to dethrone the Shah and perhaps even murder his family. The Shah responded by sending his younger brother Ali off to Pakistan. Ali was also the son of the Queen Mother, and the only member of the family who could succeed, since all the other males were of Qajar blood. The Shah had decided to protect the line, no matter what.

As July moved along, Mossadegh completed his plan for a national referendum to eliminate Parliament. Tudeh began organizing demonstrations in favor of the action. There were signs that the Tudeh hoped to profit immeasurably by the reduction of the nation to total dictatorship.

On August 10 Mossadegh announced the referendum to approve dissolution of the Majlis, and once again he would use the two-ballot box system so his supporters could watch those who were brave enough to vote against him.

For several months some of the key army officers of Iran had been in hiding, although in communication with the Imperial Palace. One of these was General Fazlollah Zahedi, whose loyalty to the Shah was so well known that he was high on Mossadegh's wanted list. He and other advisors were urging the Shah to strong action if he wanted to save the throne.

The Shah at last seemed to recognize his danger, and to realize that he must accept the confrontation with Mossadegh at this point. Of all the men in the kingdom whom the Shah might trust, Zahedi had to lead the list. He had fought for the old Shah. He had become a general at 27 under this dynasty. He had been military governor of Isfahan. He had held a dozen posts. Like many a Persian he was a born intriguer—the British had imprisoned him during the war and sent him off to Palestine for his tricks. But he declared himself totally loyal to the Pahlavis, and that was the point now.

At this moment, having escaped a trap set for him by Mossadegh, Zahedi was a man with a price of 100,000 rials on his head.

On August 11, the court calender announced that the Shah and Soraya had gone to Ramsar on the Caspian, "for a short rest." To Persians this meant the Shah was choosing to absent himself from the city on the evening of Mossadegh's referendum to dissolve Parliament, and they understood that it was the Shah's protest.

Next day the referendum was held. This time Mossadegh out did himself. The *Yes* votes were to be recorded at the Cannon Square in downtown Teheran. But anyone brave enough to vote *No* had to go to the Bhariston voting place, and this was surrounded by Mossadegh's bullies. Just a few more than a dozen people braved the Bharistan polling place, and they were stoned and beaten by the thugs. As for the vote, it was almost unanimously as Dr. Mossadegh wanted it. Two million people voted Yes to a negligible No contingent.

The way seemed paved for the Mossadegh dictatorship.

Up north, the Shah was worried. The moment of no return was upon him and he realized thoroughly that from this point there could be no going back. He was challenging Mossadegh.

On August 13 he signed two decrees. One of them discharged Dr. Mossadegh as Prime Minister for violations of the Iranian constitution. The second appointed General Zahedi to the post. The Shah handed these orders to Colonel Nematollah Nassiri, commander of the Imperial guard, and an officer who would give his life for the Shah. First, Nassiri was to drive to Zahedi's headquarters six miles outside Teheran, a village fortified and watched by apparent beggars and gardeners, all of them heavily armed. Concealed machine guns stood on the walls. He was protected by the Moqqadam tribe, one of the fiercest group of warriors in all Iran.

Driving by back roads, Colonel Nassiri arrived at the Zahedi headquarters and delivered the order appointing the general as Prime Ministor. The staff office was disturbed, the colonel was a long time in coming, and they feared something had gone amiss with the plan.

That was true, said Colonel Nassiri. The Shah had been prepared earlier in the day to make the change. But by law the Shah's orders had to be written on special documents prepared by the confidential secretary of the Cabinet. Nassiri had been forced earlier in the day to fly to Teheran, swear the secretary to secrecy by whatever means he had, and then fly back to the palace to secure the signature. That is why he was late. He must hasten on to deliver the order that discharged Mossadegh.

But to whom?

If Nassiri delivered the message to the old politician it was quite possible that Mossaddegh would ignore it and pretend it had never been written. There must be a better way.

General Zahedi decided that to prevent bloodshed he must make the document public. He might give it to a newspaper, but so venal were the newspapers of Teheran that it possibly would not be believed. It might not even be printed, but handed over to Mossadegh.

The general decided that the document must be given almost publicly to Mossadegh so the word could not be denied. He kept Nassiri at the headquarter for two days. Mossadegh was planning a meeting of his cabinet for the night of August 15. Nassiri would descend on that meeting and deliver the order just before curfew, when few people would be on the streets and it would be difficult for Mossadegh's men to raise any mobs for violence. The army would move in swiftly, and by the next day it would all be quiet.

Nassiri left the headquarters late in the evening, planning to deliver the message to Mossadegh and his minister in company at 11:30 that night.

* * *

Two of Zahedi's generals got into a staff car and set out for Teheran, intending to move in at the General Staff offices and take over. They were wearing their dress uniforms, with medals.

Nassiri approached the villa of Dr. Mossadegh, at 109 Kakh road. He got out of the staff car and knocked. Nothing happened.

He knocked again, and a police captain of guard came to the door. He would not let Nassiri in. He would not bring Mossadegh out. Nassiri had to give the documents to the officer. Then he sat down to wait.

The officers' car came to a roadblock. The driver stopped, and asked an officer what was happening.

Mossadegh knows, said the officer. There had been treason. In the back of the car the officers shouted to the driver to go on. They must reach headquarters and warn Zahedi before the Mossadegh forces could move in. Headquarters was a command post in the city.

* * *

At 109 Kakh Road Colonel Nassiri was still waiting. He waited for nearly two hours. Then out came the guard officer, to give him only an official receipt for the documents, and an order to report to General Headquarters where General Riahi, Mossadegh's commander, would see him.

Back in the car, he was driven to headquarters, and allowed inside on presenting his name. General Riahi greeted him apoplectically and began asking questions.

Why had he gone to Mossadegh's house?

Why had he chosen that particular timing?

Who was behind all this?

Colonel Nassiri would not answer the questions. He was arrested and ordered imprisoned. On the way out of the building he managed to convey a message to his chauffeur:

Warn the Shah!

* * *

At the rendezvous the generals found Prime Minister Zahedi. There was nothing to be done that night. Mossadegh's forces roamed the streets maintaining curfew until 5 o'clock in the morning.

They sat and planned, and waited.

* * *

Shah Mohammed Reza had been kept in touch with events until the rapid movements of the night. He knew that Nassiri had arrived safely at Zahedi's headquarters. He knew that Nassiri was scheduled to deliver the message of dismissal to Mossadegh. He did not know what had happened since.

For two days he had lived in hope and depression, walking long in the garden; trying to bury himself in his books.

At midnight, Soraya had gone to her apartment, but the Shah stayed up, waiting.

At three o'clock came a message. Colonel Nassiri had been arrested and thrown into prison. Mossadegh was still in power.

And then came a broadcast from Radio Teheran. It was Mossadegh himself, the histrionic spellbinder, sobbing as he told the people of Iran of the dastardly plot against himself. He said many of the plotters had been caught, and only Zahedi and a handful of others were at large. He offered 500,000 rials for Zahedi's capture.

Hearing, the Shah knew that the plan had failed. The forces of Mossadegh still controlled army headquarters and the apparatus of command. Mossadegh's swift arrest of the Shah's messenger indicated what must happen next; the old Prime Minister had no more fear for the crown if he could arrest the commander of the Imperial Guard.

The Shah could stay and fight. If he called upon the people, the tribesmen would rebel for him; he was the one symbol of authority in the land now that government was breaking down. But the Shah was still a timid man. He did not understand the source of his strength. Having given lip service to Mossadegh all this time, he did not understand that he had transferred some of this strength to the old Prime Minister. And most of all, he did not understand that his strength was retrievable.

He was worried. The Mossadegh forces controlled the radio. They controlled most of the press, and the army at this stage was an unknown quantity.

So the Shah made his decision. He would flee.

18

The Revolution

In the early morning hours as Mossadegh in Teheran moved to protect his position against forces he did not know, the Shah awakened Soraya and the two prepared for a swift and lonely journey. There would be no ladies in waiting, nor any pomp. The Shah would fly his own plane, and they would take a copilot and a personal aide. That was all. They would take what money they had and jewels to finance the journey. But they must move, and with the dawn.

They flew to Baghdad, where they landed at about noon and the Shah taxied the two engined Vickers plane to the edge of the runway, and called the tower to demand audience with King Faisal.

Faisal did not come to the airport, but he did send his foreign minister, Sayyid Khalil Kenna, who offered the Iranian royal pair the use of the royal guest mansion while they remained in Iraq. The Shah did not get in touch with his embassy, for he knew the ambassador was a servant of Mossadegh's. At last the growing enmity between Shah and Prime Minister had burst its bounds, and all the Shah could expect from the forces under Mossadegh's control would be trouble.

Tea with the King of Iraq, a night of rest, and the unhappy royal couple moved on toward Rome . . .

* * *

How right the Shah was not to call at the Iranian embassy in Iraq. Mossadegh had cabled or wired every embassy everywhere to give no help to the Shah. When he arrived in Rome, a charge d' affaires refused him the keys to the royal car that was always kept there. But an embassy secretary saved the ruler further embarassment, and the Hotel Exceslior found suites for the party.

Mossadegh had waited for this day and he moved swiftly. All pictures of the Shah were ordered out of the shops and business houses. For the first time in years the Shah's name did not appear in the newspapers—suppressed by Mossadegh's order. At the royal palace, the Imperial Guard was disarmed and replaced by Moaadegh's soldiers.

With his own man as chief of staff, Mossadegh had to gamble that he could control the army. That was the big unknown factor. And he was shrewd enough to know he could not hand over the police powers to the Tudeh, who were eager to have them. The Mossadegh revolution would become a Communist revolution if he did so.

On the morning of August 16, as the Shah flew toward Baghdad, Teheran erupted in riot. Radio Teheran and the government controlled newspapers attacked the Shah openly and announced that royal rule had come to an end. Mossadegh was the elected ruler of the country, they said.

Not so said the organs of Tudeh. A Democratic Republic was to be the new government, and Tudeh was to lead it.

Teheran was in disorder, and the local Tudeh organization, financed by Russia, ran through the streets of the city, tearing down royal statues and beating any who opposed them.

Opposition did come from the organizations put together by

the Americans: the supporters of the religious community and the supporters of the army, and those who loved the Shah. CIA Agent Roosevelt and his organizers, with the expenditure of a few thousand dollars, had put together the opposing force.

As one can see, on August 16, Teheran was alive with action on the streets: emotions suppressed for months were now released with all the fury of which Iranians were capable.

In his cell in army headquarters, Colonel Nassiri pondered the future of having cast his fate with the Shah so irrevocably. Almost immediately he felt the effects of help; that night his brother managed to send him pyjamas and a toothbrush, wrapped up in a copy of a clandestine newspaper that printed the texts of the Shah's messages to General Zahedi and to Prime Minister Mossadegh.

Nassiri had been accused of fabricating his orders to Mossadegh. That was the game: Mossadegh and his men were to pretend that the Shah had never discharged the Prime Minister.

Next morning the Mossadegh forces began to establish their case. Nassiri was called before the Judge Advocate General of the army, and flatly charged with treason. There had never been any order from the Shah, said the Judge Advocate General. Nassiri had fabricated it all.

Nassiri then produced the newspaper, and the officer dropped that line of questioning. The Mossadegh men could not make the case that the coup had been faked.

Mossadegh was seriously afraid of assassination, and kept himself locked in his villa, surrounded by tanks and machine guns and his picked police. His principal spokesman was Foreign Minister Hussein Fatemi.

After dispatching messages to all the embassies denying the ruler aid or comfort, Fatemi moved into the streets, and addressed crowds before the Prime Minister's residence. He called the Shah corrupt, and he damned the Pahlavi dynasty with as much fervor as former Empress Fawzia had ever done. He spoke of the need to proclaim a republic in the next few hours.

Inside the ring of guards, Dr. Mossadegh considered his problems. The Tudeh was demanding a part in the new government, and Mossadegh was warned.

He did appoint a council of regency aimed at securing the government until an orderly transition could be made. He assessed his support.

At this point, the country was basically divided into two factions. The army, the landowners, and the clergy supported the Shah. Of these, the army and the clergy represented the organized force, and the landowners represented big money.

Mossadegh's support came from the intellectual elite, the students, the youth who had travelled abroad and were impatient with the ancient ways and ancient poverty of their homeland, and the professional agitators of the left.

But here, at the moment of seizure of all power, the left fragmented. The Tudeh broke up into at least three factions, one representing the Moscow line, one representing a more anarchical group, and one representing the Social Democratic way of thinking. Thus the basis of activist power of Mossadegh was eroded. Tudeh was included in the proposed council in the person of Khodabandeh of the Tudeh party, and those in the party opposed to him lost much of their enthusiasm for the cause.

Outside in the streets could be heard the sounds of shouting, and occasionally of gunfire. CIA Agent Roosevelt's bands were beginning to clash with those supported by Tudeh.

Downtown on Shah Reza and the other boulevards, the mobs stormed and ransacked the shops, with particular attention to all the glittering consumer goods that most could never afford in these days of privation. And Shah Reza itself was renamed by order, the Road of the Republic. Around the University on that road, the red flag was flown alongside the red white and green of Persia.

Mossadegh's police and his army command acted as quickly as they could. They placed all the members of the royal family under house arrest, they rounded up suspect officers and jailed them.

They believed they had dispersed the Imperial Guard, weaponless. They began arresting foreigners, particularly Americans.

General Zahedi, and a handful of his supporters reasoned together that morning, as the police patrols and tanks passed by their hiding place. Was it worth the chance to try to take the nation by force? Did they have the resources?

The actions of Kim Roosevelt suggested one important line of support. That morning, General Zahedi learned also that the Imperial Guard had not been dispersed, that he could rearm them and use them as shock troops.

Zahedi decided to lead the struggle.

The first step was to print and circulate a true copy of the Shah's order to try and convince any potential supporters who were faltering. They found an old Armenian photographer who could not read Persian, and he did the job for them quickly. In a few hours, the true copy was on one of the underground presses, and a new copy of the newspaper was published, proclaiming that General Zahedi had that day taken rightful power.

Three hundred copies of the documentation were printed in all. They were rushed to foreign embassies and to the foreign press, and left in prominent places at the Bazaar and central meeting spots.

With troops to protect him, General Zahedi held a press conference that day on a barren hill outside Teheran.

Mossadegh was aroused. If he was to win he must stamp out the revolution before General Zahedi could get it moving. The rioting in the streets continued that evening of August 17, and the tempo of "takeover" was increased. Some dreadful mistakes were made then; one of them very much philosophical: Mossadegh ordered all units of the Persian army to stop using the name of the Shah in their daily prayers to Allah. The words "Persian nation" were to be used instead.

As evening came, the well-directed mobs financed by CIA moved into action. They stormed army headquarters, most of them unarmed. The guards opened fire, and killed and wounded some rioters, but the mob moved on, and the guards lost heart and fled. The mob seized weapons and secured the headquarters and its prison. They freed Colonel Nassiri and General Batmangelich, who had been appointed new chief of staff by the Shah, but whose arrest had come during the nighttime hours of crisis. And with that came the convincers for the army—there was no denying that these officers had been imprisoned because of their loyalty to the Shah.

General Riahi, the chief of staff appointed by Mossadegh, fled the area. The Shah's forces had seized an important communications center. Quickly they moved to consolidate the army bases in Teheran. They passed the word to the military college, where the students were plotting on their own to kill General Riahi, who was supposed to address them that day, belaboring the Shah.

Throughout the city, armed bands moved about seeking contact with the enemy forces. By day's end, the city was in complete chaos, and some military forces loyal to Mossadegh came up against army forces that had declared for the Shah.

The situation in Teheran was still in doubt, but Zahedi had a strong foothold, supported by his mobs and the growing number of armed troops that could be called to action.

His next step was to contact the big army garrisons at Isfahan and Kermanshah. Were they to remain loyal to Mossadegh they might tip the scales; if they turned to Zahedi, his victory was almost assured. Captain Farzanegan undertook the six hundred-mile journey to Kermanshah that night to carry the word of the Mossadegh attempt to eliminate the Shah, of the Shah's flight, and of Zahedi's struggle.

Mossadegh, of course, knew what the dangers were. His police scoured the hills and obvious places for Zahedi's hiding spot. Could they but capture the general, the uprising would fail. But Zahedi went back to his own house, or the ruins of it. The house had been destroyed and sacked by a looting mob led by the Tudeh. The Mossadegh men did not look for him here.

Mossadegh's police and armored military units guarded the roads out of Teheran to stop any word from reaching the military units outside. But Captain Farzanegan slipped through the cordon, and so did Zahedi's son Ardeshir, who went to Isfahan to rally the military there.

The curfew did not ring this night of August 17. Rioters and troops clashed in the streets.

Next morning, Tudeh forces concentrated much of their effort on the destruction of the statues of the Shah and his father which stood around the city and in the nearby towns. They pulled down the statues and destroyed some of them. It might have been their greatest mistake as they learned when they headed for Shah Reza's mausoleum outside the city, intent on destroying this as well.

The mob arrived, but found itself met by local residents, armed with picks and bicycle chains and axes and a few guns. The Tudeh came on, the villagers opened hostilities, and killed eleven of the desecrators.

This attack upon the institution of the kingdom was a serious mistake because it allowed the army forces to raise as strong an hysterical outcry as Mossadegh had ever managed in his cause of freedom and independence from foreign control. The majority of people in Teheran were not students, or even half educated. They believed in the Shah more than they believed in the Koran. They believed in ancient custom more than they believed in Mossadegh's promises. Until now Mossadegh had known, and had never tried that inevitable conflict with the Shah. Now he was committed.

On August 18, U.S. Ambassador Henderson called on Prime Minister Mossadegh in the fortress villa on Kokh Avenue. He mentioned the Shah's decree. Mossadegh denied knowing anything about it, and he berated the Ambassador in behalf of the National movement. He had discovered, he said, that the Shah, and many members of the Majlis were paid by the British and the United States.

Henderson did not flinch; he was an old hand at diplomatic dissemblement. He bored on: did Mossadegh know from this isolated point what was happening in the streets of Teheran? Did he know of the rioting and the victories of the forces of Zahedi in the military garrisons? Did he know that the Kermanshah garrison had gone over to Zahedi? Did he know that the Communists had control of the Tudeh mobs? (He said nothing about the CIA mobs). He threatened that unless the violence ceased, the U.S. nationals would all be withdrawn from Teheran, on the basis of civil war.

Mossadegh called on his armored division to restore order in the city. But the troops had been directed not to fire, unless they had specific instructions. Those were his instructions, said Mossadegh: order must be restored immediately.

When the instructions were handed to the troops in the tanks and armored vehicles, various units began to desert, rather than fire upon their fellow countrymen.

Some of life went on as usual in Teheran. Outside the city, on his big estate, General Hassan Arfa scarcely noted any activity at all. He was long retired from the military, and operating his farms as a good landholder did in Iran. On the morning of August 19, his wife drove into town, but soon returned with the news that rioting was general in the southern part of the city. Yet they managed to deliver their daily milk from the dairy cattle to market without incident. From the Bazaar came news that Mossadegh's troops were deserting him.

The pro-Shah forces in the streets now seemed to be in control, marching forth, carrying the red white and green flags of the kingdom, carrying pictures of the Shah and shouting his name. Mossadegh had freed from prison one of the most right wing reactionary party leaders in all Persia, Dr. Davoni Monche Zadeh. The promise had been that Zadeh would be of help in destroying the Shah image. But once out of jail the right winger leader turned.

Perhaps then Mohammed Mossadegh realized that his cause was lost.

By midmorning the Shah's portrait was hanging on a banner above the railroad station. An hour later, an orator with a picture of the Shah stood in Parliament Square, near the ruined statue of Shah Reza, lauding the Shah, and berating his enemies.

He began the cry:

Shahinshah

Shahinshah

And soon it rose above the square from thousands of eager throats, and it increased in volume, slowed, swelled again, as the demonstrators showed their feelings. More thousands jammed the square, the very sight of them intimidated the police of Mossadegh who had been ordered to disperse the crowd. Thousands upon thousands, standing, swaying, chanting,

Shahinshah

Shahinshah.

19

Power and Glory

If you saw them walking up the Via Veneto together you would never have realized that the slender well-dressed man in the double breasted light suit and the beautiful woman in off-shoulder polka dot gown were a royal couple awaiting word of a fate over which they now had no personal control. They walked. They drove. They ate and drank and spent much time in the privacy of their suites. They waited. They read the newspapers that told the world the Shah had been deposed, that his throne was no longer of any more importance than that of his old acquaintance Farouk of the Egyptians, who had gone down the year before, not having learned the adage that a ruler of the Middle East who would rule must control the army.

But luckily the Shah had always followed his father's adage and no matter what, had kept his relations with the army open. That last act before leaving Teheran, of appointing a general to succeed Mossadegh had solidified the bond. Had the Shah been Machiavellian, which he certainly was not, he could not have played his hand more successfully.

By noon on August 19, most of Teheran's public squares were in the hands of CIA Agent Roosevelt's mobsters. Automobiles were parading the major thoroughfares, lights burning, and showing pictures of the Shah, or in their absence, Iranian banknotes pasted to the windowshields like badges.

In the villa on Kakh Road, Dr. Mossadegh was trying to rally his shattered forces about him. He fired his chief of police, one of the army officers who had deserted his caste to throw in his lot with the national movement. In his hour of need, Mossadegh could not trust anyone who had been connected with the old army. He appointed one of his relatives to the post.

In *Under Five Shahs,* General Hassan Arfa tells the tale of the next few hours.

The fighting around police headquarters was real and fierce. Mossadegh's men knew that they must hold here; their lives might be forfeit if they lost. And they fought vigorously with their tanks and machine guns and rifles. But when General Modabber was dismissed, and the new chief came to take over, he was surrounded by these policemen.

"Are you for the Shah or for Mossadegh," they demanded.

"Everyone is for the Shah", came the cautious reply.

"Then shout Long Live the Shah", they said.

"Zendebad Shah", yelled the General, and the policemen cheered.

That is how police headquarters fell to the Shah's forces, without another shot being fired. The general drove back to Mossadegh's villa and reported.

"Everything is finished" he said. The Shah's men had won the day. He was leaving the city and Mossadegh had best rally his tanks and fight his way out if he wished to save his life.

"But what about the people who voted for me at the referendum?" Mossadegh asked.

"Gone with the wind," said the general, and then he was, too.

The mob headed for the Radio Teheran led by shrewd men who understood the sources of power. The station was guarded by policemen, but when they were accosted and their affiliation demanded, they threw up their arms and shouted for the Shah. The premises of the radio station fell without further ado.

A technician had secreted a vital part of the transmission system, which caused some delay before the announcement of "Victory" could be put on the air.

Actually the end was not yet; Mossadegh had given orders that his villa was to be defended to the last man, and General Riahi had taken them seriously. As the crowds began to attack on Kakh road, the machine guns clattered, and the dead and dying fell to the pavement. The mob backed off.

Then General Zahedi arrived at the radio station, and was carried exultantly inside as the repairs to the transmitter were being finished. He broadcast to the nation:

"I have come in person to collect the reward for my capture," he said and the crowds screamed for joy.

"Long live the Shah."

Zahedi, astride a tank, then rode to police headquarters where he faced the policemen, and they, too, praised the Shah.

As midafternoon neared, the city people were rubbing and washing off the slogans for Mossadegh and the insults to their Shah.

General Arfa and other loyal leaders moved around the city stopping at the squares to make speeches to the crowds, telling them that the Shah had triumphed, and receiving the cheers and even embraces of the people.

At police headquarters, General Zahedi supervised the release of a dozen high-ranking officers who had been jailed by the Mossadegh forces, and sent them off to posts where they could help quell what remained of the opposition. General Bagmantish went to headquarters and arrested General Riahi. Armored vehicles were assembled, including a brigade from out of the city, and sent toward Kakh road. An officer was sent ahead to announce the coming of superior force and to give Mossadegh fifteen minutes to surrender.

Inside the villa, Mossadegh wept and waited. The Tudeh leaders offered to defend the town if he would give them guns. He refused—he knew the kind of defense he would receive if Tudeh were armed—he would lose no matter who won.

His officers came to report the constant stream of defectors. He appointed a new chief of police, not knowing that police headquarters had actually fallen. Foreign Minister Fatemi arrived to announce that the Shah was about to broadcast from Rome. Mossadegh turned on the radio just in time for Fatemi to hear that a crowd "had torn the traitor Fatemi to pieces in front of the house of Mossadegh."

Wishful thinking—but perhaps only for the moment. Foreign Minister Fatemi recalled suddenly that he had denied the Shah everything when the Shah fled. Fatemi turned pale, and disappeared over a back wall of the villa.

At 3 o'clock in the afternoon, the armored units from army headquarters appeared in front of the Mossadegh villa. The Prime Minister must now decide: was there to be a battle of his tanks and machine guns to the death? One of his officers suggested that he accept his downfall as premier.

Mossadegh refused.

Mossadegh then said he was invoking the Hague convention to stop the fighting.

Outside, the Shah's men laughed.

The firing began. One of Mossadegh's officers tried to raise a white flag of surrender on the roof, even as Mosaadegh was demanding that the soldiers protect the house.

Suddenly in came a soldier with a report from the wall. Two Sherman tanks had arrived and were ready to begin their destructive battering of the wall.

Someone who understood royal politics in Iran handed Mossadegh a revolver and suggested suicide.

Mossadegh refused.

Still in his pyjamas, he struggled into a raincoat, and climbed a ladder over the wall that separated his villa from that of his friend and postmaster. He took refuge in the cellar and hid there. Aides went out secretly to find a vehicle for his escape.

At 4 o'clock in the afternoon it was all over. The castle had fallen. Mossadegh was in hiding, only a handful of his supporters dared brave the streets, and the fighting was ended. General Zahedi cabled the Shah in Rome that order was restored in Teheran once more. He did not yet have the information, but similar uprisings had occurred in all the major cities and towns, and the Mossadegh forces had fallen everywhere before the mobs and the army troops loyal to the Shah.

In a meeting room of the Excelsior Hotel in Rome, the Shah called a press conference. He had put a brave face on his departure from Teheran, and later he claimed it was all part of a plan. But the fact was that he had fled because he did not know what to do.

Now he knew.

The press questioned him. What was the Shah going to do about Ambassador Nuri, the Persian envoy to Italy, who had been "not at home" and who had prevented the Shah from having even the keys to his car.

"Nuri is no ambassador of mine," said the Shah.

The old temporizing days were apparently gone. Knowing the sources of power, knowing that he had the power, the Shah now prepared for the first time to rule. He spoke loftily of the constitution of Iran and the authority of law.

Then, the press conference ended, the Shah began conferring with the first secretary of the Embassy in Rome, who had been able to convince his ruler of his loyalty. After that conference, the Shah and Soraya went to dinner in a restaurant, like any tourists in Rome.

Next morning a telegram from General Zahedi reported Teheran was quiet. The revolution was over, and the General requested the Shah to return, using the name of the Persian people in his plea. The people had shown their devotion, and were willing to pledge their eternal faithfulness, the General had written.

Another press conference was held, and the afternoon dailies of Rome, which had predicted two days earlier that the Shah was finished in Iran, now trumpeted the news of the triumphal return of the Emperor of Emperors to his homeland.

The rule began right then. The Shah chartered a large plane for journalists, and took as many as he could to Teheran with him, to see the aftermath of chaos and the return to imperial rule.

Soraya had to stay behind in Rome. She was not well, and the Shah had much to do.

Once again the Shah was a personage of importance. The newspapermen crowded around the royal suite, for he had little protection from them. He had to deal firmly with them, and with his newfound strength he did so.

Princess Ashraf called from the airport. She had flown to Rome on hearing the news in her exile, and the authorities had detained her because she had no visa. The Shah, the powerful ruler of his country, was able to arrange the necessary protocol with a telephone message.

At midnight on August 20, the Shah and his party departed for Iran; the ruler dressed in full general's uniform, to remind all of the source of the power he would wield upon his return.

20

Consolidation

When the Shah returned to Teheran, there were a thousand things to be done. But first of all, the treason of the past must be so thoroughly obliterated that it would never again raise its head in Teheran.

Mossadegh was arrested within a few days. He came in to Zahedi's office to give himself up. Others were picked off or out of their places of hiding one by one. The Tudeh went deep underground, and hid out Foreign Minister Fatemi for seven months before he was captured.

In the intervening period, the Shah learned a great deal about the manner in which Mossadegh's revolution had been run. He learned that earlier a hundred Tudeh adherents had infiltrated the army. By the end of the Mossadegh regime some 600 officers had adhered to the National Front, and they were cleared out. Some were tried and executed. Many were given forms of clemency. Fatemi and others who had showed *lèse-majesté* were sentenced to death and executed. Dozens of sentences were commuted; Mossadegh got off with a three-year sentence and the Shah showed his leniency (and his control) by commuting the former Prime Minister's sentence. Mossadegh retired to a villa and was reduced to political impotence from that day on.

One important finding of the victors, was the extent of the Tudeh preparations to take over the government from Mossadegh and turn it into a Communist regime. CIA Agent Roosevelt's opposite number had been as active as the American agent. He had been unlucky, for the Soviets had to contend with the basic loyalty of the people of Iran to the king figure; a tradition going back for thousands of years. The Shah's agents now discovered caches of arms and plans of the Tudeh for seizure of power. Once warned was once armed, and the Shah began to strengthen his secret police and the palace control over the sinews of power in his land.

The rebuilding program must depend on some immediate assistance from abroad, for the events of 1952 and 1953 had bankrupted the Iranian treasury. No money was coming in from the oil industry, and Mossadegh had inflated and debased the Persian currency.

The crisis in Iran had been heightened by a decision of President Eisenhower and Secretary Dulles that no more aid would be given Mossadegh because of his anti-foreign intransigeance and refusal to negotiate the settlement of the oil question.

The Shah now proceeded to promise settlement. The Americans turned about quickly, and began funneling assistance into the country in the form of supplies, technical material, and credits. The oil issue was settled by purchase of the old Anglo-Iranian properties by the Persian government, compensation to the British of some £25 million, and the establishment of an International Consortium to operate the refineries and fields until the Persians learned the oil business. Oil production began to rise—three million tons in 1954 and 27 million tons in 1956. The next year, 1957, saw Iran surpassing its old pre-nationalized oil production record with 36 million tons.

The Shah had improvements on his mind. His management or

even participation in public affairs had been virtually forbidden by Mossadegh, but with the old man gone the Shah took these planning powers for himself. He wanted to do a number of things simultaneously. One was to improve education and health, one was to establish the oil industry of the nation in the hope that this would be the beginning of industrialization. One was to strengthen a middle class that had suffered harshly under the Mossadegh policies of economic limitation in favor of national fervor.

And for reasons of state as well as reasons of ego, the Shah wanted to become a world figure of renown.

The reorganization and rebuilding of Savak, the secret service, was a prime task. Within a year after the downfall of Mossadegh this was done, so successfully that a Tudeh organization was discovered nesting within the army, and about 600 officers were arrested. Many were tried, many were condemned, and many were executed. The Shah had already determined on one policy which he continued to follow: unlike his father he used leniency as a political weapon. Scores of those condemned either to death or long sentences were amnestied, on the theory that amnesty saps a man's courage without making a martyr of him. One who has been given amnesty for a political crime knows well that it will not occur again. That tends to give a conspirator pause. Further, those who had been allied with Tudeh were never again allowed in positions of political importance. If they stayed in Iran, they must make their livings in the private sector.

As for internal affairs, the Shah was wise beyond his attainments. He recognized where others did not the sources of Iranian discontent. Eighty percent of the people of Iran are tribesmen and peasants. A handful of these people and a number of rich in the cities lived in real splendor, but the average Iranian lived in poverty, in a mud hut, without plumbing, running water, or electricity. Even in the cities and towns people burrowed into the sides of hills to make caves for their homes, where they sweat in summer and froze in the chill snows of Iran's winters.

How to change this without throwing the country into the

hands of egalitarians, was the Shah's problem. He wanted what he called a "constitutional monarchy" with a parliamentary system, but one carefully controlled. "Not in the pattern of factions and cliques," he said. He would allow two major parties, for there was no place in his Iran for small parties. That reaction was a definite reflection of what he had seen happen in the Majlis, when Mossadegh had welded all the dissident groups together under the banner of anti-foreign nationalism.

Iran's democracy was not to be a western democracy, although many of the western words were used. The concept was quite different:

"We wish to avoid at all costs the recurrent experience in some democratic countries where the people give the governments the opposition they deserve."

Thus, he established a nationalist party, which supported the government programs that he advocated, and an opposition party, the people's party, whose task was supposedly to offer constructive criticism of the government programs. In carefully controlled elections, the voters would elect the members of the Majlis, and half those of the Senate. The Shah would appoint the other half of the Senate. The Shah would dissolve Parliament at will. The Shah would appoint the Prime Minister. The Shah would rule, not simply reign.

In the 1950s, with the waves of equality sweeping the world that had just freed itself from colonialism, the Shah's program seemed unlikely. He could expect the continued opposition of intellectuals, to whom freedom is like oxygen. He could expect surges of opposition from the clergy, whose leaders sensed that every change the Shah made toward western modernization worsened the state of Islam in the land.

Knowing his people, he could expect continued government by assassination.

It came. In November 1955, the same organization that had assassinated General Razmara and brought about the Mossadegh crisis, made an attempt on the life of Prime Minister Hussein Ala, the Shah's good friend and advisor. When the plot was uncovered by Savak, the Shah discovered the complicity of the Mullah Nawa Safavi, and the plan for assassinations of any number of officials, until the aims of Fedayan Islam were achieved. That organization was wiped out, its leaders were tried and executed, and the Shah hoped thus to have brought the opposition under control.

Savak concentrated on three areas of life: the clergy, the educational community, and the army where purity must be maintained at all times to keep the army strong as a base for the Shah's power.

The Shah then focused on securing the support of various nations to assure his independence. His father had always found Great Britain to be the bete noire of Persia, but times had changed. The British lion was reduced in strength. The old concepts of empire had disappeared in colonial aspiration at the end of World War II, and a whole new world was taking shape. The most power hungry nation in the world in the 1950s was the U.S.S.R. seeking to encircle itself with friendly governments. The Soviet encouragement of Tudeh, was shown to be a part of that program. The United States intervention in behalf of the Shah naturally put him under deep obligation to Washington. It also convinced him that his future lay with the west, not the Soviets.

After the death of Stalin in 1953, Soviet Russia's intense effort was concentrated at home, and relations with Iran became better. At the same time, Secretary of State Dulles was flying around the world organizing various defensive pacts against the Russians. One such was the Baghdad Pact. The United States pressed the Shah to enter this alliance. The military were for it, of course. So were the landlords and the growing middle class. The intellectuals were against it, and so were most of the followers of Dr. Mossadegh, for they remembered the isolationist theories of the past with longing.

But Iran did join. The Shah cast his lot with the Western World, and pledged himself to ties that bound Iran with Britain and the United States.

Whatever solidity Iran possessed in this period could be attributed to the Shah in his new found power. The elections of 1954 were carefully supervised, and after that he brought out his old Seven-Year plan. The agreement on oil, the agreement on regional defense, the program of U.S. technical and financial assistance all brought stability. In 1955, Iran made agreement with the U.S.S.R. which liquidated all the old claims of each country coming out of World War II. The stage was set then, by the next year or so, for the emergence of a development plan, backed by a steady, though insufficient foreign trade balance. In 1956, fortunately, a new oil deposit was found near Qum, which aroused interest in the Iranian reserves, particularly since only one sixth of the country's area was under contract to the international consortium.

The Shah decided to build National Iranian Oil Company, and to encourage foreign countries to send their representatives to bargain for exploration rights, and to bring in technicians. Inherent in this was the training of Iranians, for it was his dream that long before the oil resources of his country were exhausted, Iranians would be drilling, piping, refining, and selling their oil for the benefit of themselves.

Always, the Shah was conscious of the need for social reform, at least enough betterment coming each year to convince the majority of people that Shah-rule was superior to any other.

"We have managed," he said after he had put National Iranian Oil Company squarely in business, "to set a new pattern for developing Iran's resources without striking any discordant notes, without creating an internal class struggle, or an international crisis."

Not quite so successful at first were the Shah's essays into international diplomacy. He went abroad to Britain and the United States. In Britain, the tradition of royal politesse awed this ruler as it had awed many before him. In the U.S. he was regarded as one of the lesser assets of the Eisenhower administration. The huge increases in assistance that his generals wanted were not forthcoming.

In 1956, Soraya and the Shah went to Russia where Khrushchev treated them better by far than Stalin had treated kings. They travelled about, dined at the Kremlin, and argued with Khrushchev about the Soviet policies that had turned the Shah to the western world.

His approach in these conversations with Khrushchev was revealing: he ended by giving the Russian leader his word "as a soldier" that he would never allow Iran to become involved in any aggressive schemes against the U.S.S.R.

There were troubles in these years in the Middle East. Iraq's kingdom fell into difficulties, and in 1958 the generals staged a coup. Britain and France launched an ill-timed assault on Egypt in the troubles over the Suez Canal. Iran stayed out of them; the Shah was promoting his own interests. His basic interest in Iraq was to settle the troublesome question of the Kurdish tribesmen, who moved back and forth across the Iran-Iraq borders, fomenting trouble and sometimes revolution. In time this would all be settled, more or less amicably, and many of the Kurds would retire from robbery to raise their herds on Iranian soil and take advantage of the social reforms that were promised.

Yet in all that was occurring, the Shah was well aware of the same needs of his country that he had expressed to the Americans at the time of the Teheran conference, fifteen years before. Little had been done in those interim years to bring Iran into the twentieth century. The ruling Shah was determined in the days after Mossadegh that this would be his course.

Television sets at one of Teheran's largest factories.

The consumer goods business includes gas cookers and hot water heaters.

Iran now exports these coolers and heaters to the Middle East.

Mercedes designed the minibus, but it is assembled in Iran.

Mercedes is the most popular name in motors in all Iran.

The famous Peykan, Iran's most popular auto. It is a Hillman reproduction, made with Hillman dies.

These young Health Corps women are preparing to go into the field.

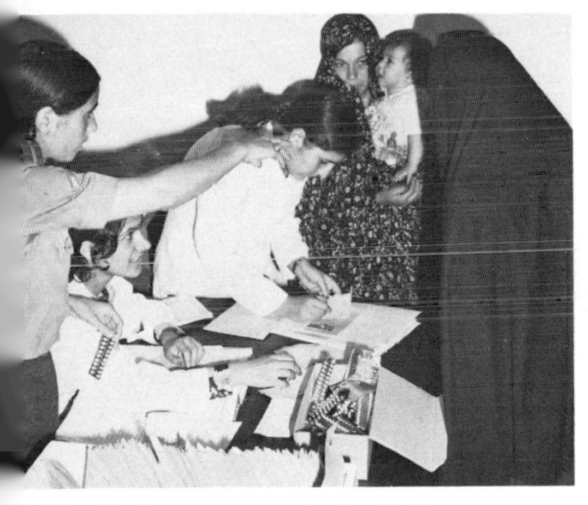

Health Corps women in the field.

The sign says For Children—a Better Life.

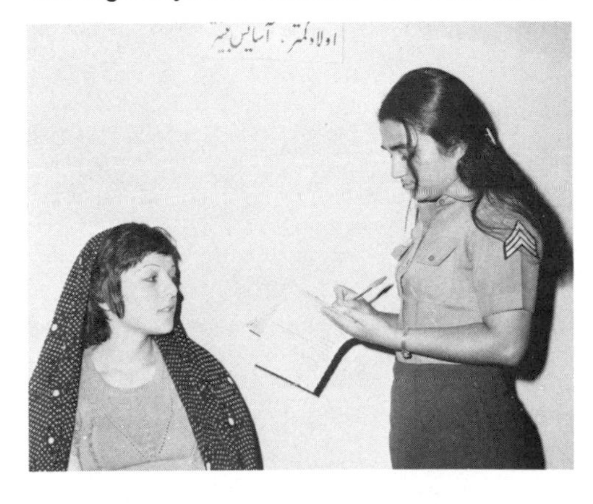

Coming with vaccines.

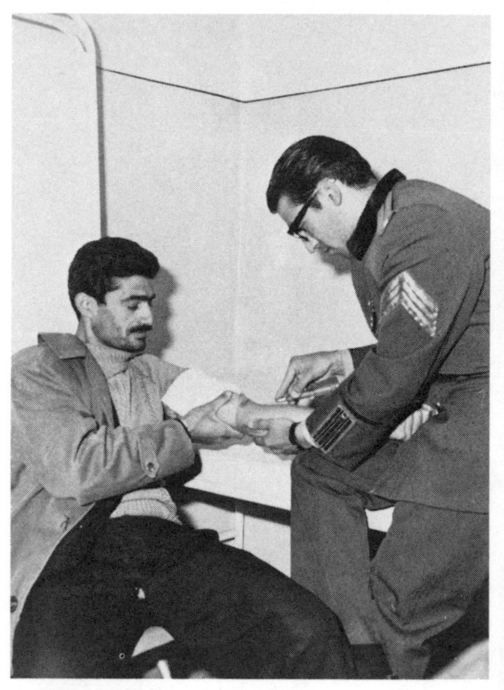

An inoculation.

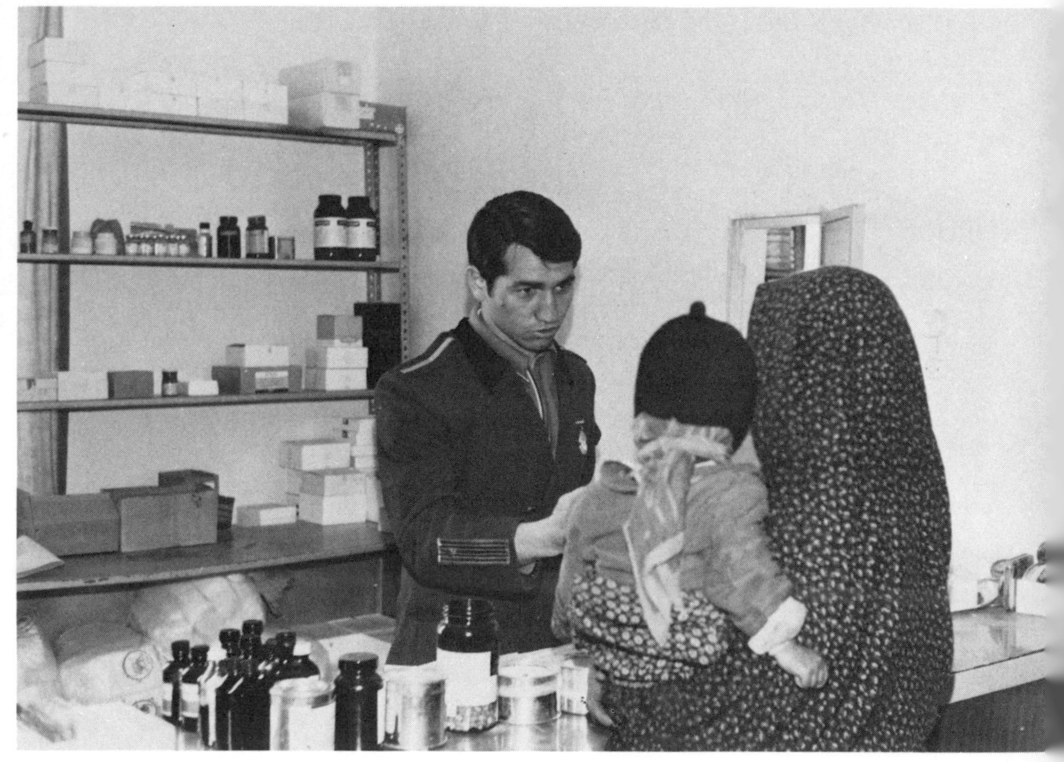

Bringing health to the villages.

Working the fields.

Persia has a successful orchard industry.

Cane sugar is an important product.

The equipment may be Rumanian, Russian, British, or American.

21

The Fate of Soraya

After the Shah had left Rome to return to Teheran, sharp-eyed reporters had quizzed Soraya impenitently about her gynecological state.

Was she pregnant? And if not, why not, they seemed to be asking in that disrespectful way of Roman reporters.

The Queen was silent in 1953. She flushed and said nothing.

She was silent again in 1954 as Iran waited for an heir. The matter had become even more urgent by then, for Prince Ali, the Shah's only brother by the Queen Mother, had been killed in an accident abroad, and there was *no* heir apparent to the Peacock Throne. The Shah would have to change the Constitution that forbade his Qajar half brothers from ruling, or he would have to take another wife.

It was conceivable, under Moslem law, that the Shah could have taken another wife who would bear him an heir, and retain Soraya as his queen. He was very much in love with her and she with him; that all the world knew. Perhaps that is why drove him from the idea. Even more, the Shah, though a professing Moslem, was of the new school. He was a thoroughly modern person, Europeanized in many respects, and those close to him in the Palace said the concept that he would take two wives was completely out of the question.

In the fall of 1955 Soraya made a visit of her own to Rome. How things had changed! In 1953 she and the Shah had come into Ciampino airport in his big two-engined Vickers, but with only three pieces of luggage between them. Sorayas's dress had been torn in back and her green eyes had worn heavy natural shadows that day.

On September 30, 1955, she arrived again, cool and calm, those green eyes shining, and with fifty pieces of luggage in her train. She brought servants this time to attend to her needs.

She was 23 years old; she had been married to Shah Mohammed Reza Pahlavi for four years, and she still had not borne a child.

The official story was that she had come to Rome to visit the coutouriers. That was logical enough. Soraya was one of the best dressed women in the world; the Shah believed in spending money to impress his own people and the jet-set and remainder of royalty that existed in the ambience he liked to frequent.

Soyara did make the rounds of the couturiers, and for her slender figure they always had gowns that would fit, or for that matter, men and women would stay up half the night to make her what she wanted.

But Soraya was also consulting doctors. Four years of marriage and no pregnancy was ominous for the future, now that the Shah was 35 years old, and bound to produce an heir to save the line.

Could it be that the typhoid fever of her engagement period had affected her child-bearing? Could it be that she was sterile from birth? Could it be that anxiety and worry had caused in fertility? The doctors considered every possibility.

Soraya stayed on in Rome, visiting friends and buying. Then she went home, and the same questions from the press got the same sad-eyed, tight-lipped failure to answer.

It had been a very happy marriage, marred only by the dreadful events of the days of Mossadegh, which came six months after their second wedding anniversary. In the crisis of the days of coup, she had been her husband's mainstay; the one person he could trust implicitly. She cared nothing for politics, and everything for her husband. She loved being queen; she was in fact quite imperious, and she and the fiery Princess Ashraf often clashed, particularly when Soraya insisted that Ashraf pay her the formalities of her position. Ashraf, the Shah's twin sister, could hardly be blamed for her attitude since it was an accident of the womb that had relegated her to the position of princess royal.

But it was a happy home. Or homes.

Soraya spend money on "the little" conveniences. She had begun with the winter palace in Teheran, having it scrubbed and renovated, and rebuilt, painted and redecorated. She bought new furniture. She ordered rugs from the rugmakers, beautiful creations of the finest silks, to bring more splendor to the palace.

And when she was finished with the winter palace, she began on the summer palace, then the palace on the Caspian, and the hunting lodge in the mountains.

She and the Shah traveled everywhere, and she proved to be the loveliest jewel in his kingdom. She impressed royalty and commoners alike with her regal bearing, her beauty, and her intelligence.

The task of the Empress of Iran was to supervise the social services. When there was a school or a hospital to open, Soraya did the honors.

The Shah studied the problems of oil and visited the oil fields. He opened factories, and went into the fields to visit farmers and inspect the new tractors and cultivators. The royal couple entertained in the city for the nobility and the diplomatic colony. They went to Switzerland for holidays and to London, and as far afield as the United States.

In the spring of 1958, all was not well at the palace in spite of the affection the pair had for one another. The Shah's advisors were whispering: It had been too long, they said. Soraya had no child and Soraya must now be adjudged to be barren. The Peacock Throne must have a successor.

The Shah listened. He had barely begun his program of rebuilding Iran to bring it into the twentieth century. He could see how far he had to go, given the most amenable of societies. And his was not that amenable. Constantly he maintained control by using the iron hand and the velvet glove. The Savak had infiltrated every level of the society, with special attention to the universities.

The Communists had been reduced to hollowness, but Mossadegh's sympathizers were not so easy to change, and they could not be eradicated, for they were in fact nationalists of a type. The Shah tended to be tolerant of the National Front adherents, and to the followers of the extremists among the clergy. He could look with a certain equanimity on the riots in the streets, from behind the guarded gates of the palace; the army was the key and he had no fears about the army.

The Shah was an absolute advocate of education, and in the early 1950s he had increased the educational potential of the country enormously. But it brought its own troubles. He sent students abroad to study; they became bemused with the technological achievements of the western (and eastern powers) and they also became dissatisfied with the political system at home. They wanted a greater equalization of power; and wanted to come home and be the leading lights of their country. Some did not want to come home unless they could have life on their own terms.

So the Shah learned quickly enough that the country was, as Historian Hafez Farmayan put it, in an extremley delicate structural poise. All the more important then, that he add every bit of stability to the system he had chosen to impose on the nation.

An heir was an absolute necessity.

One day in the early spring of 1958, the Shah gave Soraya the news. For reasons of state—and for no other—he was going to have to divorce her. She must leave Iran, never to return. She could go anywhere in the world she wished and settle down. The Shah would bestow on her all the property she had amassed in Iran since their marriage. She could keep all but the crown jewels and the royal jewels.

So in a few weeks, Soraya left the palace for the last time and was flown to Rome, where she had chosen to live out her life. It was reported that she had approximately a million dollars in capital, plus an income of $4,000 a month. Soon she had an impressive villa on the Appian Way, one of Rome's most fashionable districts, and she also spent considerable time in West Germany, where her father was now the Shah's ambassador to Bonn.

For months the Shah corresponded with Soraya, and poured out his woes to her. It was the cruelty of fate that had parted them; it was the will of Allah.

Soraya's mother accompanied her most of the time, as a duenna to assure that the former empress would not become an object of gossip in the society of Europe.

Soon enough, however, there was talk everywhere about the Iranian pair. For the Shah's agents had been instructed once more to seek a proper empress for him. Thus the Iranian throne was in the news of the world's capitals week after week.

Princess Ashraf, Princess Shams and all the ambassadors went looking for a suitable candidate. For whoever found the right one might aspire to the utmost influence at the court of the Peacock Throne.

The applicants came and went. It was much like the story of Cinderella, with the prince wandering about, seeking the girl whose foot could fit the glass slipper. But in this case, the glass slipper was almost precisely Soraya's.

The Shah set down the conditions; the girl must be kindly and Western educated, socially oriented, and able to take on the role of the nation's mistress and mother. All these tasks had been performed by Soraya and almost to perfection. What the Shah wanted was a carbon copy but with only one small change—the new empress must be able to produce a boy child.

Shahnaz was the one who found the new Empress. It was ironic that the daughter of Fawzia, cast off because she produced but one girl child, had found the next empress.

For Shahnaz and her husband were in Paris, and representing the Shah there diplomatically. In the course of the search, Princess Shahnaz met a young student of architecture at the Sorbonne, one Farah Diba. She was attractive, she spoke several languages. She was intelligent. Except for the fact that she was French-oriented instead of German-oriented like Soraya, she was a copy of the younger Soraya. And as for the French aspect of it, the Shah's Frenchified education in Switzerland made that more welcome.

Farah Diba had other attributes. Her father's father had been a student in Russia, and had served as an officer in the days of the Qajars, a man of a famous old Azerbaijani family, but with impeccable references to the crown over a 40-year period, when others were rebelling against the Shah's authority. Her father was educated in Russia and in France, had studied political science in France, and then become a loyal officer in the army after taking the course at the French military school at St. Cyr.

How useful it could be to have an Azerbaijani occupying half the Peacock Throne. It would end any lingering doubts about sometimes recalcitrant province's future. Many a royal marriage has been made for less.

Farah Diba came home to Teheran for the summer holiday and was entertained by Shahnaz and her husband. The Shah was asked to come. A few discreet and quiet meetings were held, and then the Shah proposed. It was very much a royal proposal, made for kingly reasons. What wretchedness the Shah was going through could only be guessed, but all this time he had been writing wistfully to Soraya off in Rome.

Now there was one last chore: Soraya must be informed. The Shah did not have the courage to do so himself. The informing was done by her father, the Ambassador to Bonn. And then there was one last letter, in which the Shah told his former empress himself that it was all true. The girl had been found.

The dream had ended.

22

Long Live The Empress

In her own right, Empress-elect Farah Diba had attributes that would make her a valuable asset to the Peacock Throne. Unlike Soraya, she never had to be taught proper Persian, for she had lived most of her life in Teheran, on the elevated plateau of the Iranian nobility. Her father's army duties had been largely legal in nature; it was a happy well-to-do family until her father died of cancer when she was 10 years old.

Afterward the family was still well-to-do—rich by western standards. Farah attended private schools in Teheran, ending with the well known Razi school which specialized in French culture. Her knowledge of Persian language and culture was unexceptionable.

Her forte was art, and when she was grown enough to look about for a field of interest, she decided to go to Paris, to the Ecole Speciale d'Architecture, where she studied for two years. She studied hard. It was a demanding institution, and she fared well. Then she met Princess Shahnaz and the royal romance was begun.

It was certainly not a love match, that much was plain. The Shah had actually met Farah months before when he was in Paris and the Embassy had held a reception for the monarch, inviting the more respectable Iranian residents of the French capital. He could not even remember her, and she teased him about his oversight. But it was no oversight, he was seeking a consort who could bear him a son and then participate in the activities he planned for the social development of Iran. Personality or personal like had very little to do with the selection.

The Shah's situation was delicate to say the least. He had already been married twice with great pomp and conspicuous spending, and it seemed quite out of order to make a spectacle of this marriage. After all, it might turn out as unfortunate as the other two had been. If Farah could not produce a male heir. . . .

So the proposal of the Shah and the acceptance of Farah were kept quiet in the palace. She went back to Paris to buy the trousseau. She went to Dior and other shops, buying dresses ten and fifteen at a time. She went to other institutions to acquire all the necessities of an empress. Meanwhile jewels were being made for her, a coronet and diamond necklace and many another bauble.

Although the engagement was not formally announced, the couturiers of Paris let the secret out, and in late October, when Farah attended the Paris celebration of the Shah's fortieth birthday at the embassy, everyone seemed to know. Toward the end of November her preparations were complete, and she returned to Teheran, where the Shah made it public, and wrote one last loving letter to Soraya, announcing his forthcoming marriage, and telling her that she could not hear from him again, but that he would never forget her. Nor would the sovereign ever let his former queen be in want, he promised.

Soraya reacted sharply and in an intensely feminine way. As the newspapers headlined the announcement of the Shah's wedding, she went out, notably unchaperoned for the first time, with the well-known Prince Raimondom Orsini, and let her picture be taken dancing cheek-to-cheek with him in the 84 Club, one of the favorite jet set spots.

Next day Roman society was agog. Her mother, Countess Eva

Esfandiari was in town and should have been along. His mother, Princess Luisa Orsini Aragona, was in town and also should have been there. By the unwritten laws of Rome's high society, the two young folk's presence alone on the dance floor indicated an immediate engagement. It was supposed to be announced that week, and the prince indicated he might or his family might, have something to say at a cocktail party for Soraya which he was giving in a day or two. Or perhaps, said others, they would wait until the Christmas holidays, when Soraya and her family were going to St. Moritz for a skiing holiday.

The reaction in Teheran was all that Soraya could have hoped. From her father in Bonn came the word: the Shah was distressed. The Shah wished her to delay any announcement of engagement or marriage until after his own wedding to Farah on December 21.

At least she was not forgotten.

The Shah's wish must be obeyed. He was, after all, still her ruler if no longer her husband, and he was the source of her monthly income—although her capital was enough if she chose to defy him. But the gesture was important here, and it was made. Soraya departed in mid-December for St. Moritz without making any announcements about a forthcoming marriage to Prince Orsini.

The royal wedding itself was a quiet affair, although none of the regality required for the throne was absent. Farah had as beautiful a wedding dress as any queen had ever worn, with eight little palace girls in diadems and white to carry her train. And the train was 2.5 meters long, made of 40 meters of white satin. Dior had made the dress, with mink garnish on the hem and the train, and Dior had also prepared a pearl embroidery holder for the bride's corsage, after a Persian miniature of the 18th century.

The palace guards were in evidence, all polish and attention. The couple met in the throne room, as had Soraya and the Shah, and they went then to the wedding room in the palace, where the high priest Imami received them and performed the simple ceremony. But only 30 persons in all were present, members of the imperial family, high officers of the court, and the bride's relatives. The Shah wished to keep quiet about this part of his affairs until the matter of an heir was settled.

A brief honeymoon away from Teheran, and the bride settled in to learn her new duties as first lady of the Persian empire. She appeared with the Shah at the annual celebration of the youth scouts, and he made her president of the Persian Girl Guides. That was not only symbolic, it was downright pleasant. In her youth, Farah had been an enthusiastic Girl Guide, camper and hiker who spent many a happy holiday in the Iranian mountains.

She appeared with the Shah at sporting events and at reviews and embassy celebrations.

In the spring, they went to Pakistan to pay a state visit to President Ayub Khan. Farah was glittering in her presence, as a Persian empress should be. The next, she was hostess at the palace in Teheran to King Hussein of Jordan, and splendid at the court dinner in a lamé gown and diadem and the red white and green ribbon of her country.

That was April. Then came the announcement that all Iran had awaited. The Empress was expecting in October.

The court schedule was cut sharply as the doctors took every precaution to make sure nothing went wrong with the royal birth. And nothing did go wrong. On October 31, 1960, the palace announced the birth of a baby—a boy!

They named him Cyrus Reza and made sure the world and all Iran knew that Persia now had its Crown Prince, and that the line of the Pahlavis was safe for another generation.

Crowds lined up for blocks around the Mother Protection Hospital, where Farah had gone to give birth. They cheered and shouted and clapped their hands for hours. Outside in the towns and villages, hundreds of sheep were ceremonially slaughtered to celebrate the wonderful event. In tribal territory, the warriors danced and sang and pledged their fealty anew to the Light of Lights, who had proved he was man enough to lead them.

In a week, the royal limousine came to the hospital to collect

Farah and the new heir, and again the streets to the palace were lined with crowds trying to catch a glimpse of the Empress and the Crown Prince. Guards surrounded the limousine. These were different times than those old days when the Shah had delighted in moving out among the people as nearly incognito as he could. Terror and assassination were abroad in the world, and Iran's history in this regard was such that the Shah now kept a very tight security. He had learned from the assassination attempt and the days of Mossadegh.

But banners and flowers were the order of this happy day and the guards kept their profile low while Farah's was raised high. Three million carnation lined her path as she returned to the royal palace, now the proven empress of all the Persians.

23
Time of Trial

A photograph of Shah Mohammed Reza Pahlavi taken in 1960 showed a taut, slender figure, almost gaunt in the face, with worry lines and hair graying beyond his 40 years. For as the Shah had learned in the past seven of those years, heavy is the head that wears the crown.

Dr. Mossadegh was still alive, under house arrest, but always a threat to Shah-rule by his very presence. Yet, to eliminate him, particularly after so much time had elapsed, would be to court revolution. So Mossadegh remained in his villa and cultivated his garden, while the Shah moved about vigorously and tried to remove all traces of National Front rule.

Oil production was progressing very satisfactorily, having achieved 45 million tons in 1959, or 45 times what it had been under Mossadegh's rule-or-ruin regime. That production provided the backing for the Shah's extensive program of social reform, through economic use of the nation's resources, and encouragement of the development of consumer industries to build up a middle class. The Second Seven-Year-Plan, now in effect, called for every kind of change from religion to eating habits.

In the seven years since Mossadegh, the country had roiled with tensions as the Shah brought changes. He had perfected his police state, and he saw that it was not enough. "Police measures might by themselves succeed for a month, or a year or two years in limiting subversion," he said, "but eventually the pressure or absence of social justice would tell the tale."

So the Shah was open enough, even in the face of his known enemies and detractors within the kingdom. He operated a police state—now he would proceed apace to match the police power with social justice.

In 1955 he was ready to step up his reform program. He began. But there was much to be done.

Parliamentary elections were held every two years, and although they were controlled and no subversive elements were allowed to surface, the elections always brought stress to the political community. Parliament, after all, still belonged to the moneyed classes. Ninety percent of the deputies were landlords or bureaucrats. There was not one single poor peasant representative in the House.

In 1957 the Shah told Prime Minister Manuchehr Eqbal to set up a two-party system, as noted earlier. This was to be the first step in parliamentary reform, and parliamentary reform, in the Shah's eyes, must coincide with the rewards that western technology was expected to bring to Iran. The Premier's party was the Nationalist party. The opposition was the People's party.

Organization of the parties was handled in a purely Iranian fashion. Deputies were *assigned* to one party or the other, with two-thirds of the seats assigned to the Nationalists and one third to the People's party. The lists were taken to the Shah. He approved, and that is the way the Majlis was split. The Shah made it quite clear that he had engineered this split as a part of his experiment in westernizing the government. It was, in other words, politics by royal decree.

How would it work?

The elections to the Twentieth Majlis and the way that body comported itself would provide much of the answer.

The Shah set the date for new elections. He wanted young people in the Majlis, he said. Bowing to his will, the two parties found candidates, many of them young people whose fathers had served in the Majlis or were government officials.

On June 20, Premier Eqbal promised that no election ballots would be changed over during the night of election—it was to be a "free" election this time. That news was so unusual that many did not believe it. It was quite out of the Iranian tradition.

The Shah encouraged all to speak up on political issues, expecting in his innocence that the debates would be conducted on high moral grounds.

Instead, he quickly learned that the mudslinging was prodigious. As soon as the various politicians and factional leaders were sure the Shah meant what he said, and that they could talk their heads off without losing them or going to jail for subversion, the melee began. Representatives of the teachers, of workers, of the religious movement, and other elements of the country began castigating the government for its failure to deliver what they wanted.

Radical groups decided to upset the elections, and rioted at the polls that summer. This first brought out the police and then the charge that the Shah had interfered with the elections after having promised not to do so. Ali Amini, the leading independent, and a high-born aristocrat, insisted that the Shah cancel the elections.

The Shah dismissed Prime Minister Eqbal over the argument and appointed a new premier, Jafar Sharif-Emami, a trained engineer, who might be expected to put the government on a straight line. As for the election, it was called ended by Shah-fiat, even though the results in Teheran had not yet come in. From the provinces, and from the Teheran election returns—100,000 out of the two million people in the capital—it was declared that the Nationalist party had won 106 seats, the opposition party 47, and the independents three seats. Hardly what Britons or Americans would call a democratic result.

The Shah was not dismayed by the criticism of westerners or his own intellectual community: he was upset by the undertone of violence that he had hoped to avoid by granting a part of the loaf of freedom. He was frankly experimenting with the western forms. The two-party system seemed to work in the United States and in England; perhaps it would work in Persia.

It was not working very well.

The Shah called new elections for December.

They were as unsatisfactory as the last. The corrupt deals were scandalous. The Minister of Interior was known to be buying and selling votes. So were other political leaders. And as usual, the worst of it was in Teheran.

By February, the Shah declared the elections to be finished and convened the Twentieth Majlis with something less than ecstasy in his heart. The main job of this parliament, he charged in his speech, was to reform the electoral process so that the will of the people might somehow be heard.

Meanwhile, he was busy with his administrative program—the Seven Year Plan—that was supposed to bring Iran alive economically. He was making sure that the publicity only he could give was adequately disposed by his presence at crucial places at crucial times.

He opened a school for the blind. No longer would blind children grow up to beg on the streets. He inaugurated telephone communications in three towns in southern Iran. It was not much progress, but better than none. He distributed 34 of his personal villages to small farmers.

The beginnings were small—an anti-tuberculosis center at Resht, a deep well for any number of villages and irrigation in southern Teheran. But they were beginnings.

Soon Iran had its first bureau of standards, and radio telephone communication to the outside world. And it began to have schools. All those promises of the past were being brought to fruition.

A village school was opened near Yezd. A textile industry school was opened in Isfahan. On the Shah's birthday, 28 schools were opened in one day, and the next month nine technical schools began taking students.

This was meeting the basic need of the people—education—so they might progress in a thousand ways. In the past, education had been limited to the upper classes and the small middle class. But the Shah was determined that the teaching of reading and writing should be available to all his people, from the city office workers' children to the sons of the shepherd of the most nomadic of the tribes.

Industrialization was another of his dreams, and this year he saw some results. A factory was opened in Karaj to manufacture railway ties of concrete—a useful method of shoring the railroads in the desert. Power stations were opened in 15 towns, and street paving was completed in seven others. Electric signals were installed on the railroads. A sugar factory began operating near Teheran, and a plant to make sesame seed oil opened.

In a country as arid as Iran, water was of prime importance for power and for irrigation. The development was earnest as construction began on the Shahnaz dam, one of the major projects to harness the mountain rivers. An irrigation canal that ran hundreds of miles through the dry lands was opened. It added greatly to the age-old underground water system developed by previous emperors.

Sefid Roud dam was now under construction, and work was moving as quickly as the contractors could manage. In Tabriz, a system of water mains was laid out, and a new system of fresh water was brought to Rey, a town just outside Teheran.

The very nature of these improvements indicated the tremendous distance Iran must travel to enter the twentieth century.

The Shah tried to bring his own understanding of western ways into play; to create a climate of progress, and break as many links with the ancient past as necessary to bring about change. From the United States, he brought a firm headed by David Lilienthal and Gordon Clapp to study development of Khuzistan province as an integrated parcel. Lilienthal and Clapp had done just this kind of work in managing the Tennessee Valley Authority in the U.S. Power and irrigation became the keys to industrialization in a planned economy. It was precisely what the Shah wanted for Iran. The start in Khuzistan would provide a pattern for building everywhere. And the major project was the construction of the highest dam in the area, and one of the highest in the world, at Andimeshk on the Dez river. Its completion promised to transform the whole region, and the irrigation and power provided would speed the industrialization of all Iran and help make the country self sufficient in agriculture.

In the spring, after admonishing the Majlis to reform the electoral laws and checking on his projects, the Shah set out on one of his many trips. These travels had several purposes. First, they brought surcease from the heavy routine of work that he laid out for himself. He would get up at 7:30 in the morning, breakfast alone and read the Persian newspapers, the Paris edition of The Herald-Tribune, perhaps the Rome Daily American, and the British and French papers that had been flown in. He would also have translations of Italian and German press reports.

At 9 o'clock he would be at his desk in the palace, meeting with the Minister of Court. Then he would begin to see his ministers. Four or five of them had constant access to the throne and they usually brought questions from several of the lesser ministries.

Two mornings a week the Shah met with the heads of the army, the navy, and the air force. The head of Savak (secret police) had a special relationship, for the Shah was now altogether security conscious. He had become a careful man because he wanted to survive.

Sometime during the morning he would try to get an hour with the head of his secretariat, to instruct him in answering communications and the preparation of the mountain of paper work that was assembled every day.

Persians lunch late and most government offices close at 1 or 2 o'clock in the afternoon during the torrid summer weather. The

Shah would lunch about 1:30 with the Empress, or some of the royal family, or a minister or a foreign dignitary, depending on his calendar. Most Persians make the midday meal their main one; not the Shah, he lunched lightly, for he had a full afternoon schedule as well.

He might take a brief nap, and then read the newspapers for another hour. One afternoon week he spent with his High Economic Council, the central planning agency for his reform program.

During the rest of the week, there would be reports to be read, for only the Shah could stand back and assess the progress being made as he pressed on a sometimes laggard, sometimes unwilling country the necessity for change.

And one day a week he met with his Council of Ministers—his cabinet—and instructed them in what must be done, then listened to their plaints and suggestions.

Besides this, there were various official appearances. He frequently managed to see a peasant group and hand over the land titles to them personally (in the presence of reporters for he had a well developed sense of public relations.)

An historic milestone for Iran was the opening of the newly created Bureau of Standards, and still another step forward was on the day the Shah cut the ribbon opening a new hospital in Teheran. Seventy years earlier there had been but a single hospital in the capital city, how there were 25.

If there were no official duties pressing, or trips or meetings, then the Shah spent an hour in late afternoon riding or playing tennis or volleyball or some other sport.

He kept remarkably fit. He was an abstemious man who did not drink at midday and only sparingly in the evening. Then he would dine with Farah and any members of the family who were at the palace, or there might be a dinner of state. The most noteworthy entertaining at the palace was saved for crowned heads from abroad or their equivalent. That year, for example, Queen Elizabeth and Prince Philip spent four days in Iran on a goodwill trip, and the festivity was almost constant.

Such strain was part of the reason the Shah and Farah went away several times a year.

Another reason for the many trips was observation. Even a king, flying his own big plane and surrounded by every courtesy and every protection, can learn from travel. For one thing, outside the country, the Shah learned much from reporters. The very questions they asked showed the interest people had in Iran.

Invariably, the Shah was quizzed in the "Democratic west" about the restrictive nature of Iranian society. Sometimes patiently, sometimes with a bit of an edge in his voice, he answered questions about the secret police, the house arrest of Mossadegh, punishment for crimes against the state, and queries about the torture and manhandling of prisoners.

The western reporters had virtually no understanding of the basics of Iranian culture and practice, and for an Oriental potentate, the Shah showed remarkable patience with them. He also learned from them how to shape his public relations program.

A third reason for these foreign trips was to show the flag, and build up Iran's position in the world. When the Shah came to power in 1941, Persia was notable for its ancient culture, and to the British for its oil, to the Russians for its caviar. By 1960, after the oil nationalization and the Shah-revolution over Mossadegh, the kingdom was becoming a leader in the muddled affairs of the Middle East. The oil potential was great. That made Iran important and would make it even more important in the years to come. The economic activity level was high; the pumping in of moneys from various international redevelopment sources brought foreign businessmen seeking contracts and profits. This was not necessarily the route Iran would follow. This was the doing of the immesnely active Shah. And his travels abroad, with all their pomp and purple ribbons and state dinners, medals and parades, were constant reminders to the world of Iran's existence.

There was another reason for his travels—it was purely personal. The Shah was as great an egotist as any national leader, and he liked to move among the powerful people of the world. As a stripling he had sat with Roosevelt and Churchill and Stalin. Now he dined with President DeGaulle and the Queen of England, and a succession of U.S. Presidents and Secretaries of States. He visited dictators, and other kings, and they paid him the homage he would pay them in turn. As Shah Mohammed Reza Pahlavi put it in his autobiography, he *liked* the job of Shah; the glitter of the palaces and the life of luxury that was a definite part of it.

In June of 1960, the Shah and the Empress set out on a visit of state. Their major goal was Norway, where they were regally entertained by King Olaf and Princess Astrid, and visited all the historic shrines and places that were proper. The king entertained them and they reciprocated at a festive dinner at the Grand Hotel of Oslo, where the diplomats appeared in their gold braid and black and national sashes. The Shah wore his black uniform coat trimmed with gold braid and medals, his blue trousers striped with crimson, and Farah was in a Paris gown of organza, interwoven with silver and embroidered with pearls, and a shimmering ermine coat, her glossy black hair topped by the tiara of her rank.

But as the Shah and his Empress feasted, events were taking a sorry turn in Teheran.

The teachers, led by a rising nationalist leader named Mohammed Darakshesh, had struck in May. They wanted more money, but above all they wanted proper recognition for raising Iran's standing above the other states of the desert regions. There had been demonstrations, and violence in front of the Majlis, and a teacher had been shot down. Prime Minister Sharif Emami had taken the blame. He had retired, and Ali Amini had been named to the post, promising to bring the reforms more quickly and to bring teachers pay and perquisites to the level they demanded.

Amini had asked the Shah to dissolve Parliament again. The elections had been rigged, he had said, and they were meaningless. Further, these deputies in the Majlis were not behind the Shah's reforms; they were landlords who would oppose land reform, and bureaucrats who would oppose the fight on corruption.

So before taking off on his trip, the Shah had dissolved the Parliament, and left Amini to keep the pieces together.

But new problems arose.

The ghost of Mossadegh came back to haunt the Shah. The teacher troubles had been only the tip of the iceberg that was moving through Persian political waters. The National Front was rekindling old fires, and the dissolution of the Majlis had brought to the fore all the elements of dissatisfaction of the last seven years. In the Bazaar, the name of Mossadegh was heard once again, even though the old man was still confined to his villa.

Prime Minister Amini was purging the recalcitrant elements from the Shah's government and with full royal support. A half dozen generals had been deposed for corruption or foot dragging. Leading civil servants were discharged for refusing to accept the Shah's land reform program. And all of these people were looking about for a source of power. General Teymour Bakhtiar, the former Savak chieftain, now deposed, was sought by some as an alternative leader to Mossadegh, who was too old.

The rumor of coup was in the air, the CIA operatives in Teheran were warning, and the warnings came to the Shah in Norway. He cut short his visit, and hastened with Farah to Rome, where he might have instant communication with his loyal Prime Minister, Amini, by that new radio telephone establishment he had dedicated a few months before.

24
The Last of Soraya

What a wrench it was for Soraya to have her Shah in Rome, so close to the via Appia, but a million miles away in every regard but geographical.

Soraya was still wedded to the throne although never again would she lay eyes upon her beloved. And cruelly, the Shah was now standing between his former queen and what little happiness she might salvage from her disrupted life. For months she had been seeing Prince Orsini almost every day. They had gone horseback riding, automobiling and skiing and dancing together innumerable times. It was said around Rome that it was certain they would marry soon; for Orsini was perfectly satisfactory to Soraya and to her family. And she was regarded as an eminently proper spouse for him, for she had been divorced through no fault of her own. Besides that, the Roman Catholic Church would have little difficulty in looking the other way over a Moslem marriage, especially if Soraya would become a Christian, and there were indeed indications she would.

But there was a difficulty—the Shah.

Orsini had not lived a totally blameless life, in this city of *la dolce vita.* A year earlier a pretty French model named Monique Bertounesque had sued him as the father of her 2-year-old daughter. Mlle. Bertounesque wanted the Prince to acknowledge his paternity and provide for the child.

The Iranian court took the position that such a scandal would reflect badly on Teheran, and the Shah refused to give his permission for the marriage. Soraya might have done as she pleased; she might have married Orsini defiantly. But Soraya's father had a high position in the diplomatic service; Soraya's relatives were welcome at the court. If she defied the Shah her family would suffer more than she. The Shah's allowance to her was not a serious matter; Orsini expected it would cease upon their marriage, and the Orsinis were not exactly penniless Italian nobility.

For months Orsini had been seeking approval by the Shah for the marriage, and Soraya had indicated that she was ready to wed but only if he could secure it. He asked for an audience. There was no reply. He offered his excuses regarding the paternity suit. There was no reply. He gave full details of the impressive Orsini geneology. Nothing came back. He offered a financial statement. The Shah was not impressed.

By the time the Shah and Farah arrived in Rome and had they been willing to see Orsini, it probably would not have mattered. For the Prince—even a prince—must eventually give up in the face of such royal refusal to acknowledge his existence. So the romance had cooled.

The Shah remained in Rome a few days in the face of the CIA warnings of trouble, then decided it was safe to return since the threatened coup of his generals had not materialized. Anything else he could handle.

From this point on, Soraya began going with one man after another. For a time she was involved romantically with Hugh O'-Brian, the American cowboy television star. They talked of marriage, but Mama Esfandiari broke up the affair. It would be most unseemly, no matter what the Shah thought, for Soraya to marry a cowboy—even a television cowboy. The Shah was never called upon to adjudge that case. O'Brian slipped away to the hills of Hollywood and Soraya went on, the beautiful lonely ex-queen. If the Orsinis, who had given the world five popes and 40 cardinals were not good enough, then there was no chance for an O'Brian.

Then Harold Krupp, the brother of Alfred and cousin of the Krupps who built the armaments industry of Germany, came into Soraya's life. Was he suitable? Apparently not. The romance died.

Next came Gunther Sachs, another German industrialist, and this time an announcement came from Soraya's family in Munich that there would be a wedding. But there was none. Sachs disappeared, too, from Soraya's presence.

Soraya continued to move from one emotional crisis to another. Then in 1963 it seemed she had found a new interest. She signed a contract with Film Producer Dino de Laurentis. She hoped to play opposite Maximilian Schell, another actor she had apparently been in love with for a short period. But that romance had chilled as well, and now de Laurentis had to find a new leading man.

The movie was to be "The Secret," the story of an Italian princess who falls in love with an American NATO officer. The names of Cary Grant, Burt Lancaster, Robert Mitchum, and Kirk Douglas were all mentioned for the male lead. But apparently they turned down the role because Soraya wanted top billing, and Soraya as an actress was an unknown quantity.

Then Paul Newman turned down the role and plans to produce the film were dropped. But not Soraya's will or hopes. A year later she did play in a motion picture—"Three Faces of a Woman," opposite Italian actor Alberto Sordi. She was an American millionaire's daughter; an heiress pursued by an ardent Latin lover in one episode.

In another episode the co-star was Irish actor Richard Harris, De Laurentis played the last co-star role himself.

Soraya worked hard, finding the role more demanding, she

said, than that of Queen of Iran. And why not? For as Queen of Iran she had played herself; now it was putting on red wigs and makeup and affecting strange accents for an international audience.

A few months later the film was released and shown at the Teatro Nuovo in Milan. It was a dreadful failure.

In the first place, Soraya's queenliness got in the way. She refused to play conventional love scenes of the Bridget Bardot type. The most passionate scene showed the co-star kissing her hand. And in the boudoir scenes the bed was always in the distant background—a far cry from the usual film fare of continental audiences.

In the second place, so unsure was she of her histrionics that de Laurentis cut out almost all her lines, and she ended up being a clothes horse wearing twenty-three changes of costume.

Everyone knew the former Empress of Iran knew how to wear clothes.

That was not enough.

In a few months she met Franco Indovina, a prominent Italian film director, for the second time. He had directed one of the episodes in "Three Faces of a Woman." They fell in love, and it became a very serious affair. He was living apart from his wife and two children. They soon began to share a villa, and Soraya began talking of using her capital to form a motion picture company. Apparently her own role would be that of capitalist, not actress.

It was a happy life. Franco Indovina applied to the courts for a legal separation from his wife. If matters worked out properly, he and Soraya planned to marry. The days of empire seemed a long time ago.

And then, one day while flying to Sicily in an Italian airline plane, the plane crashed at Palermo and Franco Indovina was killed.

Soraya was desolate. This had been the affair of her life; as important to her older years as the days of empire had been in her youthful years. Her whole life changed, and she retired from a world that had suddenly grown cold. She alternated between the villa on the Appian Way and Munich. She answered few letters and she saw few people.

And she did not remarry. She remained as always, the sad empress, the reminder of the terrible demands of royalty upon the human breast.

25

The White Revolution

The Shah, who returned to Teheran after that second brief nervous sojourn in Rome, was a far more composed and confident ruler than he had been earlier. He had surmounted attempts at assassination, attempts at coup, attempts at subversion and his luck continued to hold.

After the dissolution of the Twentieth Majlis, he ruled by decree. He and Amini agreed that this approach would best serve the peaceful revolution the Shah wanted to bring to his country.

First of all was the important matter of land reform. Vitally important and necessary to all else the Shah proposed to do for his people—the most difficult single act. For in all past history the Majlis had been dominated by the landowning class. With the Majlis in session, it is doubtful if land reform could ever have been enacted, it would have been opposed by the landowners, and that included the clergy, who held huge tracts in the name of Islam.

The Shah's aim was to break up the big estates and thus abolish forever the feudal system of land management. Peasants were to own the land, and no landowner, if possible, was to keep more than he could manage. It was in this way the resources of the nation would be redistributed and the peasants gain a stake in modern Iranian life.

In January, 1962, came the enactment of the law by decree.

Land reform began in Azerbaijan, in the Maragheh district. The government broke up the big estates and paid the landowners a stipulated price for the land. Then the land was made available to the peasants to work it, for purchase. This meant the establishment of a new banking system, cooperatives for buying seed and selling produce, and the building of extension services to teach the peasants modern farming methods.

The landowners and the clergy said it would never work. The change in the social system of Persia would be too drastic, the peasants would fritter away their new land and be unable to manage it if they could hold it.

The Shah ignored his critics, and on March 13, 1962, he travelled to Maragheh and handed over hundreds of land deeds at ceremonies where hundreds of peasants for the first time received gifts at the personal hand of the Shah. He had already tried this out in a ten-year period on his own estates. He knew it worked. It was now up to government to make it work.

The Shah's reforms and rebuilding of the national economic structure were expensive, and Iran frankly could not afford it. Nor were the huge loans it needed immediately forth-coming from the outside world. The United States provided tens of millions of dollars each year in various credits, but Iran still suffered. Amini resigned as Prime Minister in a quarrel with the Shah over spending and the budget. He was replaced by Asadollah Alam.

Alam's task was to speed land reform. In some provinces it was not easy, and in Fars the Qashqai tribesmen rebelled when told they were losing some of their tribal lands to individual owners. The rebellion began with the ambush of a young land reform officer in his jeep. When the Shah heard that this young man had been murdered, he moved with an alacrity that would have been praised by his father. He sent in troops, and declared martial law in the province. In a matter of months the resistance was crushed, the land reform program was put into effect, and martial law was removed. The casualties had been 109 tribesmen and nine government men and soldiers.

The Shah had adapted a tenet of revolution to spread the land reform movement across the land. He was able to convince the majority of huge landholders that to keep their holdings as they were was to bring about destruction, eventual revolution, and the loss of everything. He promised the landholders new sources of investment for their capital to bring profits and riches, and they were generally satisfied that what he said was true. So month after month the class of landed farmers grew, until by 1968 practically every estate had been cut up, and the holder of 5,000 hectares of land was regarded as a large landowner, where before 50,000 hectares had not been enough to arouse comment.

With the immediate success of the land reform program, the Shah expanded on his other reforms. The occasion was the organization of a National Congress of Peasants. The Shah attended, and he exuded the charm of which he was capable. He was chosen honorary chairman, and in responding, he made a speech to the Congress, outlining a revolutionary program for the whole country.

He spoke of the land reform law, and the peasants agreed that it had brought the seeds of a new life to them all. Then he outlined other major changes.

- a law nationalizing the forests of Iran. No more would the timber of the country be lost to burning or to sale abroad for private profit.
- the sale of state-owned factories to private businessmen. This change would give the old landowners a satisfactory method of investing capital, and would also provide capital for land reform. Until then, the land reform capitalization had been the most difficult part of the project, for

the landowners wanted to be paid, but the poor peasants had no capital. The establishment of farm credit services required heavy capitalization.

- twenty percent of the net profits of factories and industry would hereafter be shared among the workers in the industry.
- universal suffrage would be the aim of the electoral laws to be reformed.
- a nationwide literacy corps would begin, to bring the skills of reading and writing to every village in the land as soon as possible.

The peasants, of course, greeted this speech as historic and applauded wildly. Not so all in the kingdom, particularly the Mullahs, who once again saw their base of power under attack, first by universal suffrage, which would affect the status of women vitally, and second, by universal literacy which would remove the power of the mosque schools, even from the remote areas of the country.

When he had finished outlining the program, the Shah announced a national referendum to ratify it. Shah Mohammed Reza had learned a good deal in the Mossadegh years, and particularly the use of the national referendum to buttress one-man rule. If the *people* backed his program, then when a Majlis was reconvened, how could it deny him without going against the people?

Thus was the Shah's famous White Revolution born of the land reform program that year.

His announcement came at the Congress on January 9, and it nearly precipitated a national crisis. On reading about it in the newspapers, the Mullah Ayattollah Behbehani sat down to write an angry letter to Prime Minister Alam.

The Shah might do what he wished with his own lands, and if the landowners were foolish enough to give up their holdings that was their business. But let the Shah not touch the lands of the church, said Behbehani. It was the will of Allah that the church keep its lands.

The Shah learned of this protest. He could not back down, for the church was now by far the largest landholder in the whole of Persia, and to allow the church to keep its property would be to defeat his whole program.

He conferred with Alam about the reply. When it was sent, it was like sending a bomb.

In the first place, said the Prime Minister, the church was no different from any other institution in Iran. That was a major blow. For hundreds of years the Mullahs had virtually dictated the social policy of the country. First Shah Reza had stripped them of power, and now Shah Mohammed Reza proposed to strip them of the source of the security they retained.

Alam was brutal. The conditions were no better on a church farm than on any other, he reminded the Mullah. It was well known scandal in all Iran that the people in charge of the religious estates diverted huge sums to their own use. The corruption here was as evil as in any corner of Iran. The religious community was lucky, said the Prime Minister. The Shah was forbearing and would not expose these embezzlements, but he was determined to put a stop to them. The peasants *would* have the religious lands. If there was worry about the future of the church, there need not be. The Shah had graciously guaranteed the needs of the church from the imperial revenues.

The letter precipitated sharp reaction. Behbehani and his associate Mullahs knew their backs were against the wall this time, and they were ready to fight. They organized religious demonstrations against the land laws, and against universal suffrage, which was the other point that aggrieved the church.

The protest against universal suffrage was greeted with approval by a certain male element in the community, a conservative religious and socially backward group who still felt that women's place was in the home. So the criticism of the Shah broadened.

But counter demonstrations were organized by the women of Iran. The most aggressive of these women were teachers and public employees in the government. They staged a strike to show their protest against the Imams, and against the old electoral laws, which deprived right to vote to "women, murderers, thieves, criminals, and the insane."

The women vowed that they would have their rights, and many doffed the *chadur* that day, although for years the Shah had allowed them to retain the veil if they wished.

The Bazaar was alive these days with argument and even riot.

The Shah felt that some powerful demonstration was in order, and so two days before the referendum he journeyed to Qum, which is the heartland of the Shi-ite religious faith. Here lived the most important of the Mullahs of the country. It was here that the headquarters had been established for the resistance against the Shah's reforms.

The Shah came boldly to the holy shrine of Maasumeh the Immaculate, and he distributed with his own hands the land certificates that represented the church's holdings in this area, the peasants who worked the land now taking title.

Then the Shah spoke, warning the clergy to fall into line behind his program or risk further deprivations. "We are done with social and political parasites," he announced. "I abhor the 'black reaction" even more than the "red destruction."

January 26. Referendum day. The Shah was very careful not to arouse the religious community by waving the flag of women's rights too actively. He was determined that women were to be emancipated, but he did not underestimate the forces that would join the clergy if he made too much of that particular issue. Only on the morning of election day was it announced that women would be able to vote. Even then separate ballot boxes were provided for the women because their votes would be tabulated and reported, but not counted in this referendum. The Shah knew when to stop.

When the results were announced two days later, the Shah's program was approved overwhelmingly 5,598,711 votes cast for it, and only 4,115 against. Like all Iranian elections it was suspect of rigging; the Shah could be as effective here as Dr. Mossadegh had had been. But it was logical that a program benefiting the people would be acceptable to those it would help. And the only ones it would not help were the vested interests of money and privilege.

The Shah's way was clear. His instrument was the cabinet, which promulgated his *farmans* or decrees by which he ruled in the manner of the ancient kings of Persia.

After the referendum, the Shah issued a new decree, to every provincial governor: the six-point program was to be regarded as the law of the land. And then he had the cabinet pass a special law guaranteeing women's suffrage and the right to hold office. From that time on, the way was open for women to fight for their own rights.

For years the Shah had been pressing the Majlis to reform the election laws, and he had received virtually no cooperation from a legislative body that was filled with persons of privilege. So in 1963 the Shah reformed the election law to his own requirements.

The clergy made its stand with word from Qum that riots were to be fomented in the streets against the new election law and the change in the status of women. One summer day the rioters broke loose, beginning as usual in the southern Bazaar area of Teheran, where the clergy had their stronghold. Rioters, armed with clubs, moved northward in the city.

The rioters shouted and terrorized women as they moved and warned them that this was only the beginning if they came out of their homes into society.

On the way north the mob burned the places of business of known Shah supporters. They reached City Park, and burned the new Children's library there, an act of defiance against the Shah.

The Shah moved in without uncertainty. He declared martial law in Teheran and in Shiraz. He had the religious leaders arrested, and he gave several of the leaders the worst punishment they might receive—he banished them from Qum, the center of their faith.

The Shah continued his land distribution with great ceremony and publicity. He went to Hamadan and gave away more land certificates, and made a speech excoriating the Shi'a clergy. He did all he could to intimidate the clergy, for he was furious that the recent riots they had sponsored had cost 86 lives and put 190 people in the hospital. (The Shah's enemies said it was 3,000 dead.)

Giving away land, making speeches, furthering his reform program, the Shah spent the summer in Persia, preparing for the new elections. He organized a Congress of Free Men and Free Women, whose basic purpose was to choose proper candidates (Shah opinion) for the new Parliament. When the lists of candidates were published in September, indeed nearly all of them were persons chosen by Shah fiat at the big convention.

The Shah had been whittling. Formerly, the Majlis had been dominated by the landowners and the clergy. In the Shah's lists there were no landlords of the old power. Only one half of one percent of the candidates were clergy, compared to 23 percent in the days of his father.

But, for that matter, there were no more peasants than there were clergy. And there were two women for the Senate and six for the Majlis.

The dominant group of that Parliament, as it would be for many years, was the new elite, or the upper middle class that the Shah was encouraging in Iran. That meant well-to-do businessmen, doctors, lawyers, the foreign educated, and present or previous government administrators. Special groups, such as the infant labor movement, were encouraged by inclusion of a few members of the Majlis. (4.6 percent of the seats for labor, for example.) Industrialists were allowed a few seats also.

So the Majlis was duly elected in the kind of controlled elections that were a puzzle to the Western World, but that represented huge forward strides over the decadence of the old system. For the first time, with the wrench from power of the landlords and the clergy, the people of Iran saw a basic change in their political and economic systems. The internal enemies of the Shah said the change could never last, that the ruler was forcing the country into bankruptcy. On the right the extremists detested this government because it deprived the vested interests. On the left it was equally hated because it was not "democratic" in the western sense, for the intellectuals wanted the millenium. On the far left the White Revolution was detested because the Shah had succeeded in stealing a page from the revolutionary's book. Land distribution and the encouragement of workers under strictly controlled conditions are the mainstays of the revolutions of the twentieth century. Almost everywhere the vested interests had refused to accept the rights of the poor. But here was the Shah, the golden, glittering Shah, with his love of pomp and luxury, and his vast wealth, striking out among the other rich and taking from the rich and giving to the poor.

It was indeed a revolution.

26

Upheaval

The Shah was seeking new blood to lead his revolution. For he understood as well as anyone in the kingdom that if he failed in his efforts to change the country, the result would be something like Mossadegh's regime, but probably dominated by the Communists. In disrupting the ways of the old society he had made sure it could never be the same in Iran. On his own, he had already established that.

The leading figure to emerge from the furore over the White Revolution was Hasan Ali Mansur, a young intellectual who believed in the Shah's program, and from it formed the platform of the New Iran party. The Shah was pleased. The party not only gave him a vehicle for his reform movement, but in Hasan Ali Mansur he had a young enthusiast on whom he could count for support.

The future looked bright in one way. The economic recession that had dogged the country for three years seemed to be ending. Still, there were signs of deep trouble in the community even though the new Parliament was the best in the nation's history, the most representative, the least venal, and the most likely to do something for the people.

But it was too much to expect that the events of the past ten years would not leave scars. Mossadegh's supporters had not forgotten. Nor had the clergy.

On January 21, 1965, Hasan Ali Mansur was the victim of the old Persian technique of government by assassination. His killers were a gang of youths egged into the crime by the ferment in which Iran was caught.

A few weeks later, the liberal American journalist Sidney Lens was in Persia on a quick trip, and was fortunate enough to find some of the opposition members who were not afraid to talk to him in private. They were embittered about the Shah's establishment of the police state, for they were mostly supporters of Mossadegh. They were careful of the Savak, but the Savak did not then seem to be so perfectly organized as it would become in later years. So they voiced their complaints to the American.

The riots of June, 1963, one said, were far more serious than they had been reported to be in the United States. (That was the period when the Shah felt compelled to take refuge in Rome and did not return home until his police assured him the disorders were controlled.)

Three thousand people died in those riots, Lens was told, not just the few score that had been listed. Thousands were arrested, and the reporter's informant, a professor, said he had gone into hiding for three months after the Savak entered the university and terrorized the place. He spoke of rapes and beatings and many arrests, all of them techniques of secret police everywhere.

This professor berated the U.S. for supporting the Shah's corrupt regime. He spoke bitterly of the latter's police and army shooting down Iranians with American guns.

Then Lens went about the city and found others to verify much of the story the young university professor had told him. Savak then had 12,000 members, the opponents said. (That number was to grow over the years until Savak infiltrated virtually every level of Iranian life.) Even then, Savak controlled the society by arresting those who were unwise enough to come to the royal attention as opponents of his regime.

There was nothing particularly unusual about this; nothing new; nothing out of Persian character. Shah Reza had done the same. Mossadegh had arrested his opponents and jailed them without trials. But the difference was that in 1963 and 1964 those young men and women had been sent to the Western countries to be educated and been exposed to what were then different conditions. Government by assassination did not begin in America until 1963, at least openly. The youths educated in the 1950's in the west were not so used to violence and police methods as later generations would become when it began to be revealed that governments in the west as well as the east engaged in covert police operations.

So there was indignation in the air in Teheran in 1965 as Sidney Lens spoke to opponents of the Shah.

They declared that his reform program was primarily faked, and charged that the Shah kept for himself large chunks of the new enterprises—hotels, cement works, sugar mills, tile factories, shipping concerns, air lines.

They sneered at his land reform. Of the 22,000,000 people, the vast majority were poor, uneducated, unmedicated. They charged the Shah with taking the money from Iran and transferring it to Swiss bank accounts. They said that since 1963 the Shah had received 90,000,000 rials for 187 villages, while the state paid out 5000,000,000 rials for 5,000 villages owned by others. In other words, the Shah was robbing the nation, they said.

They were critical of the land reform program because only one-tenth of the peasants had received land. Further, they were critical because the peasants had to buy the land; they did not get it free.

They were critical because the cooperatives and peasant assistance programs were not working as rapidly as they should.

Because the economic reform program was going slowly many

thousands of peasants had flocked to Teheran. There they could not find housing, and so they moved into caves and mud shacks on the outskirts of the city, creating slums where people lived in animal conditions. Lens visited such a community, and reported it was every bit as primitive and dreadful as he expected it to be.

It was true. People did live like that in Iran, without doctors, without medicine, without running water, without electricity. I had seen it myself in 1947 on a brief stop in Iran. And there had not been much change. That was precisely the point of objections made by the educated youths who were being sent abroad in increasing numbers by this Shah.

The young intellectuals did not believe in the Shah. All his arrogance, all his Oriental potentate's rigging, caused them to be deeply suspicious of him.

They objected to the status of the poor. They objected to their own status when seen against the backdrop of what was happening in Iran. They claimed the poor were no better off. (Certainly some of them must have been by this time, the beneficiaries of the earliest land reform). They saw land speculators making fortunes all around them, including the nobility and members of the royal family, and they longed for the days of Mossadegh, who, they said, was at least leading the country along the path to democracy.

They told Lens that the Shah did not have popular support, that he was to Iran what Dictator Trujillo was to the Dominican Republic, or what Franco was to Spain. (I had seen people living in caves in Spain, too, in 1948.) They indicated that rebellion was about to break out in Azerbaijan, that the Kurds were continuing to cause trouble on the western borders. (The Kurds were causing trouble along the western borders in the 1900's and in the 1970's, and might be again in the 2000's, for Kurdistan existed as a dream of empire in the mind of every Kurdish tribesman.)

After his investigation in the early months of 1965, Sidney Lens returned to the U.S. convinced that the opposition to the Shah was real and growing, that he was operating a repressive state that must some day fall, and that the forces of discontent were such that leadership would be found to topple the Shah.

Lens's report in *The Progressive* magazine was written before the assassination of Hasan Ali Mansur; one might say the American writer sensed the coming of serious trouble. How right he was remained to be seen.

The assassination of Mansur brought about appointment of another young man to the prime ministry. He was Amir Abbas Hoveyda, a professional from the oil company, who had come into politics in this new movement, Hoveyda was as well qualified to serve his Shah as any man might be. He was totally self-effacing, totally loyal, and a man of such limited imagination that he looked upon the prime ministry as an administrative post. He was the ideal Prime Minister for a Shah who insisted on running his own government. He would have succeeded in the ancient days of Cyrus and Darius as well as he did with this more modern absolute monarch.

Hoveyda turned to the tasks of the reform program with skill and a managerial brilliance that had not been matched in Iranian politics. The program began to move ahead.

Yet Sidney Lens was right, even more trouble was ahead.

In the winter of 1964–65, Iran was the center of considerable political controversy in the Middle East. To the west, Gamal Abdul Nasser had long since put King Farouk out of Cairo and was attempting to weld the Arab states into a confederation. One aim of the confederation was to rise up and smite Israel and perhaps wipe it off the map. Iran's Shah was not sympathetic to that view. He had reasonable relations with the Israelis. He supplied Israel with oil, and in return, the Israelis helped train his secret police. Nasser quarreled with the Shah over the position of the Arabs. The Shah was determined not to become a part of Nasser's orbit. The fact that Iran was a Moslem country did not obscure the other fact that it was *not* an Arab country. And the fact was that the Shah intended to lead the Near East and not let Nasser do it. For this, Nasser called him "a wicked man and a traitor to Islam"—thus at least joining the Shah's more liberal critics in this one respect.

The troubles and controversy, particularly the assassination of

Mansur, brought rapid changes to Teheran. Most important was the Shah's gathering about him young people in whom he had personal trust. General Pakravan had been chief of Savak. He was fired, and General Fardoust, an old friend and schoolmate of the Shah's, was the new head of the secret police.

Almost immediately violence came again to Teheran. On April 10, 1965, on the heels of reorganization of the security forces, a guardsman at the Marble Palace tried to push his way through the palace to assassinate the Shah. Two other guardsman stopped him and were killed in the shootout, but so was the intended assassin. The Shah then brought in General Nassiri, a tough-minded soldier, who would help keep the order that the Shah must have if his program was to succeed and he was to avoid the sudden death that had come to so many Persian leaders in the past.

27
Line of Succession

All during the hectic years of the 1960's, the Shah's major effort was aimed at rebuilding an extremely shaky government. The increase in oil revenues and the vast addition to the spending program of the central government led to fiscal carelessness. This in turn created massive corruption. There was nothing new about that in official Iran. What was new was the Shah's approach to corruption.

Constantly, the government purged its ministries. The army high command was reorganized, and then replanned another time. Generals were turned out by the dozens. So many civil officials were accused of embezzlement that usually they were only fired from government rather than charged. For a thousand years official corruption had been the way of the nation—it was not going to be wiped out over night. And among the critics, particularly the intellectuals of the universities, there was serious doubt as to whether real efforts were being made to clean up the mess. The opulence of court life made that doubting inevitable. As long as a handful of the royal family and upper nobility lived in such luxurious splendor, it would be hard to believe that the Shah really cared for good government and the welfare of the poor. The contrast between Gulistan palace and the scrofulous beggars of the Bazaar was simply too great for the imagination.

Yet the Shah, while maintaining all his prequisities of kingliness, was making real progress in every way. The Majlis could certainly not yet be said to be a truly democratic legislative body. But the two political parties Iran Novin and Mardom, were different and did espouse different aspects of Iranian life with different attitudes. The Shah's party, Novin, held 180 seats in the Majlis, and the Mardom held 29 seats, with five seats held by a third smaller party.

The Shah used his majority in the Majlis to push through the legislation that his ministers drafted for him, but there was no question of rule—the Shah ruled with a firm hand as he had been doing.

Meanwhile, he was making his reform program viable in every department with results that sometimes seemed incongruous to foreigners. Supermarkets were springing up, and on the main streets even of Teheran, it was not unusual to see a band of fat-tailed sheep being driven passed the supermarket when their herder took them through the streets enroute to the slaughter house. The beggars were still out, even on the main streets of the city, but the number of automobiles was growing year after year, as the middle class emerged, and the automobile became a major status symbol of Iranian life.

Much of this was the result of a deliberate U.S. policy, begun under the Eisenhower administration, of assistance to Iran. It was done to keep Iran from falling under the Russian aegis. The aid program jumped from about 40 million dollars a year under Mossadegh to 130 million just afterwards, and then kept going up. Iran wanted to rebuild its defense against a potential attack, for in the 1960's, not only was Russia a potential threat, but just as much worry was caused by Nasser's aggressive efforts to unite the Arabs and take leadership of the Muslim block of nations.

The Shah continued to have the problem of internal security. It was inevitable that his growing attention to education would produce a dissatisfied intellectual community that wanted freedom. At the University of Teheran, the largest and most important educational institution in the country, there was constant unrest. The National Front had asserted its control of 90 per cent of the 15,000 students. No longer by 1967 was the figure quite so high, but the capacity of the students to create unrest was still prodigious. They did so from time to time, and when they caused trouble, the Shah was always faced with the same problem: if he used too much force in dealing with them he might create a revolutionary situation. He might also turn loyal factions against him for these students were the relatives of the elite of Iran.

One thing was working for him; the new middle class was prospering after a period of ups and downs. Real estate boomed, and with the building of dams, the creation of new villages, the growth of the economy, the middle class flourished and gained capital.

Out in the country the Shah had been whittling away at the illiteracy problem for ten years. At the turn of the decade, the rate of illiteracy had been 85 per cent. It was coming down slowly but steadily as he built new schools in the outlying cities, towns, and villages.

Most impressive to the world, and best news of all, was the steady economic growth rate the Shah's programs had brought about. The growth averaged 9.5 per cent a year, and was going up, even as the cost of living was going down due to government subsidies for such basic foods as rice, wheat and sugar, and salt and oil.

The U.S. Embassy these days was touting Iran as a fine investment opportunity for American capital. That capital was coming in, often in joint ventures with Iranian capitalists, and the Shah was getting ready to invoke his fourth development plan.

He was also preparing to crow a bit, and consolidate the gains he had made abroad and at home. No longer was Shah Mohammed Reza Pahlavi in any sense a shy or untried ruler. He had faced assassination more than twice for many a plot was uncovered before it got to the action stage. He had watched the processes of government by assassination, and the continuation of Prime Minister Hoveyda in his role after more than two years was, for Iran, a sign of growing stability. The Shah had claimed in his autobiography in 1960 that he was trying to strike a balance between authoritarian government and the pure democracy so lauded by the Western Powers, although to his mind their achievements had been questionable at best.

The improvement in Iran's situation, and the hopes he had for industrialization were still not moving as rapidly as the Shah himself wanted. If affairs continued to progress at this pace he might not live long enough to see the economic independence he planned. The fourth developmental plan called for expenditure of nearly 11 billion dollars, beginning in 1968. But the Shah knew that would not be enough.

For reasons that included economics and his own sense of dynasty, then, the Shah decided that his birthday in 1967 would be honored by the grandest party ever held in the world, a multimillion dollar affair that would serve all his purposes. It would be as good as a trade fair for Persia. It would serve notice on the rest of the Moslem world that Persia and the Shah were to be reckoned with in any leadership struggle in the Middle East. It would reward Farah, who had taken such short shrift at her marriage ceremony, purely for reasons of state. It would proclaim the succession, and name the Shah's first son as Crown Prince of the realm.

For months preparations were in the works for the celebration. A huge wide red carpet was specially woven to run from the steps of the palace through the entrance to the gardens so that the imperial party could go to greet the people after the ceremony. The ancient coach building firm of Josef Klicmann of Vienna was set to work making a reproduction of the Hapsburg imperial coach, specially for this coronation—all ivory work and gilt. It was taken apart and flown to Teheran and then reassembled.

Flowers were brought in from Holland again, and rare delicacies from Paris and Rome; all flown in tremendous quantity for the great party. Caviar was brought down in large vats from the Caspian. Jewels were prepared by the royal jewelers for the affair and special jewels for the Empress.

Her gown for the occasion was to be all silk and ermine and Persian work studded with precious and semi-precious stones. In all, the coronation was to put to shame any coronation of the past, including the period ages ago when the Peacock Throne rested in Delhi.

The birthday-coronation, was set for October 26, 1967—the forty-eighth birthday of his Imperial Majesty. From the world of royalty and celebrity came the most talked-of figures, and the hotels of the capital city were jammed with reporters of every nation who came to observe what they could of the spectacle.

Princess Farahnaz was there, splendid in her own finery, for next to the queen she was the best dressed woman in all Iran. The other princes and princesses of the realm were guests of honor, including Princes Farahnaz, the second child of Empress Farah. Prince Karim Aga Khan came a few days early to act as technical consultant, and gave the Court the benefit of the experience of his own coronation as the Aga Khan a few years earlier. There were receptions and parties at the palaces and at lesser palaces, at state buildings, and at the Royal Teheran Hilton.

The diplomatic corps was there, and so was a major representative of every nation; even those which looked with more or less genial disdain upon these Oriental trappings. But the show was really for the Iranian people, for tribesmen from the far reaches of empire, from Azerbaijan, from Kurdistan, from the Persian Gulf desert and the mountains near Afghanistan and Pakistan. The whole city, the whole country, was to be turned over to a week-long festival, much of it supported by the royal coffers. A huge crown was erected above a roundabout on Pahlavi avenue, and along all the major thoroughfares, pylons were built to illuminate the night and make it bright as day.

The Shah came from his summer palace, and the procession

brought him and the Empress down the avenues, past the crowd, in the ornate carriage, drawn by eight snow-white horses, to the Gulistan palace where the coronation would take place. The Crown Prince rode behind in a coach of his own, and the lesser members of the family came in other vehicles. The long procession moved slowly and majestically to the palace before the eyes of thousands upon thousands of Persians who cheered and applauded their ruler from behind the carefully guarded police lines.

Then came Queen Farah in a white dress with a long train that dragged across the silken carpet. She was escorted by six maids of honor.

Three minutes passed as the audience stood, and queen and prince composed themselves on both sides of the great throne.

Exactly at the end of those three minutes there arrived the commander of the army, of the air force, of the navy, and the personal chief of staff of the Shah. And then the Shah, splendid as always in uniform, in the black diplomatic costume of the day, with medals. He passed by the relatives and lesser members of the court, all in their court costumes, the women wearing long dresses and hats and their best jewels. Behind were the press and cinematographers, carefully screened, the representatives of foreign magazines and newspapers, all invited, to record this moment of history for a waiting world, and thus assure another triumph for the Shah.

Up the carpet then came a triumvirate, two generals and a private soldier. One general carried the red and gold and feathered crown of the Shah with its precious jewels. One carried the black bejewelled crown of the Shahbanou, the queen. The soldier carried the Koran.

Slowly, to the sound of trumpets they marched up the long red carpet to the Peacock Throne. The crowd stirred inside, and outside the thousands cheered as the imperial flag was raised on the pole, signifying the coronation was in progress.

The highest Imam in all the land took the Koran from the bearer, and blessed it and handed it to the Shah, who kissed the holy book.

The diplomats and the courtiers were hushed as the Shah took the great crown in his hands. The Queen stood gravely by on his right, while the young prince fidgeted on the left.

THEN THE SHAH PICKED UP THE CROWN *AND CROWNED HIMSELF.*

To an outside world the gesture seemed completely arrogant.

Why not an Imam to crown him in the name of Islam?

But there was the outsider's basic misunderstanding of Persia and the Shah.

For to Persia there was no higher authority than the Shah, and it was only natural for him to crown himself; no other had the authority or the presence or the dignity to do so, and the Shah must be superior to all others.

So the trumpets blared and the flags waved outside and a salute of 101 guns was fired to honor the monarch's honor of himself.

As the reverberation of the last shot rang in the air, Queen Farah approached the monarch sitting three steps above the crowd on the tall bejewelled throne. Her maids lifted her train, and she stepped forward.

"The most important day of my life shall also be the great day in the life of my consort", the Shah had said a few days earlier.

Now he crowned her *Shabanou,* or Empress. She was the first woman in the history of the Persian throne to be crowned empress. Always in the past the emperor had wives, many of them, but never a single consort.

And as the coronation cape of furs and jewels was placed about her, she knew that she bore a greater responsibility. The Shah was making her also regent. That bestowal meant that if perchance he died or one of his enemies took his life, the Shabanou would reign and *rule* Persia until the crown prince came of age.

This was an even graver change in the Persian social system, and marked the reality of the change in the status of women. No other woman in the world possessed the potential power over the subjects of the realm that Farah now was given.

28
Consolidation

The coronation had as much political significance as anything the Shah had ever done. Shrewdly, he had assessed the state of his nation and concluded it needed diversion. The festivities and splendor of the coronation of the Emperor and Empress certainly did lift the spirits of the people and also was the occasion to tell them of the great good works of the Shah's regime and the gleaming future that lay before Iran.

Forty-five minutes after the uncrowned Shah entered the palace, the crowned Shah left in all his regalia, the heavy crown upon his head, to pass out into the sunshine where his people could see their monarch.

Shah and Shabanou rode in their gilded coach looking like nothing so much as a Hollywood version of the Cinderella story. The richness was so tremendous, the pearls and jewels and gold and diamonds so overwhelming, that to a cynical observer the whole seemed more comic opera than reality. And several of the newspaper and magazine writers on the scene so stated in articles in the western press.

What they failed to appreciate was that this kind of show was not primarily for them, but for the ragged peasants and workers of Persia. To them the Shah represented a glory beyond aspiration, and also a hope, for in his contacts with the people the Shah unceasingly spoke of his responsibility to bring the lowly of Persia to the standards of western Europe and America. That message was getting through and even in the universities where there was growing unrest.

The Shah went through the streets to the mosque for a brief celebration there to pacify the religious, of whom there were fewer each year in all Iran.

And then the round of coronation entertainments continued. That night the Shah and Empress inaugurated the Roudaki Concert Hall with a purely Persian concert. Next came a performance by the Grand Ballet Classique de France, which had been flown in by private plane. Day-after-day the Shah and his consort appeared in splendid costume for the people. Sometimes he was in evening dress, handsome as he might ever be in long tailcoat and white tie. Sometimes he was a field marshal, or a general of the army, or the air force. Sometimes he wore his medals; sometimes just the ribbons.

One day the armed forces staged a parade for their ruler and the visitors; something to show off military precision but more—to exhibit some of the hardware that was making Iran a potent military presence in the Middle East.

The life guards goose-stepped by, reminding the world of the heritage of Shah Reza. The Shah, in a jeep, reviewed and inspected the forces, then the parade began in earnest.

A band in brilliant robins-egg blue, gold, black and red uniforms led the parade. The troops marched by, thousands of them in precise rows. The police, the security police, and the air force troops marched, too.

Heavy M60 tanks trundled by, reminding the Arabs of nearby countries that the Shah was not unready.

For four hours the Shah and Shabanou and Prince Cyrus sat in the reviewing stand watching the nation's military might. Little

Princess Farahnaz fidgeted beside her mother. The half tracks came by. The Pakistani bagpipers, bands from other countries and from every major military unit. Gymnasts and sports clubs and just plain people came from all over the kingdom to crowd the huge Amjadieh stadium for the show.

Pictures of the Shah and Shabanou stood high above the stadium, but so also did the symbols of agriculture and technology, for this was the theme to be emphasized to the people: through their magnificent Shah and Empress they were achieving the good things in life and this was only the beginning of the rise of Iran.

There were fireworks high above the city for all to see, and a national festival that began at the Royal Teheran Hilton, where people from every region of the land came in their traditional costumes and displayed their finery, their dancing, their music, their art, for their ruler. There were fezes and headbands, and turbans, and tall Karakul hats and caps; every conceivable form of headdress emphasized the color of the countryside—and also the plethora of custom and racial heritage that represented one of the Shah's major social problems. For out of this group of entities he was determined to create a new Persian nationalism that would transcend the tribal, and local enthusiasms and loyalties of 2,500 years. And he thought he could do it in less than a quarter of a century.

"Allah Bless the Shah and the Shabanou," came the cries as the dancers fluttered in and out of the shadows around the firelight in a thousand villages that week.

And the Shah, as a part of his ceremonial week, devoted many hours to inaugurating enterprises that proved precisely what he intended to do during the remainder of his reign.

He opened, with a single gesture, 383 schools throughout the land.

And soon he was finished with the fete; the Shah was back down to business—the business of running the most aggressive kingdom in the world. For in a few months he would inaugurate that fourth development plan, and for it he hoped to secure a new arrangement with the international oil consortium that would increase his oil revenues mightily. He needed the money, he said, to build dams and schools, and create new industries and new agricultural methods for his country.

The international demand for oil was growing every year as the the industrialized world kept finding more uses for this precious source of energy. The Shah was developing a theory about oil—that it must be treated as a finite resource, not an infinite one, and that the western nations were going to have to pay for oil in relation to what they charged the developing nations for technical resources and equipment.

This was so radical a departure from the old leasehold theory of oil management that the Shah and the Arab leaders (who were thinking in much the same way) went a little slow in the development.

In 1968 the Shah contented himself by increasing oil production once more. During the last five years it had been jumped 95 per cent over the past, with a 21 per cent rise in 1967 alone. It took a lot of money to pay for those parties, and also for the schools.

In reality, the parties, the villa the Shah bought at St. Moritz, the palaces, and all the relatives who had to be supported, were as nothing compared to the national expenditures needed for the Shah's development and improvement plans.

Some of this development—such as the defense establishment—was financed by bonds sold to private investors and the central bank. But most of it was financed out of revenues—something only a young and aggressive country could attempt to do in the second half of the twentieth century.

The Shah had big plans for the development of the nation, either by Iranians, or by Iranians in conjunction with foreigners and foreign technology. Foreign pharmaceutical firms began to appear in the market, foreign automobiles came in increasing numbers, and foreign electrical companies began to open plants with Iranian partners.

In the fourth plan, which would carry through until 1973, the

Shah intended to spend his ten billion dollars very wisely. For example industry and mining were to get more than ten per cent of the money of the government, and double the figure with private investment. For the Shah was attempting to create his own kind of semi-socialism. The people of Iran were so poor that much must be done for them; but the Shah was willing that others make huge fortunes in the doing if they could use their ingenuity to better the rest of the nation.

That was the rub, immediately. The students at Teheran and Shiraz and Tabriz and the other big universities were the first to recognize the inequities. The foreign visitors and foreign money were fine, but they brought desires and wastefulness and profiteering, and more opportunity for corruption than had existed even under the old Shah. Hard to believe but it was true.

In the next five years the Shah intended to double electric generating capacity. That was to be the grand accomplishment—until it was done many other improvements must be left undone.

The Shah was also playing his cards cannily. He was very much beholden to the United States, and was using the Americans to build his defense establishment. But he was doing much business with the eastern bloc of nations as well. The Romanians won a contract to put up a tractor factory near Tabriz, which was to assemble 5,000 Romanian farm tractors every year. When the wherewithal became available the factory would change over from assembling to manufacturing.

The Germans won bids for a power plant at Manjil, and their shipyards also got contracts for half a dozen cargo vessels. Siemens, the big German electrical firm, won a contract to build telephone equipment for Iran's indifferent telephone system. The British got contracts to supply civil airports with equipment. Leyland, the big motorcar and lorry manufacturers, won contracts for engines and lorries.

The Shah particularly had his eye on chemical and petrochemical developments. B.F. Goodrich of America, along with Amoco and Allied company were hard at work using the native petroleum for rarified products, and the Shah was watching the markets and pricing structures for these oils and fluids.

Privately, the Shah was already telling his advisors that the wave of the future lay in using Iran's underground resources for the most highly refined use possible—and to do the job right there in Iran.

Many a change was in the wind in this year of the coronation, and every change seemed to redound to an increase in the power and prestige of the Shah and his people. Iran, which for a hundred years had seemed a sleepy flyspecked backwash of the world, suddenly became important.

In 1968 Britain suddenly announced she was going to stop policing the Persian gulf area. For years British naval power held the balance there; what was to happen in the future?

The Shah let it be known quickly that he was prepared to fill the power vacuum. He would police the area from a new naval base at Bandar Abbas, on the gulf, where the temperature rises to 130 degrees Fahrenheit, and there is no shade in the summer. To do this, the Shah was already building naval power with U.S. help. He was going to depend on a force of frigates, [a modern destroyer with the strength of a cruiser] and he had a fleet of helicopters and another of jet fighters.

And who was the enemy?

The Shah briskly skirted that question. But the facts pointed to two potential troublemakers in the area. One was the U.S.S.R., building even then the largest and most powerful navy in the world. Detente had not yet come to east and west—and the West had cause to be nervous. But the Shah had more personal enemies. The Egyptians still regarded him as "that Iranian sheep thief". And he had his own opinions of Nasser and his generals, for several of the Iranian assassinations in the 1960's had been traced to Fedayan Islam, a political terrorist organization that had its roots in Nasser's Egyptian cellar.

The Shah was now pressing hard against the international oil consortium to raise not only production, but prices. Every move he made was toward Iranian independence. He decided to build an Iranian tanker fleet and quickly bought eight from Japanese shipyards. He took on India as a private customer for Iranian oil, and the Indians built a new refinery at Madras to handle the crude oil.

In the spring of 1969, the Shah demanded a billion dollars for the year from the consortium. The companies were shocked. They looked at the problem from the standpoint of their marketing procedures and profits. The Iranians looked at it from the standpoint of "their" oil, and the need for cash to finance the Iranian national resurgence program. That meant the Shah wanted another 15 per cent increase in revenues.

The consortium tried to hold him down, insisting they could not market so much oil. But the Shah said he must have the increase. He was currently engaged in a dispute over the Shatt al Arab, the river that separates Iran and Iraq, and he was concerned about the bellicose government of Iraq. More was needed for defense. More was needed for building.

The Shah did not get all he wanted that year. He chafed under the restrictions of the consortium. But two years later, the Shah led his negotiators and those of the Arab states in securing huge demands from the oil companies. He worked out a new five-year pact that made him the most powerful figure in the Middle East. For the next five years the companies would pay much more heavily, starting with a billion dollars in 1971. Iran's 1971 oil revenues for that year would be five times what Anglo Iranian paid Iran between 1910 and 1951.

But what the Shah had really done was to change the relationship between oil consuming and oil producing nations. Thus, for the first time in history, the producers were in charge.

And the Shah, with his oil reserves and his power, was the most important of them all.

'he Shah at work.

Prime Minister Hoveyda—the most successful yet.

At Kharg Island the Shah has his own tankers, too.

Here the Iranians refine and keep their oil products.

Abadan's refinery is famous the world over.

Shah Abbas—the great dam.

Not a refinery but an atomic center at Teheran University.

29
Awakening

In successfully completing those delicate negotiations, the Shah had changed the face of middle eastern oil politics forever. That done, he left in March for his annual skiing vacation in Switzerland. So pleased had he been with St. Moritz, that years before he had bought property. Now he owned a ski villa, the biggest and most important and most pretentious ski chalet around. That was his style—always flamboyant.

At St. Moritz, Farah made a few tentative passes at the slopes, pristine in her ski garb, and then retired to snow bunny pursuits. But the Shah, no matter what one thought of him (and many an oil man was thinking harsh thoughts these days as well as many an Iranian student), was a thorough going athlete. He skiied and he skiied. At night he dominated the entertainment. The rich and the film stars gawked at his chalet and wangled for invitations. The most prosperous and prominent of them got them.

In international affairs the Shah had made it quite plain he was an independent, although personally, closely allied to the United

States. But his independence was underlined by various arrangements with the U.S.S.R. For instance, the export of natural gas from Iran's northern fields began in 1961 and the U.S.S.R. was the major customer. In addition to Rumania, he was trading with the Czechs, who were supplying a good deal of industrial equipment. Yugoslavia, Bulgaria, and Hungary all had trade or exploitation arrangements with Iran on a barter basis. He dealt with France, and the Italians supplied him with plastic extruding machinery, particularly for a developing refrigerator and stove factory on the outskirts of Teheran.

By 1971, the Shah's positive foreign policy was firmly established when he said Iran would control the Persian gulf. Iran would also lead the oil exporting countries in social reform, showing the Arab states the way to progress. For after all, before the coming of this Shah, Iran had scarcely been better off than any of those countries, and several of them were much richer per capita than the Iranians.

The Shah had a frank and outspoken outlook on the affairs of the world. He spoke of Iran and the Arab states as "fourth class" powers, but he also made it very clear that he intended that Iran should become a "first class" country. He meant it, too. He envisaged a day when Iran's military and economic strength put her up with the giants.

To an outsider, the Shah's vision must seem a bit exaggerated, at least in the middle of the 1970s. It could certainly be true that Iran would in time become totally self-sufficient; an exporting industrial power with a huge market place in the Middle East, Africa and the Far East.

"Why can't we work harder and become more rational, not only in our emotions but in our minds," he asked, "and recognize that the future society must be based on technology and know-how?"

As for the Shah, by 1971 there was no doubt that he was accomplishing this aim. Teheran was booming. So were the growing industrial centers of Iran, including old Isfahan, which now boasted so much more than reflecting pools, mosques, palaces and gardens. A steel mill was there to belch forth smoke and produce native steel for native industry.

In 1973 came the 400 per cent increase in the price of oil. Those in the petroleum business who had been watching the signs could have anticipated this move, and some did. It was natural enough: the oil producing and exporting countries had for years been saying that the price of their vital raw material was lagging far behind the cost of the industrial products they must buy with it. Nonetheless, the western nations were shocked by the change —it upset their economies completely, and triggered both inflation and the coming of a depression to the industrial powers.

The depression did not concern Iran seriously, or the other nations that were eager to develop. On the contrary, the need for markets sent hundreds and thousands of westerners scurrying to the Middle East to sell their wares, from petrochemicals to ordinary ladders for building. The quick and the quick-witted began to pick up contracts, but it was not simple. In some cases bribery increased. The giant industrial firms, in particular, were always ready to put up as much as 10 per cent in bribes to get a good, fat contract. Even where there was no bribery, the honest Iranian officials looked carefully at all bidders and all contracts.

"Many will come in the next few years," a senior oil company official said one day. "and few will be chosen. We are interested in quality and performance and the technology we might gain from every relationship."

So the industrial world, by 1973, was beating a path to the Shah's door, and Iran was in the driver's seat (just as were Saudi Arabia and the other oil-producing nations). The U.S. was the leading exporter of personnel and industrial might to Iran, meeting every conceivable need of an expanding economy. Germany and Japan were next, with Britain fourth, and France and Russia next.

The growth pattern was excellent. Wilfred Jenks of the International Labor Organization, called the Shah "one of the great architects of social policy of the 20th century". The Shah was fairly well pleased with his own success. But not entirely. As he ordered the Fifth developmental plan (1973–78) he hoped to make Iran one of the world's half dozen great powers within a few years. But the inflation and the difficulties at home were giving him pause.

For even as presidents and foreign ministers and heads of great western corporations doffed their hats and came to Iran for business reasons, the Shah was aware that in a very few years either the industrial nations would develop alternative sources of power or the oil would run out. He estimated perhaps 20 years to complete his developmental program before the crisis came. Could he do it?

Much depended on the price of oil. If it kept high, higher in proportion to industrial needs than the goods he must buy, then he might make it. If the price dropped, then he must increase production *if he could.* But glutting the market for a year or two years would not solve the problem—the price would drop again.

Around the globe the press indicated nervously that the world had turned upside down; that the oil producers were in charge, and the worriers of the industrial powers wrung their hands. But the Shah knew he was walking a tightrope.

What he wanted, and the major reason for his massive public relations campaign in the world markets, was to create an illusion of strength, hoping it would draw strength. And then he had to increase his exports, for after oil, the next most important Persian export was still the figured carpet, a handmade product, created in 1973 in almost precisely the same manner it had been made a thousand years before.

Iran was producing 60,000 cars a year, most of them of a Hillman prototype. Years before, the Shah's people had brought Hillman in and established an assembly plant. By 1975 they hoped to be producing almost all the component parts in Iran. Of course, it was still a Hillman design, but it was a Peykan—in Iran—and nearly every worker and many a peasant aspired to own one.

Other possible export items were water heaters, refrigerators, water coolers, and television sets, and by 1974 many of these were being exported to some eastern Europe countries and to neighboring Arab and moslem states.

In all this production, it was apparent that more than money would be needed, and one story of the spring of 1975 tells it all.

In 1974, a British corporation that manufacturers industrial seals won a contract to supply seals for the National Iranian Oil Company's Teheran refinery. In due course the engineers and workmen of the company came to Teheran and installed the seals, remained a few days to see that they were working properly, and returned to England.

A month or two went by, and then from Teheran came an outcry. The seals were leaking. They were inferior, the British had attempted to gyp the Iranians.

Outside London, the chief engineers of the seal company knew what had happened. The seals required a certain maintenance and they had not gotten it. The installing engineers had worried about the problem at the time. For although the Shah was sending teachers out to the villages to bring modernity to the country, even the highly vaunted Literacy Corps program could not produce miracles. The trouble at NIOC was that the Iranian engineers would not soil their hands with the seals, and the Iranian technicians did not have the training to do the job.

So a trouble-shooter was sent to Teheran. In a month he had all the seals back in working order, and was ready to leave. But when he left, he knew that he would be back again in a matter of weeks.

And he was.

When the complaint came to the company again in February, 1975, the trouble-shooter engineer was ready for it. He said he would go back, at the NIOC's expense, if they would permit him to train the engineers and technicians of the Teheran refinery in the care of these seals. NIOC agreed, and the engineer returned to Teheran for another round. He did his job, but even as he did it, he sensed the continuing aversion of the Iranian engineers to actually do the work. They were gentlemen, they did not work, they supervised—and the engineer knew he would be back again and again. Only when he did not have to return another time would the Shah's problems be on the way to solution.

The same story can be told of chemicals, of oil production, of training to fly the hundreds of Bell helicopters that the Shah was buying for his armed forces. In the Paykan auto factory one day when the motor assembly line broke down, the workers tackled the jam with a crowbar. *That* approach, of course, did not resolve the problem. The assembly engineers were many hours in cleaning up the debris and getting the line started once again.

The Shah maintained that the key to the lock on Iran's potential was education. One of the serious parts of his Shah-People Revolution, which came out of the White Revolution, was centered on bringing education, health, and welfare to the villages where very few knew how to read and write. The system was to assign young men to serve six months of their involuntary military service as literacy corps men. They went to the back villages and taught the children to read and write. Girls were later brought into the program and taught in larger villages. Out of the literacy corps developed a health corps, and a developmental corps that built sewage systems and water systems.

And in 1973, as he planned the expenditures for the coming five years in his race against time, the Shah told his government it must spend $36 billion in that five-year period of the fifth plan.

The trouble with that, said a political scientist one day in Teheran, was that it simply was not working as well as it should. Corruption, as was so often the case, was dreadful. How dreadful was illustrated by a former government official, a man of impeccable family as far as the Shah was concerned, who came from a long line of government officials. He had been practicing law abroad. But in the 1970's, the Shah appealed to Iranians everywhere to come home and help in the development of their country. This man heard the call and came, expecting that his services would be used on a high level. Instead he was installed as a counsellor to one of the ministries in Teheran. One of his tasks was to pass on the legality of various schemes offered by officials within the ministry.

Soon this Iranian lawyer was the most unpopular man in the ministry.

"They brought me nothing but crooked, self-serving schemes," he said one day. "They were out to cheat the government and make themselves millionaires."

The lawyer resisted. He lasted about six months, and then he was assigned to an out-of-the-way agency where he could not longer interfere in the get-rich plans of his compatriots.

The Shah knew. The Shah had always known as well as his father that he was surrounded by nobles and servants who felt, by Iranian tradition, that an official position was a license to steal. He instituted prosecutions and one official of the sugar trust was arrested in 1974 and brought to trial in 1975. But the Shah had been prosecuting for years; still, by 1975, the corruption was not erased from Iranian life any more than the 1 o'clock end of the working day.

In the spring of 1975 there were other problems. The Shah's two-party political system was not in good order. Iran Novin was getting too strong, and some members of that party seemed almost to challenge the Shah's authority. If one thing was certain it was that he was not ready in 1975 to brook any interference with his developmental program. Something had to be done. He started planning.

As far as the corruption was concerned, he also took a long-range approach. He conferred with David Lilienthal, one of the American public figures he respected most. Lilienthal assigned a team of advisors to study and work with the Ministry of Interior on an anti-corruption campaign.

Another of the Shah's problems was more deep-seated. Millionaires were being made every month in Teheran. One young contractor in Tabriz told his relatives he was making more than $2,000 a day by putting up brick houses for a growing middle class that had the money to pay for them. As this middle class prospered and grew fat, would not the citizens demand more rights.

"The trouble with the Shah," said one former government official, "is his basic assumption that he can make vast economic changes in this country without making political changes as well."

It was ridiculous, said this man, that there should be as there were, as many as 8,000 candidates for 200 Majlis seats—with everyone knowing which were going to win.

The Shah-People Revolution was all right as far as it went, a half dozen educated Iranians remarked during conversations in the spring of 1975, but it was far from perfect.

Was it real?

It was real enough, but corruption was always getting in the way.

On the matter of distributing land to the poor: once the original grants were made the system tightened up. A farmer could only get about a 50 per cent mortgage, and this precluded many a young man from buying his own land. The farm cooperatives were highly touted as providing operating funds for farmers, but these funds could be measured in terms of hundreds of dollars; not large enough to be effective. And if a farmer got $200 for a loan, he was quite likely to go off and buy a television set with it, take a visit to a shrine, buy a new carpet, or get himself a second wife. The old ways die hard in Persia.

For real loans, the farmer was apt to get heavily in debt to the government and then have to go to the money lenders in the Bazaar and pay *10 per cent a month* interest. That way lay disaster, as many a former-landholder now knew.

And the much praised Literacy Corps:

Good as far as it went, but in a country still less than half literate, with a dozen languages native to the people, only those whose native tongue was Persian really got the benefits, because Persian was so difficult a language it took more than four years to teach its fundamentals properly.

And what of education at the university level?

The Shah was opening more universities and persuading more youths to seek higher education at the technical and university levels.

It was excellent, said the literati of Teheran, one after another except for a few problems. For one thing, there was little freedom of thought at the universities for the secret police were everywhere.

That spring some 180,000 students took the entrance examinations for the state universities, but only 10 percent of that number could be admitted to the big universities. Unless the families of the other 90 per cent had the money to send them to private universities, they would be frustrated young people—potentially dangerous to the Shah.

In that spring of 1975, the parks of Teheran were filled with these youth, studying hard in the warm sunshine for those dreaded examinations. In a way, the spring entrance examinations of that year exemplified all of Iran's problems: going far, going fast, and perhaps unable to assimilate the tremendous efforts that were being made.

30
Looking Ahead

In the spring of 1975, the Shah and his family went to the big stone chalet in St. Moritz for the family's annual vacation. The Shah relaxed and enjoyed his stay, but even as he did, he was planning; and back in Teheran, Prime Minister Hoveyda was planning, too. For they were about to make drastic changes in the political system of Iran.

When the Shah returned to Teheran, Prime Minister Hoveyda was ready. At a huge rally in Aryamehr stadium the Shah and his minister announced they were dissolving the whole political structure of Iran and creating one huge party—the Rastakhiz, or Resurgence party. All with political interest were invited to join.

Thus the Shah was taking another leaf from the book of the Communists and then going them one better, for while the Communists called their parties "mass," the fact was that once in power the Communist governments limited membership in the ruling party. What the Shah was speaking of was something like Mossadegh's National Front for he was sick of the party bickering that seemed to hold up progress of his reform movement.

Next day, he and Farah left on another of their visits of state, even as a controversy in Teheran began to develop—one that would indicate the severity of the basic problem the Shah faced in trying to bring his country forward at what some regarded as breakneck speed.

A happening back in 1955 graphically spells out the difficulty of Iran's problems with progress. In that year, a British consulting engineering firm and a Swedish contractor were awarded the contract to build the main terminal of Mehrabad airport.

They built a fine new terminal, one of the most modern in the world, and all seemed well. They had made surveys and plans, and the British engineers had done all they promised. The terminal was finished in 1959 and the contractors collected their fees and left.

When it had come to the roof, the plans called for corrugated iron, but the contractors and the Iranians agreed this was not feasible. So the roof was covered with five centimeters of concrete and two of asphalt.

All went well for several years. Then in 1970, 11 years after the building was completed, the Iranians decided the roof needed treatment, so they added three centimeters of new asphalt to the top of it. They apparently thought nothing of the strains and stresses involved.

Still, all was well until the winter of 1974–75. In December a record winter storm dumped 15 centimeters of heavy, wet snow in 75 minutes, and on December 5 one of the pillars of the terminal roof caved in; the roof fell and 18 people were killed and nine injured.

The Iranian commission blamed the foreigners for constructing an inefficient building. That was the Iranian way these days, and the government had become so adamant in blaming others for mishaps, that some firms were beginning to shy away from bidding on Iranian projects, lest they become more troublesome in the long run than profitable in the short.

Fortunately for the Shah, the worsening recession in Europe

and the U.S. made the western businessmen eager enough to do business that they would stretch many points.

On the day that the government committee reported its findings in the airport accident investigation, the Shah was in Paris being wined and dined by French officialdom in the manner he liked so much. From there he was to fly to Venezuela, to have talks with President Carlos Hernandez Perez, about the future of oil pricing. The Shah was feeling the pinch of inflation; his billions in oil revenue were not buying what they had bought even a year before in generators and buses and technical skills from the west.

On the day he was flying to Paris on the first leg of his trip, several of the big new Leyland double decker buses (the kind one sees in London, but painted blue instead of red) were breaking down in the streets of Teheran. And the reason: just like the airport; just like the Teheran oil refinery problem: a basic lack of understanding about modern machinery and the need for preventive maintenance. Some of those buses in Teheran were less than a year old. Give them another year, said one western mechanical engineer, and they would be ready for the junk heap.

When the Shah flew away that day, he was seen off at Mehrabad airport by various members of the royal family, including Princess Ashraf, and by Prime Minister Hoveyda, Minister of Court Assadollah Alam, Senate President Jaafar Sharif-Emami, Majlis speaker Abdullah Riazi and by a clutch of generals.

And then—as always when the Shah was gone—Teheran settled down to listen and to read about his activities and to wait. Nothing of importance was to happen, or could happen when he was away.

The royal family made no commitments. Foreign visitors cooled their heels in anterrooms. The Ministry of Court put out only information about the Shah's trip abroad. Other ministries referred ticklish questions to the Prime Minister, who put them in his "hold box".

On the streets of Teheran, countless thousands of cars jammed up or sped about, lending credence to a foreign theory that in less than five years the absolute saturation point of Teheran traffic would have been reached. The Mercedes—the status symbol of Teheran as the Rolls is to London and the Cadillac to New York —was conspicuous in its presence by the thousands. Mercedes and Paykans and Peugeots and Citroens were on the streets, mixed with a few Chevrolet and Chrysler products, and drivers swung offensively at one another to dodge away at the last moment. Police gave out tickets, and the busy yellow jitney taxis swarmed about, going in every direction, as the buses, all crowded to overloading, threaded their way among pedestrians and cyclists and huge Mercedes lorries.

But the action in the streets of Teheran was misleading; in the government all was in abeyance except routine business. The big decisions went begging for the next three weeks. The Shah was gone, long live the Shah!

On Sunday, the Shah had already been gone for two days, but that did not mean his likeness disappeared from the front pages of the newspapers. Indeed, the Shah's photograph, this time with Imam Jome of Teheran, was in the middle of the front page.

The *big* story was an interview the Shah had granted to the editor of the new party's newspaper before he left the country. The interview provided nothing new; just a rehash of the old; but the Shah had long felt that his presence must be emphasized to the nation every day, no matter where he might be or what he might be doing. This day, as he winged across the Atlantic toward Venezuela in his private jet, the press released the names of those who had gone with him.

The foreign minister went. There were ladies in waiting, military attaches, a master of ceremony, the Empress's press and public relations man, the Shah's doctor, the Shah's press man, and half a dozen deputy ministers.

Prime Minister Hoveyda stayed in Teheran and entertain the Prime Minister of Guinea. Little came of that meeting.

While in flight to Venezuela, the Shah learned that King Hussein of Jordan was in Florida, so he turned north and made an overnight stopover in Jacksonville. Next day, it was on to Caracas for a four-day meeting of state.

The streets of Caracas were decked with Iranian and Venezuelan flags. Back home, the newspapers reported this, and also told their readers about a big article in the Saudi Arabian newspapers lauding the Shah.

The newspapers of Monday had little to report about their leaders so they reprinted the earlier news of him all over again. Next day, it was news about Premier Hoveyda opening the first international energy and petrochemical fair in Teheran, and about the Shah being met at the Caracas airport by President Perez. Before leaving Florida that morning, the Shah had inspected several different types of jet aircraft brought for him to see by the U.S. Navy. He was considering buying more planes for the Iranian air force. The newspapers also printed a story quoting the Shah as urging more funds for support of scientific endeavor.

And so it went. Any other nation would have sent its prime minister or foreign minister to discuss the oil problem with the President of Venezuela. But not the Shah. His prime minister stayed home and did the ceremonial work, while the Shah inspected sugar plantations in Venezuela and made the decisions.

Hoveyda chatted with the French Minister of Economic Affairs in Teheran. The Shah went to dinner at the Presidential palace, and he and Perez agreed that the industrial nations were going to have to pay more and more for oil.

Next day, the Shah was presented with a replica of the sword which Simon Bolivar used to liberate Latin America. Prime Minister Hoveyda held a reception and called for Iranian students abroad to come home and help their country. Empress Farah spent much of her time entertaining and being entertained by Senora Blanquita Rodriguez de Perez, the first lady of Venezuela.

On Thursday the Shah visited more industrial plants; received a medal from Perez, and decided that they should protect the value of oil by turning more of it into petrochemicals. Perez gave a banquet which the press described as a scene from "The Thousand and One Nights".

Hoveyda was in his office that day working on his papers. But another face of Iran was represented by action: Hossein Hamadanian, the Isfahan man charged with sugar trust frauds, was released from jail on 60,000,000 rials bail (almost a million dollars ($800,000 £). Hamadanian's ability to put up the stiff bail was an indication of affairs in Iran—and he was not really regarded as a very rich man.

On Friday it was honor guards and cheering crowds in Mexico City for the 23 man and woman imperial delegation from Iran. The Shah and President Luis Echeverria wined and dined and talked business—mostly about steel. The Shah, just before leaving Caracas, had promised to raise the price of oil in September. The truth was that with Venezuela and the other OPEC nations all thinking along the same lines, he could do it. His point was that inflation was destroying any advantages the oil-rich nations had in the world.

Next day, the Mexican press came out with editorials and news articles about the Shah. "The most economically powerful man in the world," said *El Heraldo de Mexico.*

There was a lot of truth in what *El Heraldo* said. The Shah's deputy, Manuchehr Eqbal, was speaking before the Ninth World Petroleum Congress in Tokyo. The world was listening as Eqbal parroted the Shah's demands for more oil produced at higher prices.

For the next ten days life was truly at a standstill in Teheran. Princess Ashraf told the press how much the new political party would mean to the men and women of Iran. The Prime Minister kept seeing visitors and making statements about the progress of the new party.

The Shah kept entertaining, being entertained, and making policy wherever he went. He had gone into the shipping business with Venezuela when he was there, and in Mexico he decided to finance Mexican steel mills. He and President Echeverria also called for better distribution of world wealth. The Shah promised to support Panama in its dispute with the United States over ownership of the Panama Canal. Twenty years earlier, no Shah of Iran would have been heard in the world had he taken it upon himself to criticize the U.S. and line up with any who opposed her. But times had changed; economics had made of the Shah a real power in world events.

He then went on to Washington, where once again he was wined and dined and treated like the lion he had become. For had he not known seven U.S. Presidents? And all of them but Gerald Ford were gone, while he, the Shah, lived on.

The Shah then returned home to be greeted at the airport by Prime Minister Hoveyda with the bad news about the assassination of the two U.S. officers in Teheran that very day.

The trip abroad and the assassinations were symbolic of the situation in which the Shah found himself in his fifties, as the mature, powerful monarch of Iran, and the chief political figure of his country.

To accomplish what he must, he had to educate his people. As they were educated they would become more and more critical of the corruption and incompetence of his government. His destruction of the old party system indicated his understanding of the danger.

Time was running out in the 1970's. Perhaps 200,000 youths would be graduated from high school in 1976, and what was to be done with them? An unfulfilled education was a dangerous instrument.

In the spring and summer of 1975, the opposition to the Shah became more vocal. From Vienna came charges by students that nine revolutionaries held in the Shah's jail had been murdered in a staged escape attempt. On the walls of the London underground, Iranian dissidents chalked the words—"Death to the Shah".

And as the months rolled on, and the economic climate of Europe and the U.S. wilted under many strains, the Shah's timetable was so badly disturbed that the fifth development plan had to be revised—downward. However, that was not entirely unhelpful to the Shah—if one thing had been proved in two years it was the incapability of his government, as existing in 1974, to spend the big sums wisely. In the end, slowdown might be beneficial.

But the Shah's clock moved on. He had begun the march of new times in Iran, and there was no turning back. By his own statement, the police state could survive for only so long, and no longer. The educated public he needed to develop Iran as an industrial power might yet unseat him and destroy the Pahlavi dynasty after only two generations.

In 1976, how much time did he have?

Notes and Bibliography

I am indebted to a great number of persons who assisted in one way or another in the research for this biography of the Shah. First of all, thanks go to my two publishers who underwrote the cost of it all: Paul Eriksson, of New York, and Leslie Frewin, of London. Sid Goldberg, of North American Newspaper Alliance, gave me aid and comfort, and also commissioned some articles for his service that helped pay the cost.

In Rome, George Weller, retired foreign correspondent of the Chicago Daily News helped with reminiscences of his 25 years in the Middle East and lent me his invaluable research files on Iran. Without them I should have had countless hours more of digging. Reynolds Packard, retired correspondent of the New York Daily News, helped me immeasurably with his recollections and his files on Soraya, the Shah's second empress, and on the Shah's two important visits to Rome when it appeared that he might be overthrown.

In Teheran, I am in debt to scores of persons, from Haskell

Nasarian, innkeeper of the Commodore Hotel, to half a dozen deputy ministers who gave me their time. (In modern Iran, with all its economic power, the ministers of government have suddenly gained great reluctance to see reporters and writers, unlike the past.) But on a less rarified level, government authorities and various persons were as helpful as they could be in the tradition of Persian hospitality. Most helpful of all was Kazem Hekmat-Shoar, of the Ministry of Information, who arranged scores of interviews for me in the spring of 1975. Others in Teheran who were helpful were: Dr. Kazem Vedi, deputy minister of the Ministry of Education; K.R. Graham, of Clima Products, London; Dave Grierson, of Sealol of London and Uxbridge, England; the proprietor of the Perspolis Bookshop on Takhte Jamshid Avenue; M.J. Moss, managing director of Carless Chemicals Trading, Ltd., of Middlesbrough, England; Dr. Elisabeth Müller, publishing director, IPC Business Press Ltd., London; J. Rohall Jr., Petrochemicals consultant, W.R. Grace and Company of New York; Dr. Mehrangi Dolarshahi, president of the International Council of Women and a member of the Iranian Majlis; Dr. Rolf H. Müller, Direktor IME Industrie Management Europa, of Berlin; A.S. Mozayani, assistant general manager of the National Iranian Oil Company; Abdolhamid Emami, M.D., director general of the Health Corps Organization and rural Health Centers; Hossein Baniahmad, director general for public relations, Ministry of Health, and a former newspaper editor of Teheran who knows a great deal about journalistic history; various personnel of the Cyrus Gallery of Persian Arts on Ferdowski Avenue, and of Cyrus Carpet, who have many tales of tribesmen and the carpet trade.

I am also grateful to Linda W. Ladd, of Bell Helicopter, International, which is teaching the Iranians the care and use of helicopters; M.H. Bahadori, director general of agriculture in the Central Province; Kazem Abbassioun, M.D. who told me much about Iranian history; K. Malek, M.D. F.A.C. O.G., one of the returnees from America, who discussed the opportunities in Iran for trained persons; Alex Volkoff, of the Voice Of Iran, a very knowledgeable young Canadian; Dr. E.V. Tehrani, of the Ministry of Agriculture, a veterinarian who showed me sheep and told me of the difficulties of controlling rapid consumer spending; John W. Macy, Jr., director of the Development and Resources Corporation, which is David Lilienthal's working company in Iran, dedicated to the elimination of official corruption.

I had long talks with many others. They include Zaven J. Simonian, deputy minister for Urban Planning and Architecture of the Ministry of Housing and Urban Development; Dr. K. Vadie, vice minister of Education; Andrew Avramides and Charles Dougan, of Ashland Oil International Ltd.; J. Kutchemeshgi, M.D. of the Ministry of Health, A.M. Barzin, advisor, University of Teheran; Qasem Eftekhari, professor of political science University of Teheran; one political scientist who was reluctant to be identified; Dr. Teredun Kavoosi, director of general research of the labor ministry. Mohammed Mirfassihi was very helpful, on several questions. Husshain Mehrain, counselor of the minister of economics went into the economic planning of the government in grave detail. Abul Hassan Abuzar explained to me the works and limitations of the Iranian Chamber of Commerce. A. Farid, of the National Iranian Oil Company, went into detail about the manner in which the oil company deals with foreigners.

Miss Atifeh Husseini spent countless hours as my Ministry of Information guide, answering questions and leading me around the Teheran which had grown so much in 28 years it was almost a new city to me. In the village of Valadabad, a few miles from Karaj, Mohammed Hasan and Nasery Salehsehady showed me some of the changes in Iranian village life since the last time I was there. At Sardarabab I visited the local Literacy Corps school with its 35 pupils from a village of 200. Twenty-eight years ago whatever education the children received was from the local Mullah, and consisted largely of memorizing the Koran.

Cyrus Farahmandi, of the Ministry of Information's foreign press department, though a very busy man, received me cordially. Dariush Sheibani, an engineer with the National Iranian Oil Company, took me hiking in the mountains of a Sunday, when Teheran people do that kind of thing for health and entertainment. Mrs. Touran Alti, general director of the Girls Education Corps told me a good deal about the Iran of the nobility and well-to-do, and as much about the ever strengthening position of women in Iran.

Abolfazil Kaveh, of the Boys Youth Corps, was helpful and so were Professor Arasneli and Dr. Abasinian of the Health Corps. Hossein Lotfabadi, of the University of Teheran, gave me some information about changes that he had seen. Naser Soltani, of the Azmayesh Manufacturing Company, had me shown around that company's big factories where refrigerators, stoves, cooling units and television sets are made. I saw for myself that the industrialization of Iran was moving along. P.R. Borzin showed me around the University of Teheran, and told me something of the modern history of the University. On one of the days I was there, the University was closed by nervous security police, and we had an interesting encounter with the guards.

Eric Pace, of the New York Times was helpful, and his wife was equally so. Hamid Enayat, of the University of Teheran, discussed history with me. Manouchi Talieh gave me some information about power resources and allied subjects. Joe Mazandi, of United Press International, was helpful. David Stronach, of the British Institute of Persian Studies, recalled the old Persian days of years ago and told me an interesting tale about his servants.

J.P. Anderson, of Bell Helicopter and several other Bell men and women, were helpful in talk about foreigners in Iran in the 1970's. Abdul Aziz Baluch did some translating for me from the Persian. William DeMyr, of the United States Information Agency, was most helpful in steering me to people and places.

Dr. H. Morshed and Dr. A.M. Sardari led me around the maze of the nation's health services.

N.O. Ameli, FRCS FICS, Dean of Dariush Kabir medical school, showed me around his school's teaching hospital, as did several of his aides and proved to me the improvement in modern Persian health practices. Mansur Valamini, a technician in the experimental center near Gharchak, showed me improvements in sheep breeding at the Khorin sheep station. We also visited the village of Khairabad. Mike Matoba, the sculptor, told me of his experiences with the Shah and the royal family. Hans Roose, Lance Borden, and Bill Pray were helpful in my first few days in Teheran for orientation. Veil Saadeh, director of training at the Teheran refinery of NIOC, told me something of the difficulties of technical training. K. A. Kaighobadi was helpful in discussing NIOC policies. I saw the village health program in action at the village of Soltanabad, with the help of Dr. Aminhi Parsa, of the University of Teheran, and Dr. Karim Fattih. There I met midwife Taherhe Jalalpar and other technicians, as well as many patients. Soltanabad may be a showplace, but 28 years ago it was a dirty little village without even its own well.

Dr. Andre Sardari was helpful in several ways, and so were a number of persons who were not eager to be mentioned, for the control and ever presence of Savak is such in Teheran that I was constantly aware of nervousness on the part of those who spoke to me, and few of them wished to pursue the acquaintance beyond a purely official one, although I could tell they were eager to do so if they had dared.

Mrs. Parvin Amini of the Plan and Budget organization was most helpful in explaining the planning program of the Shah's Shah-People Revolution. I am grateful to Baghman Bigi, Karim Ezzatkah, Mrs. Belija Khatibi, and Nairges Berenje; Mrs. Tayib Safaie, Abbas Emmami, Ali Zahedi, and J. Kuchemeshgi.

As for written source materials, there was no paucity of information about Iran, and I list them in their importance to my book efforts.

Pahlavi, Mohammed Reza Shah, (His Imperial Majesty) *Mission for My Country,* Hutchinson, London 1961

Frye, Richard N. *Persia,* George Allen and Unwin Ltd., London, 1968

Upton, Joseph M. *The History of Modern Iran, An Interpretation,* Harvard Middle Eastern Monograph Series, 1970

Arfa, Hassan, *Under Five Shahs,* John Murray, London, 1964

Gregory Lois, *The Shah and Persia,* Christopher Johnson London, 1961

The Royal Road to Progress, A Survey of Achievements of the Shah-People Revolution, Ministry of Information and Tourism, Teheran, 1974

Krause, Walter W., *Soraya, Queen of Persia,* Macdonald, London, 1956.

Farooqi, Mohammed Ahsan, *Reza Shah Pahlavi,* Upper India Publishing House Ltd., Lucknow, 1939

Wilbur, Donald N. *Iran Past and Present,* Princeton University Press, 1948

Arberry, A.J. *The Legacy of Persia,* Oxford University Press, 1953

Rodkin, Angela, *Unveiled Iran,* Hutchinson, London, undated.

Yar-Shater, Ehran, *Iran Faces the Seventies,* Praeger, New York, 1971.

Basic Facts about Iran, Ministry of Information and Tourism, Teheran, 1974

Iran's Fifth Development Plan, 1973–78-Revised. A Summary, Plan and Budget Organization, Teheran, 1975

Iran's Fifth Plan, a guide prepared by Kayhan Research Associates, Teheran, undated.

Chubin, Shahram and Zabih, Sepehr, *The Foreign Relations of Iran,* U of California Press 1974

Sackville-West, V. *Passenger to Teheran,* Penguin London, 1943

Middle East Journal, Autumn 1967, Iran's Economic Upsurge.

Middle East Journal, Spring 1969, Political Organization in Iran.

Journal of Politics, February, 1970 Modernization and Reform From Above: Iran.

New Statesman, November 30, 1973, America's Friend the Shah.

Economist, December 29, 1973, Shah Goes to the Brink.

Spectator, May 19, 1961, Re-Assessing the Shah.

Economist, November 5, 1960, Son for the Shah.

Economist, February 2, 1963, Day of Triumph for the Shah.

Middle East Journal, Wenter, 1962, Shah's Proclamation on Reform.

Middle East Journal, Autumn, 1964, Problems of Iranian University Students.

Economist, May 28, 1966, Alone on the Peacock Throne.

Journal of Politics, August, 1955, Experiment with Civilian Dictatorship in Iran, the Case of Mossadegh.

Economist, May 9, 1959, Shah's Task.

Asiatic Review, October, 1943, Some Aspects of the Situation in Persia.

International Affairs, April, 1946, Some of the Problems Facing Persia.

Middle East Journal, January, 1950, Iranian 7-year Development Plan.

Round Table, December, 1952, Persia, the Keystone: Anglo-Persian Relations since 1946.

Public Opinion Quarterly, winter 1952, Political Extremists in Iran.

Spectator, July 25, 1952, Shah and the King.

Files of The New York *Times,* 1941–1975

Files of The Times of London, 1941–1975

Files of Kayhan, April, May, 1975

Files of Teheran Journal, April, May, 1975

Files of Journal de Teheran, April, May, 1975

Special Report on Iran, New York Times International Edition, December 4, 1961

Special section, Iran's Economy Today, New York Herald Tribune, Paris edition, September, 1963.

Index